CAPTAIN MARVEL

Rise of Alpha Flight

WRITERS: *TARA BUTTERS & MICHELE FAZEKAS*

ARTIST: *KRIS ANKA*

COLOURS: ...SON

LETTERS: ...GNA

ASSISTANT EDITOR: ...ACHAM

EDITOR: ...T

EDITOR IN CHIEF: ...NSO

CHIEF CREATIVE OFFICER: *JOE QUESADA*

EXECUTIVE PRODUCER: *ALAN FINE*

PUBLISHER: *DAN BUCKLEY*

COVER ARTIST: *KRIS ANKA*

Do you have any comments or queries about Captain Marvel Vol. 1: Rise of Alpha Flight? Email us at graphicnovels@panini.co.uk
Join our Facebook group at Panini/Marvel Graphic Novels

TM & © 2016 Marvel & Subs. Licensed by Marvel Characters B.V. through Panini S.p.A, Italy. All Rights Reserved. First printing 2016. Published by Panini Publishing, a division of Panini UK Limited. Mike Riddell, Managing Director. Alan O'Keefe, Managing Editor. Mark Irvine, Production Manager. Marco M. Lupoi, Publishing Director Europe. Brady Webb, Reprint Editor. Charlotte Harvey, Designer. Office of publication: Brockbourne House, 77 Mount Ephraim, Tunbridge Wells, Kent TN4 8BS. This publication may not be sold, except by authorised dealers, and is sold subject to the condition that it shall not be sold or distributed with any part of its cover or markings removed, nor in a mutilated condition. Printed in Italy by TERRAZZI. ISBN: 978-1-84653-733-2

marvel.com
© 2016 MARVEL

MIX
Paper from
responsible sources
FSC® C016466

MARVEL GRAPHIC NOVEL

CAPTAIN MARVEL #1

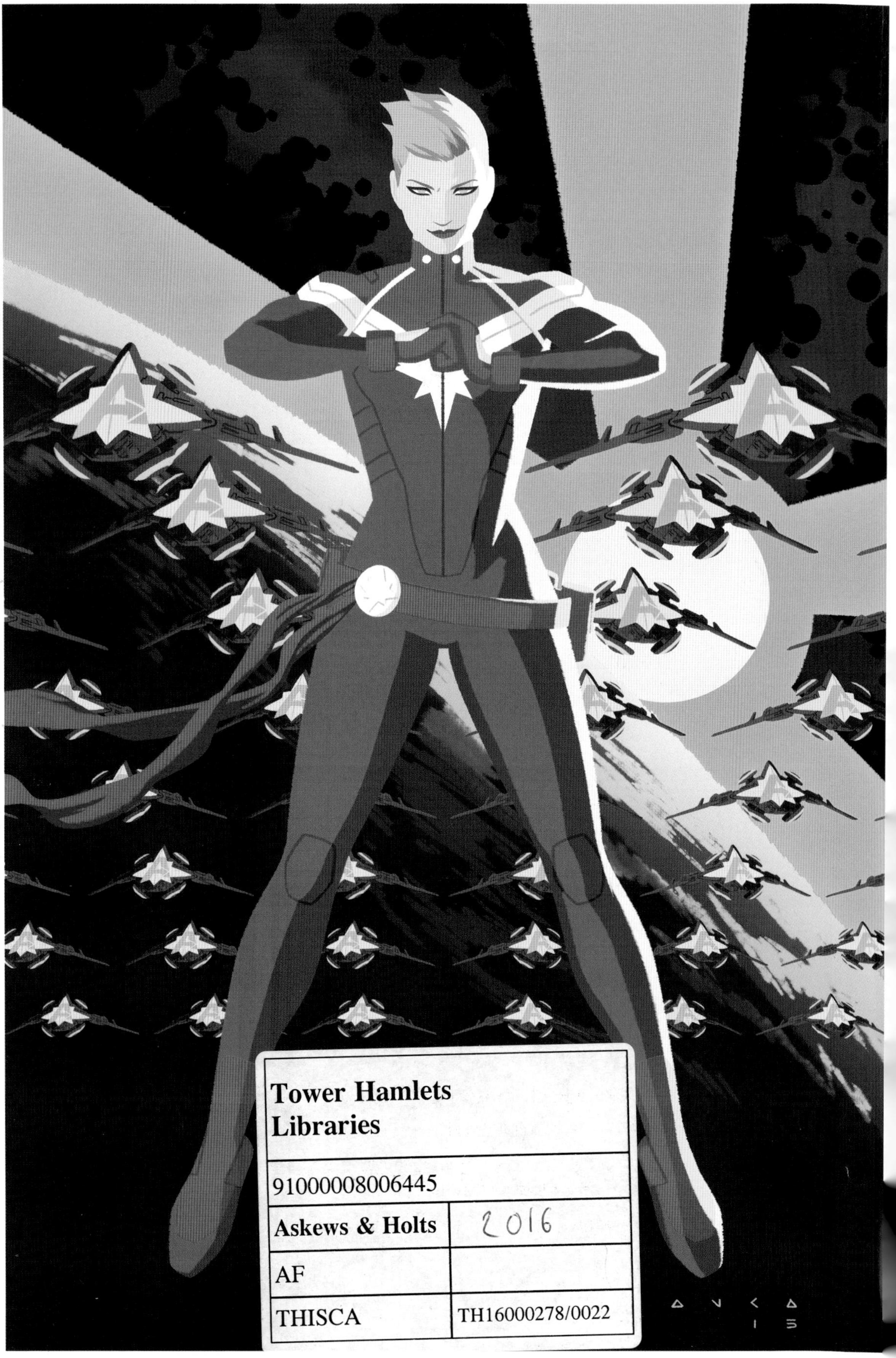

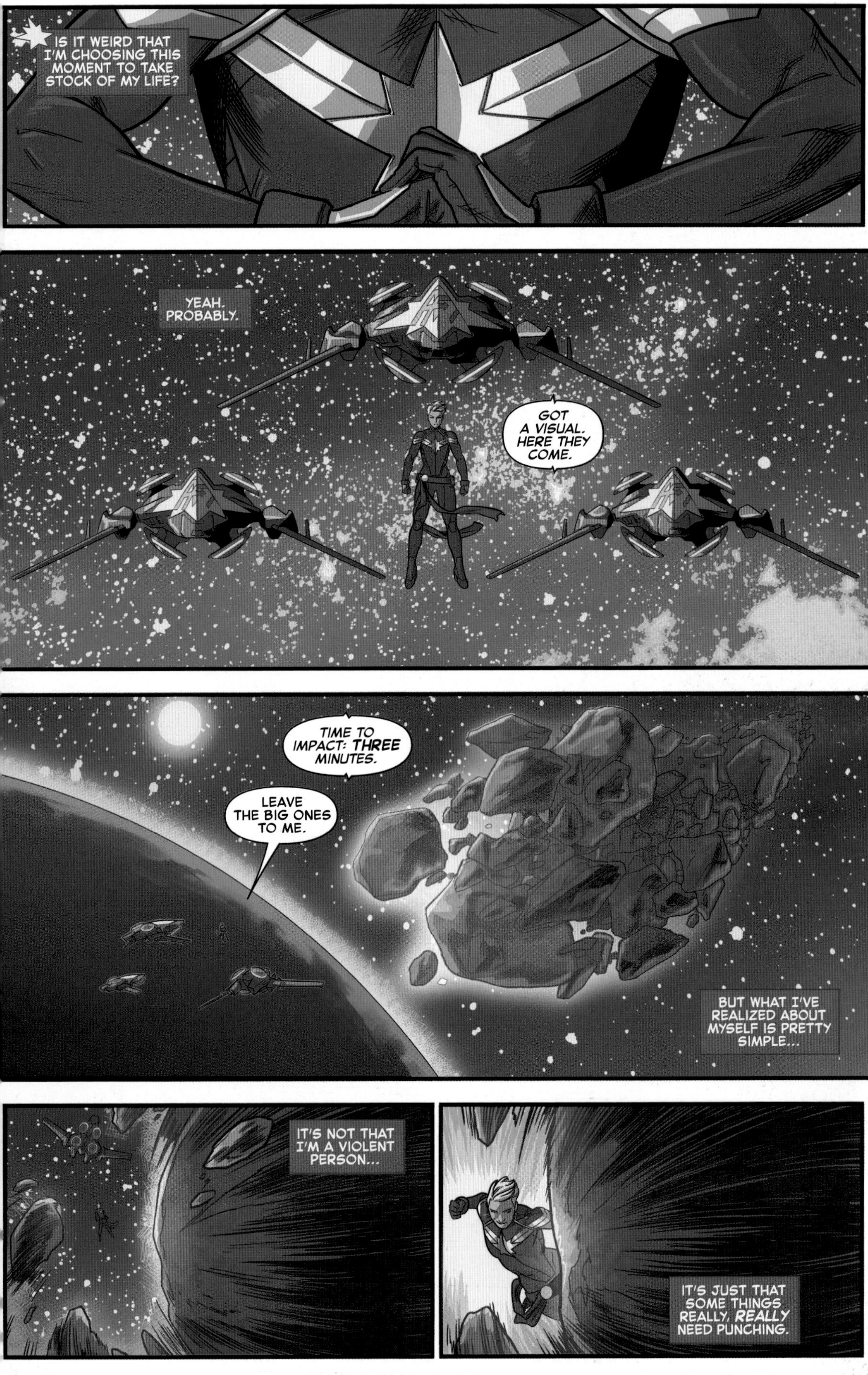
IS IT WEIRD THAT I'M CHOOSING THIS MOMENT TO TAKE STOCK OF MY LIFE?
YEAH. PROBABLY.
GOT A VISUAL. HERE THEY COME.
TIME TO IMPACT: THREE MINUTES.
LEAVE THE BIG ONES TO ME.
BUT WHAT I'VE REALIZED ABOUT MYSELF IS PRETTY SIMPLE...
IT'S NOT THAT I'M A VIOLENT PERSON...
IT'S JUST THAT SOME THINGS REALLY, REALLY NEED PUNCHING.

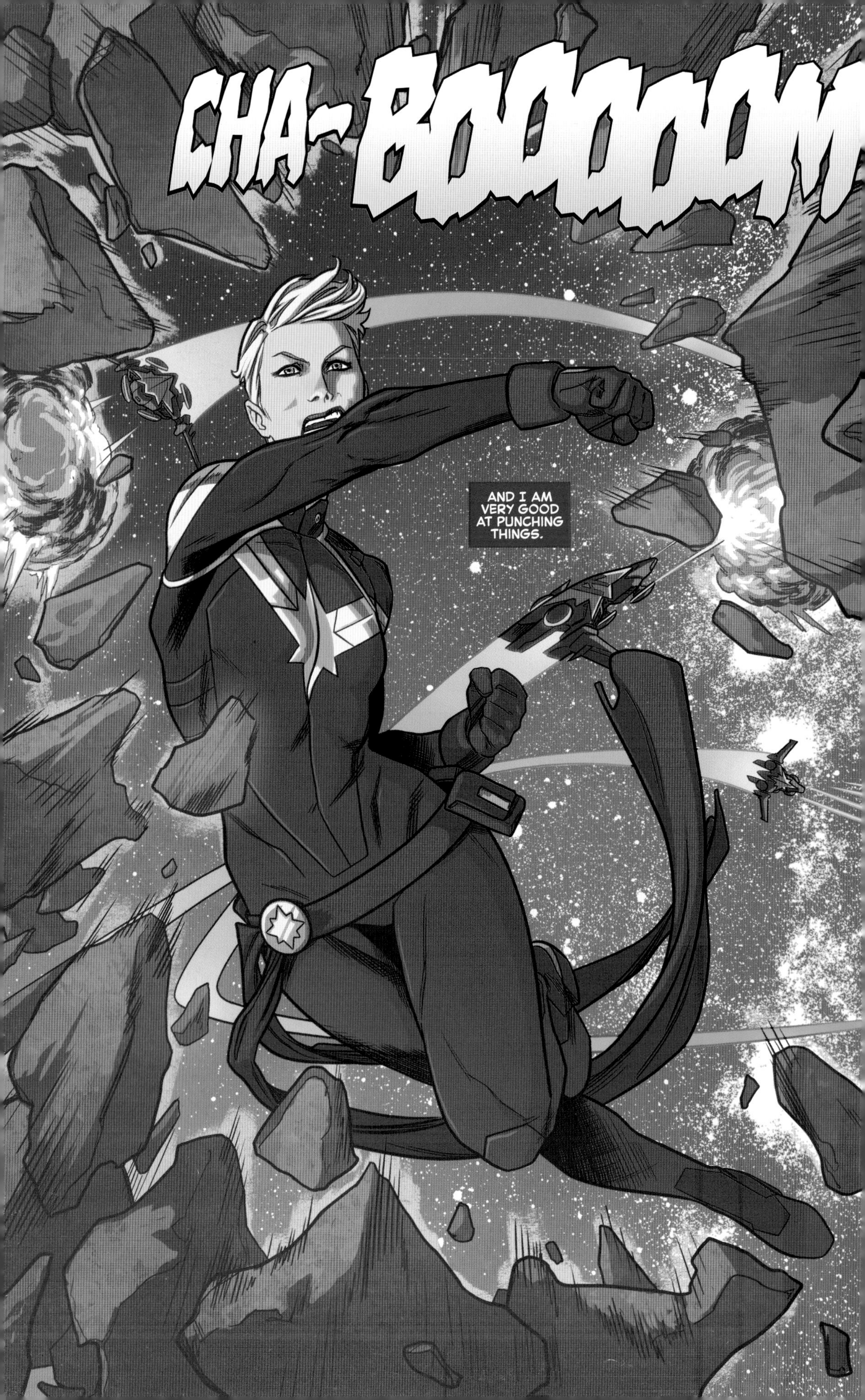
CHA-BOOOOOM
AND I AM VERY GOOD AT PUNCHING THINGS.

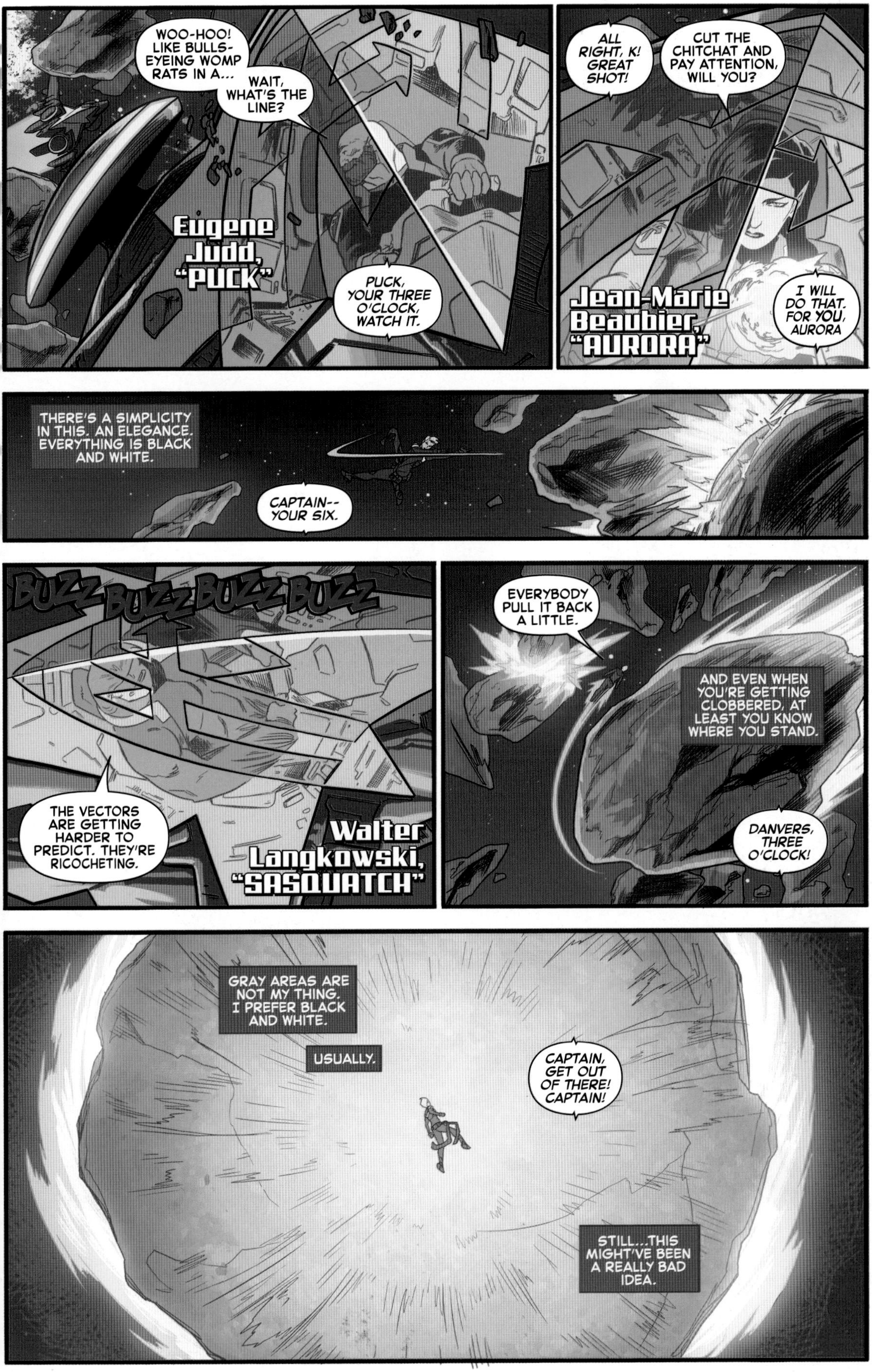
WOO-HOO! LIKE BULLS-EYEING WOMP RATS IN A...
WAIT, WHAT'S THE LINE?
Eugene Judd, "PUCK"
PUCK, YOUR THREE O'CLOCK, WATCH IT.
ALL RIGHT, K! GREAT SHOT!
CUT THE CHITCHAT AND PAY ATTENTION, WILL YOU?
Jean-Marie Beaubier, "AURORA"
I WILL DO THAT. FOR YOU, AURORA
THERE'S A SIMPLICITY IN THIS. AN ELEGANCE. EVERYTHING IS BLACK AND WHITE.
CAPTAIN-- YOUR SIX.
BUZZ BUZZ BUZZ BUZZ
THE VECTORS ARE GETTING HARDER TO PREDICT. THEY'RE RICOCHETING.
Walter Langkowski, "SASQUATCH"
EVERYBODY PULL IT BACK A LITTLE.
AND EVEN WHEN YOU'RE GETTING CLOBBERED, AT LEAST YOU KNOW WHERE YOU STAND.
DANVERS, THREE O'CLOCK!
GRAY AREAS ARE NOT MY THING. I PREFER BLACK AND WHITE.
USUALLY.
CAPTAIN, GET OUT OF THERE! CAPTAIN!
STILL...THIS MIGHT'VE BEEN A REALLY BAD IDEA.

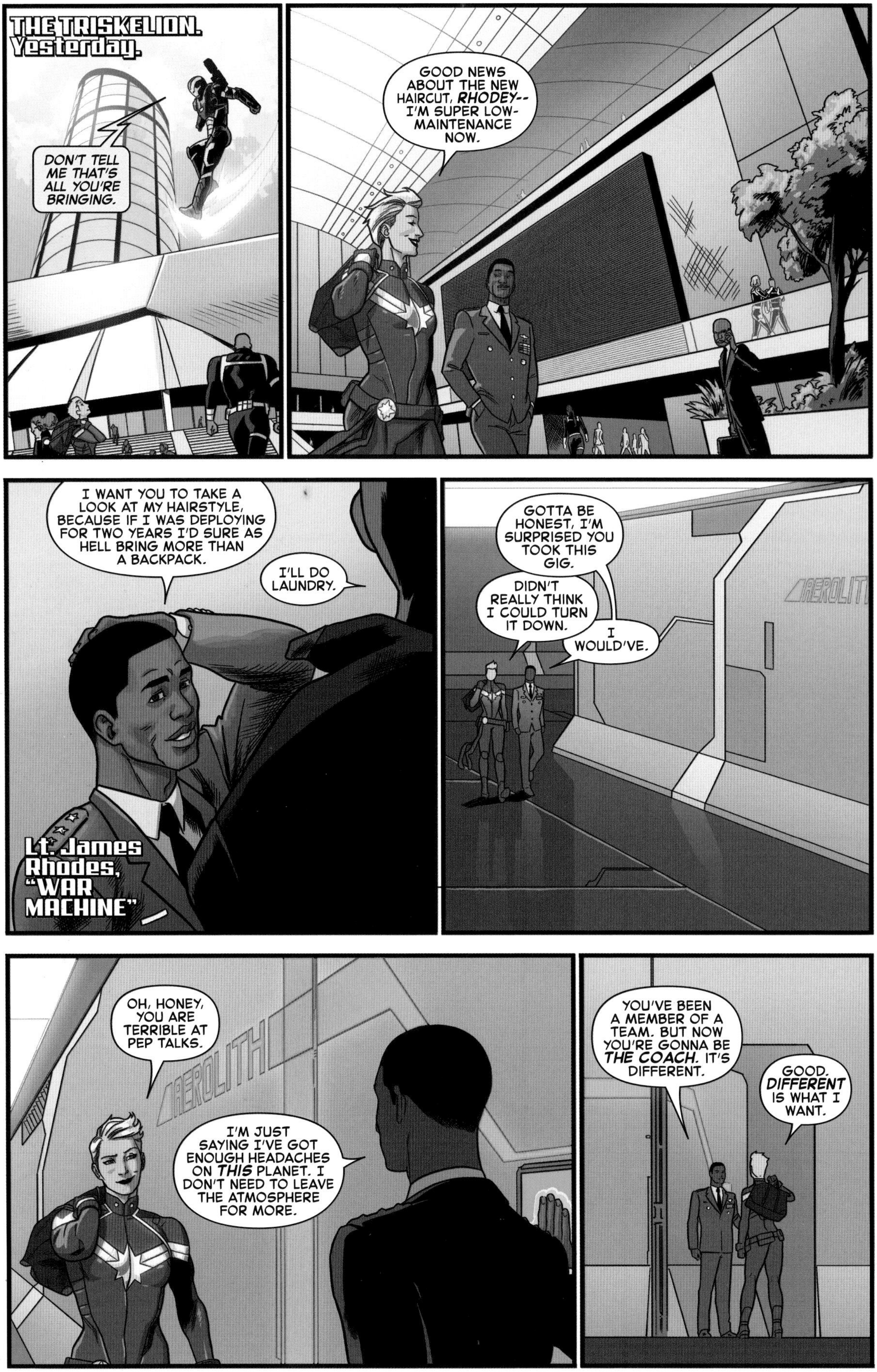
THE TRISKELION. Yesterday.
DON'T TELL ME THAT'S ALL YOU'RE BRINGING.
GOOD NEWS ABOUT THE NEW HAIRCUT, RHODEY-- I'M SUPER LOW-MAINTENANCE NOW.
I WANT YOU TO TAKE A LOOK AT MY HAIRSTYLE, BECAUSE IF I WAS DEPLOYING FOR TWO YEARS I'D SURE AS HELL BRING MORE THAN A BACKPACK.
I'LL DO LAUNDRY.
Lt. James Rhodes, "WAR MACHINE"
GOTTA BE HONEST, I'M SURPRISED YOU TOOK THIS GIG.
DIDN'T REALLY THINK I COULD TURN IT DOWN.
I WOULD'VE.
AEROLITH
OH, HONEY, YOU ARE TERRIBLE AT PEP TALKS.
AEROLITH
I'M JUST SAYING I'VE GOT ENOUGH HEADACHES ON THIS PLANET. I DON'T NEED TO LEAVE THE ATMOSPHERE FOR MORE.
YOU'VE BEEN A MEMBER OF A TEAM. BUT NOW YOU'RE GONNA BE THE COACH. IT'S DIFFERENT.
GOOD. DIFFERENT IS WHAT I WANT.

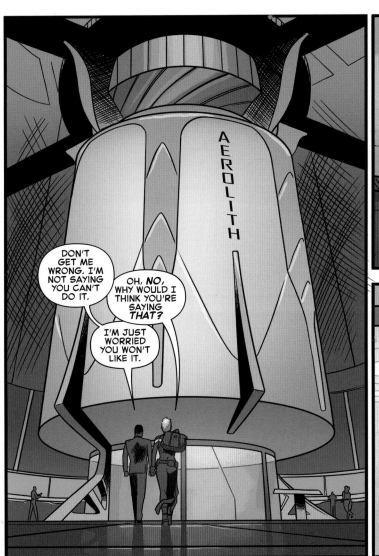

DON'T GET ME WRONG. I'M NOT SAYING YOU CAN'T DO IT.

OH, *NO*, WHY WOULD I THINK YOU'RE SAYING *THAT?*

I'M JUST WORRIED YOU WON'T LIKE IT.

AEROLITH

DOES THAT MATTER?

DOES BEING *HAPPY* MATTER? YEAH, LITTLE BIT.

MY ADVICE TO YOU IS THIS-- IN THE FIELD YOU GOTTA MAKE FAST DECISIONS. SNAP JUDGMENTS. GIG LIKE THIS...THAT DOESN'T ALWAYS SERVE.

SHRSHHH

THINK BEFORE I SWING?

SOMETHING LIKE THAT.

YOU KNOW, YOU DON'T HAVE TO EXILE YOURSELF. YOU'RE THE ONLY ONE WHO CAN FLY BACK DOWN ANY TIME YOU WANT.

IT'S NOT EXILE. IT'S COMMITMENT. YOU CAN ALWAYS COME UP AND VISIT.

I JUST MIGHT DO THAT.

GOING *UP?*

DING!

SHRAMM

HE'S WORRIED I WON'T LIKE IT.

AW, RHODEY LOVES ME.

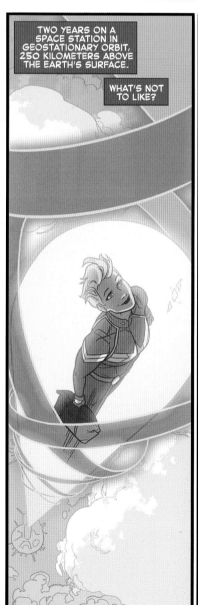

TWO YEARS ON A SPACE STATION IN GEOSTATIONARY ORBIT, 250 KILOMETERS ABOVE THE EARTH'S SURFACE.

WHAT'S NOT TO LIKE?

IT SOUNDS CRAZY. BUT I'M NOT LYING WHEN I SAY I DIDN'T FEEL LIKE I COULD TURN IT DOWN.

EARTH'S FIRST LINE OF DEFENSE, THEY'RE CALLING IT.

I LIKE BEING ON A TEAM. BUT MORE THAN THAT, I LIKE A MISSION. A PURPOSE.

AND THE BEST WAY TO FIGHT THREATS AGAINST THE GALAXY...

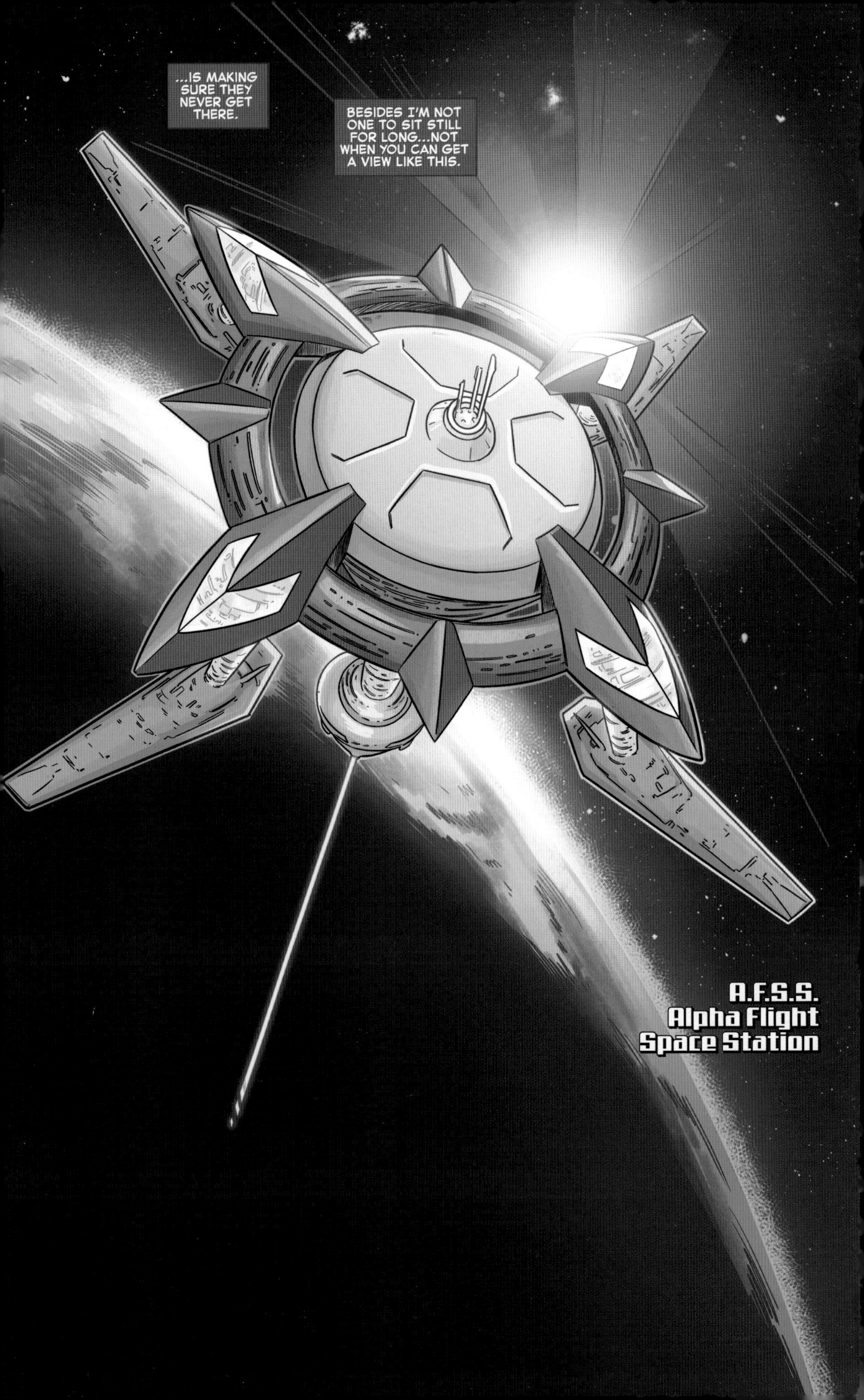
...IS MAKING SURE THEY NEVER GET THERE.
BESIDES I'M NOT ONE TO SIT STILL FOR LONG...NOT WHEN YOU CAN GET A VIEW LIKE THIS.
A.F.S.S. Alpha Flight Space Station

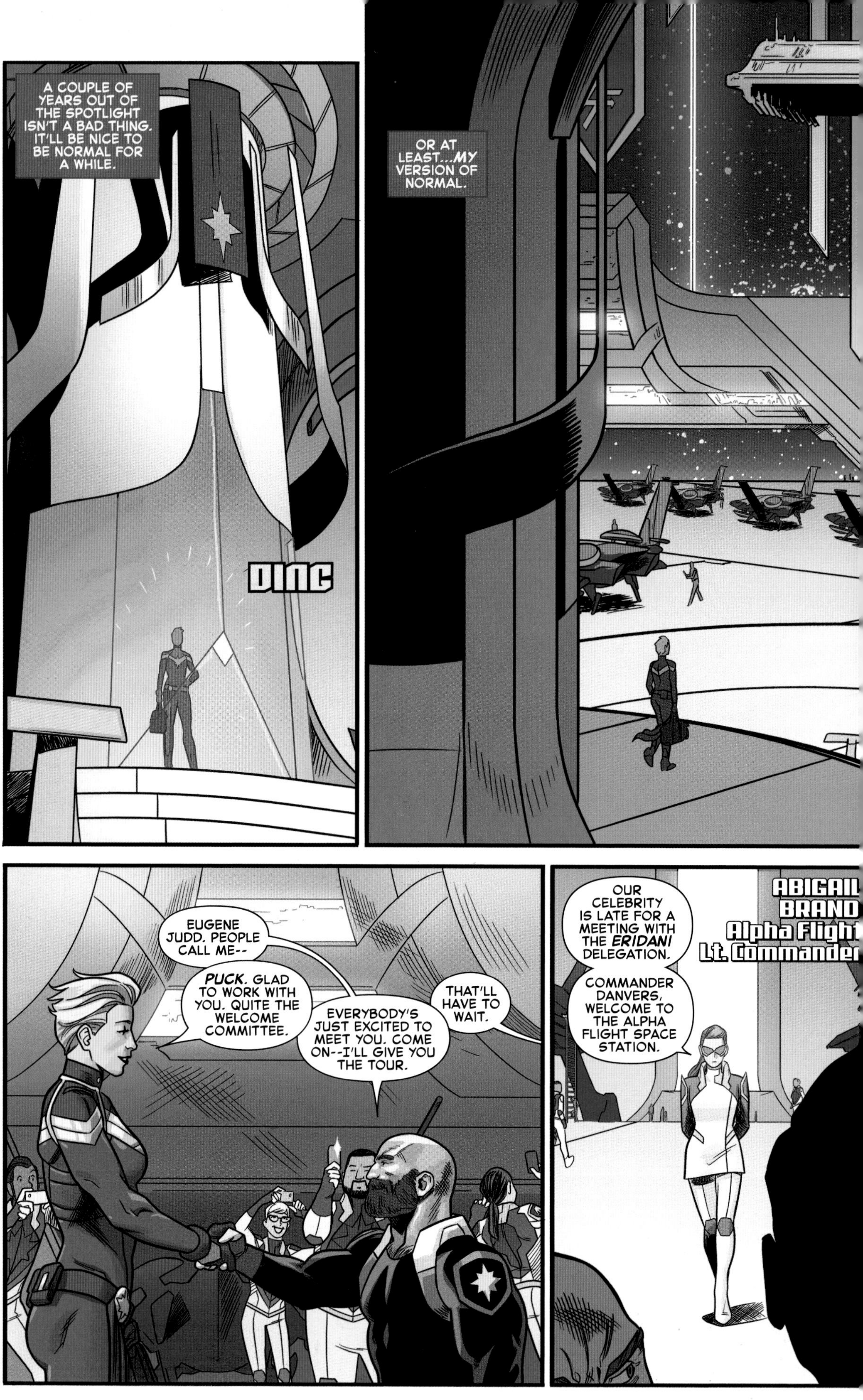
A COUPLE OF YEARS OUT OF THE SPOTLIGHT ISN'T A BAD THING. IT'LL BE NICE TO BE NORMAL FOR A WHILE.
DING
OR AT LEAST...MY VERSION OF NORMAL.
EUGENE JUDD. PEOPLE CALL ME--
PUCK. GLAD TO WORK WITH YOU. QUITE THE WELCOME COMMITTEE.
EVERYBODY'S JUST EXCITED TO MEET YOU. COME ON--I'LL GIVE YOU THE TOUR.
THAT'LL HAVE TO WAIT.
ABIGAIL BRAND Alpha Flight Lt. Commander
OUR CELEBRITY IS LATE FOR A MEETING WITH THE ERIDANI DELEGATION.
COMMANDER DANVERS, WELCOME TO THE ALPHA FLIGHT SPACE STATION.

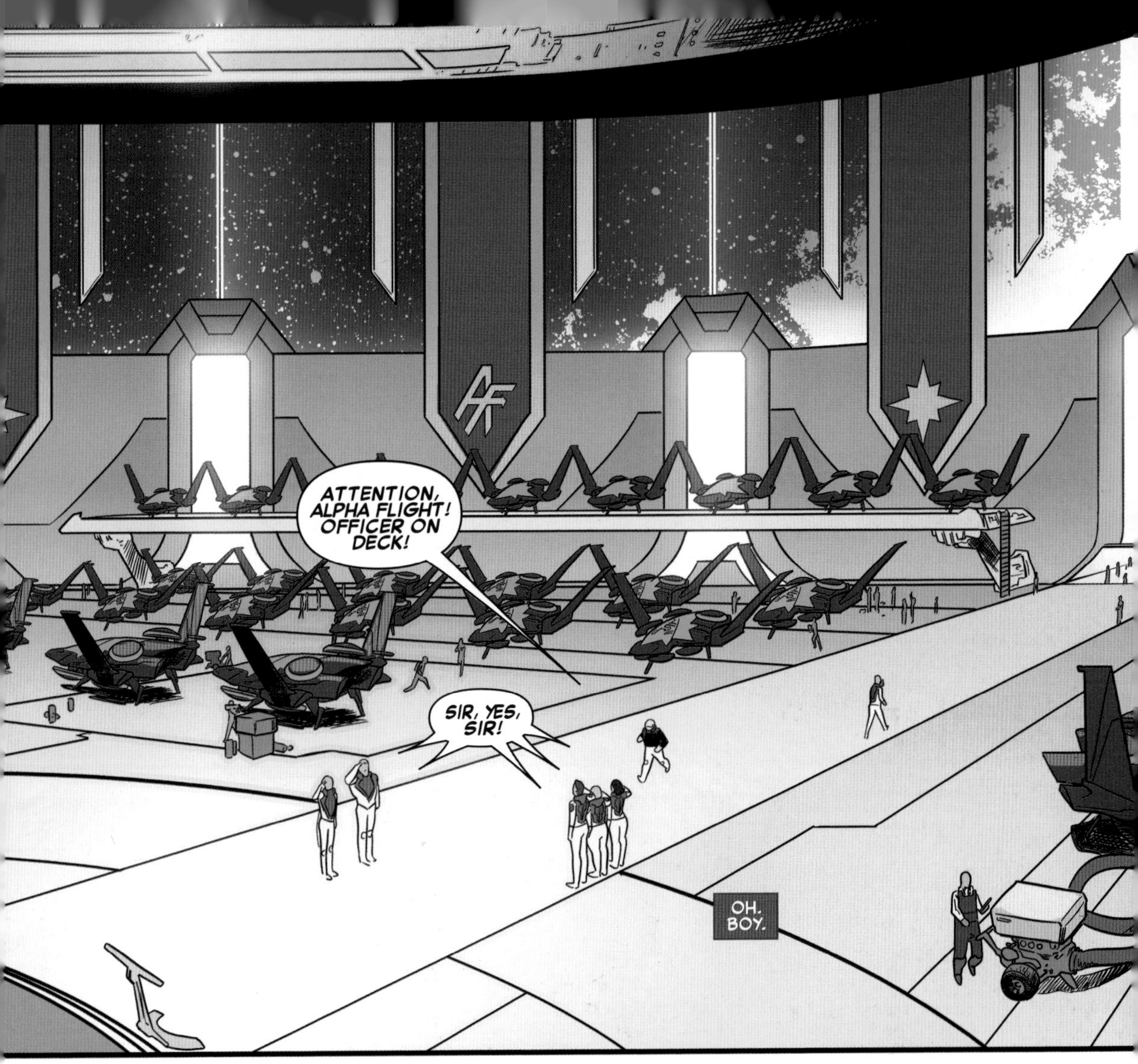
ATTENTION, ALPHA FLIGHT! OFFICER ON DECK!
SIR, YES, SIR!
OH. BOY.

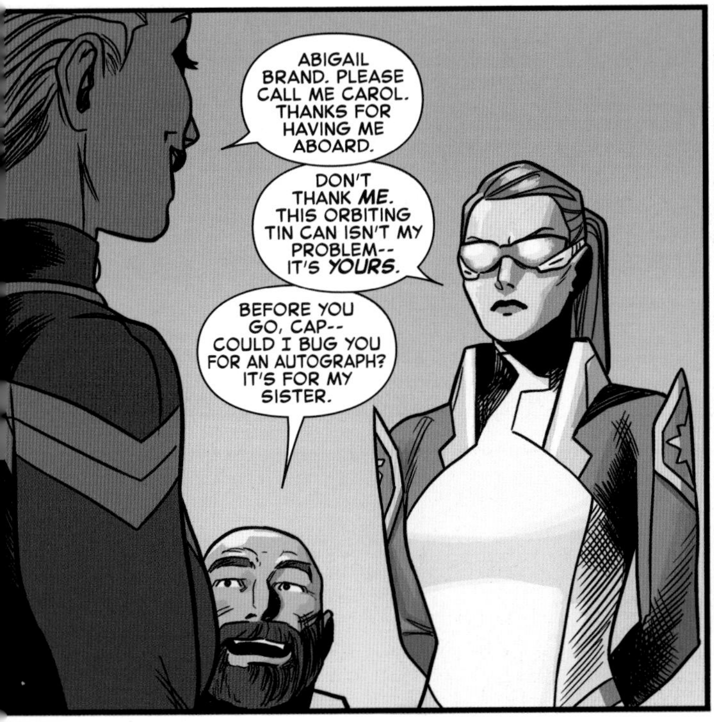
ABIGAIL BRAND. PLEASE CALL ME CAROL. THANKS FOR HAVING ME ABOARD.
DON'T THANK *ME*. THIS ORBITING TIN CAN ISN'T MY PROBLEM-- IT'S *YOURS*.
BEFORE YOU GO, CAP-- COULD I BUG YOU FOR AN AUTOGRAPH? IT'S FOR MY SISTER.

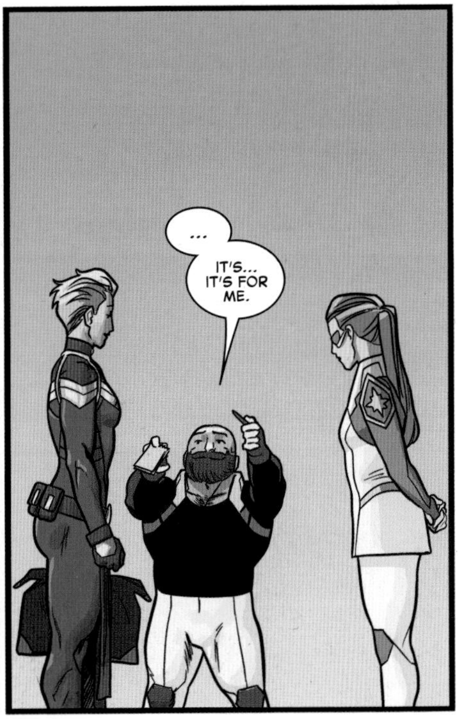
...
IT'S... IT'S FOR ME.

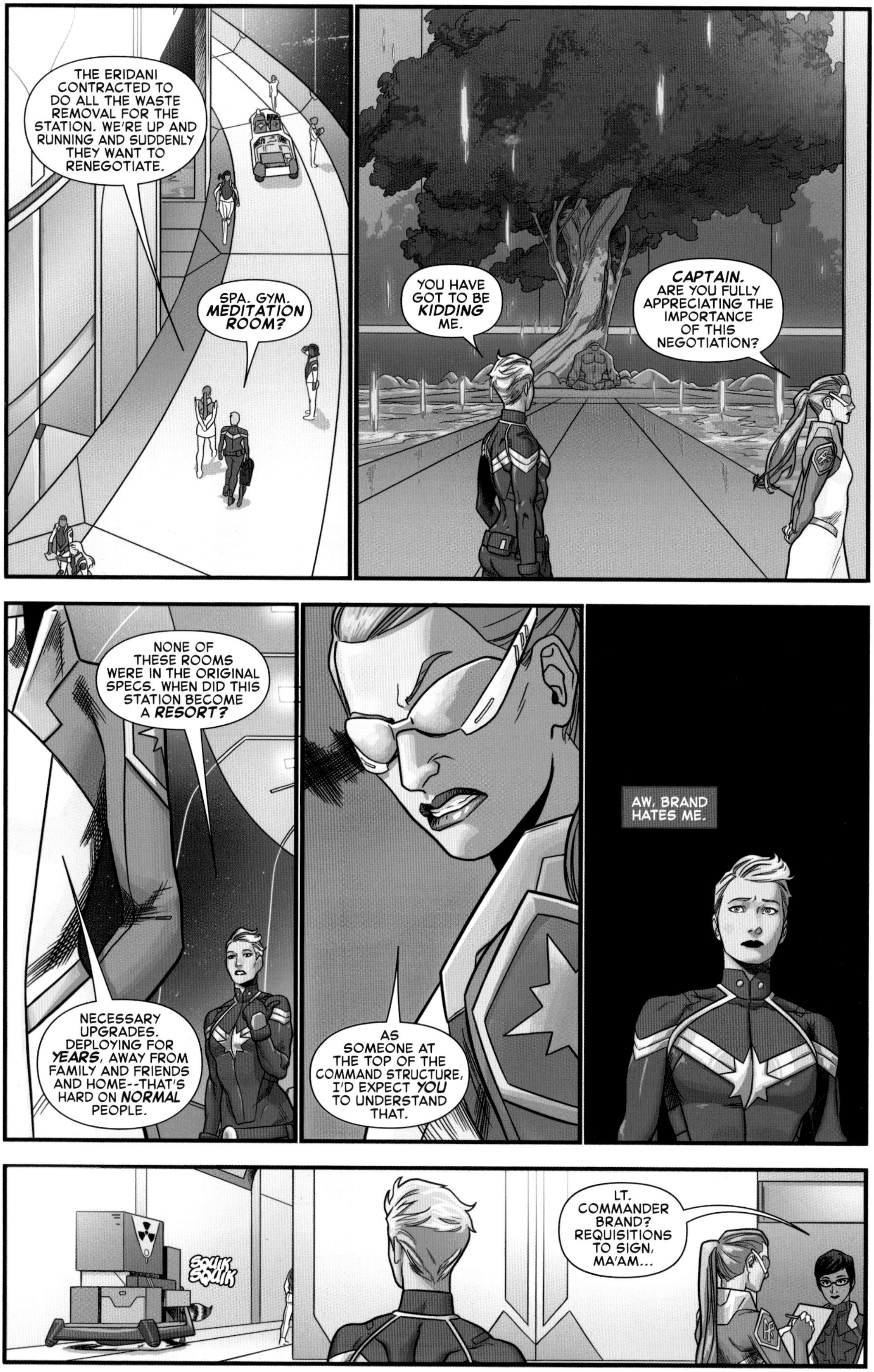
THE ERIDANI CONTRACTED TO DO ALL THE WASTE REMOVAL FOR THE STATION. WE'RE UP AND RUNNING AND SUDDENLY THEY WANT TO RENEGOTIATE.
SPA. GYM. MEDITATION ROOM?
YOU HAVE GOT TO BE KIDDING ME.
CAPTAIN. ARE YOU FULLY APPRECIATING THE IMPORTANCE OF THIS NEGOTIATION?
NONE OF THESE ROOMS WERE IN THE ORIGINAL SPECS. WHEN DID THIS STATION BECOME A RESORT?
NECESSARY UPGRADES. DEPLOYING FOR YEARS, AWAY FROM FAMILY AND FRIENDS AND HOME--THAT'S HARD ON NORMAL PEOPLE.
AS SOMEONE AT THE TOP OF THE COMMAND STRUCTURE, I'D EXPECT YOU TO UNDERSTAND THAT.
AW, BRAND HATES ME.
SQUIK SQUIK
LT. COMMANDER BRAND? REQUISITIONS TO SIGN, MA'AM...

DANVERS! WHAT'S SHAKIN'?

FIRST DAY ON THE JOB.

AH. SORRY. HATE FIRST DAYS. LITTLE HELP?

GUARDIANS AND ME ARE ON A PITSTOP BEFORE WE DEPLOY. JUST NEEDED SOME SUPPLIES.

SO YOU'RE STEALING A BUNCH OF STUFF.

NO. NO--WELL, YEAH.

YOU KNOW I LIKE YOU, ROCKET, BUT AS COMMANDER OF THIS STATION, I FEEL LIKE I CAN'T LET YOU *STEAL* A NUKE.

COMMANDER? OF THE WHOLE SHEBANG? NO KIDDING. WEIRD.

WHAT'S SO WEIRD?

JUST SURPRISED IS ALL. CAPTAIN MARVEL TAKES A DESK JOB. AREN'T YOU GONNA BE BORED?

IT'S NOT A DESK JOB.

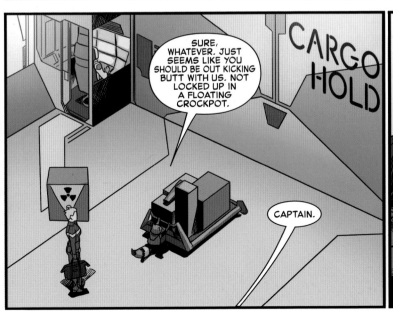

SURE, WHATEVER. JUST SEEMS LIKE YOU SHOULD BE OUT KICKING BUTT WITH US. NOT LOCKED UP IN A FLOATING CROCKPOT.

CARGO HOLD

CAPTAIN.

THE DELEGATION IS WAITING IN THE CONFERENCE ROOM.

...

DESK JOB.

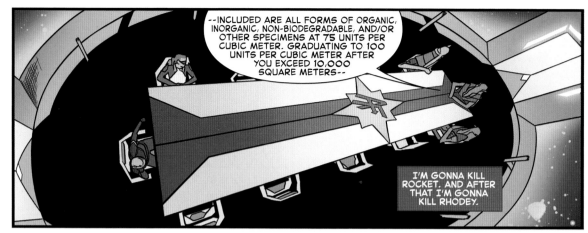

--INCLUDED ARE ALL FORMS OF ORGANIC, INORGANIC, NON-BIODEGRADABLE, AND/OR OTHER SPECIMENS AT 75 UNITS PER CUBIC METER. GRADUATING TO 100 UNITS PER CUBIC METER AFTER YOU EXCEED 10,000 SQUARE METERS--

I'M GONNA KILL ROCKET. AND AFTER THAT I'M GONNA KILL RHODEY.

--IN THE EVENT THAT RADIATION LEVELS OF INDUSTRIAL WASTE EXCEED 50 MICROSIEVERTS--

THE GREAT CAPTAIN MARVEL, TALKING ABOUT GARBAGE.

ARE WE BORING YOU, CAPTAIN MARVEL?

OR WOULD YOU PREFER THE ALPHA FLIGHT SPACE STATION BE AS POLLUTED AS THAT PLANET YOU CALL HOME?

EXCUSE ME?

THE CAPTAIN'S ONLY JUST ARRIVED AND IS ACCLIMATING TO HER NEW POSITION. PLEASE DON'T BE OFFENDED BY HER BEHAVIOR.

YOU KNOW WHAT'S OFFENSIVE? GETTING GOUGED ON SERVICES THAT HAD BEEN PRE-NEGOTIATED A YEAR AGO. NICE TO SEE THE TRASH BUSINESS IN SPACE IS MOBBED UP, TOO--

DANVERS!

HOW DARE YOU SUGGEST--

SEE? I WAS LISTENING.

COMMANDER. SENSORS HAVE DETECTED A MASSIVE ASTEROID COLLISION--DEBRIS WILL BE IN RANGE IN LESS THAN TWENTY MINUTES.

ENSIGN, YOUR TIMING IS IMPECCABLE.

CAPTAIN, THE ALPHA FLIGHT CAN HANDLE IT, YOU ARE NEEDED HERE--

YOU CAN HANDLE THIS, BRAND. BESIDES HE LIKES YOU BETTER.

ALPHA FLIGHT... ASSEMBLE.

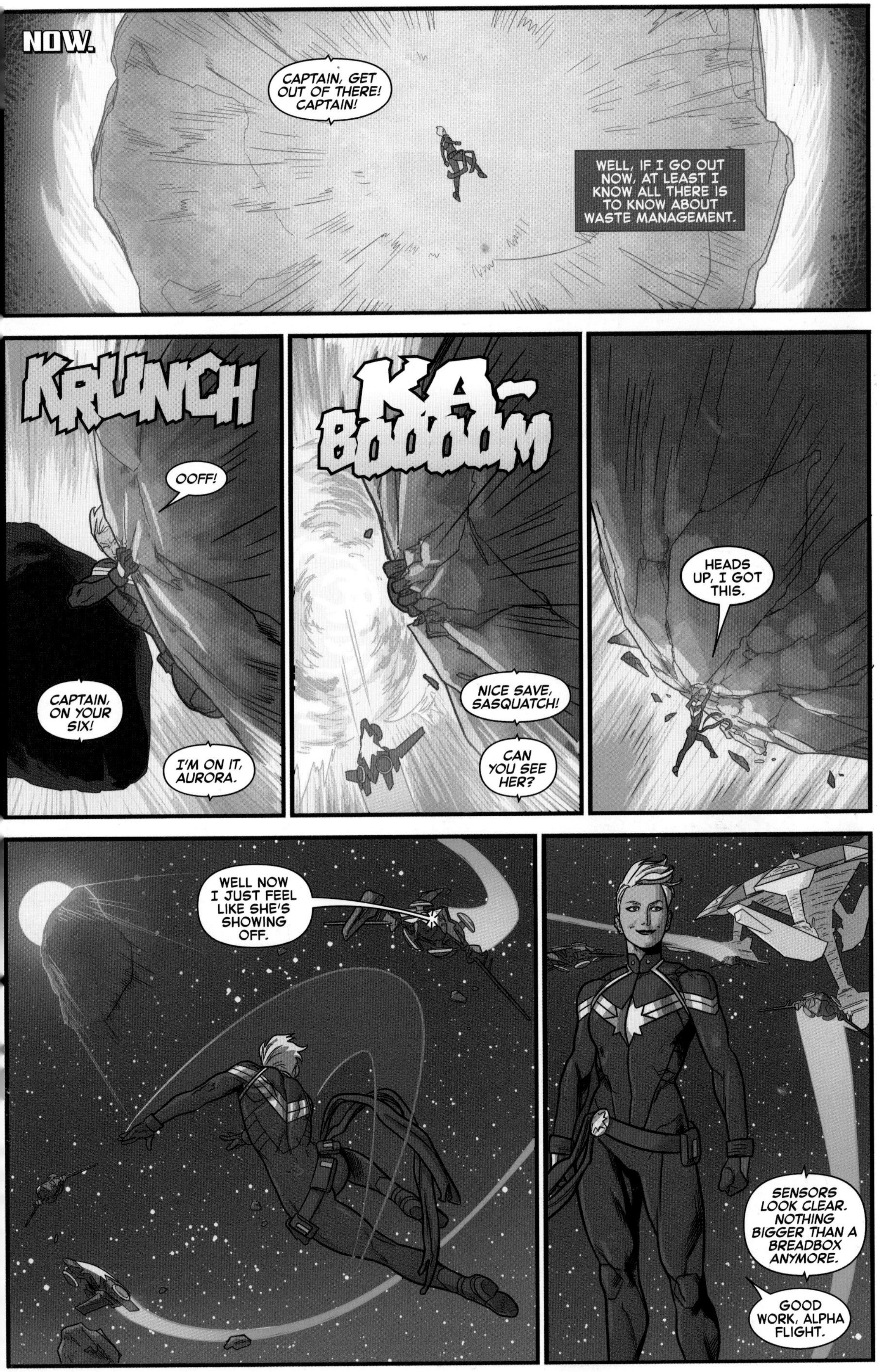
NOW.
CAPTAIN, GET OUT OF THERE! CAPTAIN!
WELL, IF I GO OUT NOW, AT LEAST I KNOW ALL THERE IS TO KNOW ABOUT WASTE MANAGEMENT.
KRUNCH
OOFF!
CAPTAIN, ON YOUR SIX!
I'M ON IT, AURORA.
KA-BOOOOOM
NICE SAVE, SASQUATCH!
CAN YOU SEE HER?
HEADS UP, I GOT THIS.
WELL NOW I JUST FEEL LIKE SHE'S SHOWING OFF.
SENSORS LOOK CLEAR. NOTHING BIGGER THAN A BREADBOX ANYMORE.
GOOD WORK, ALPHA FLIGHT.

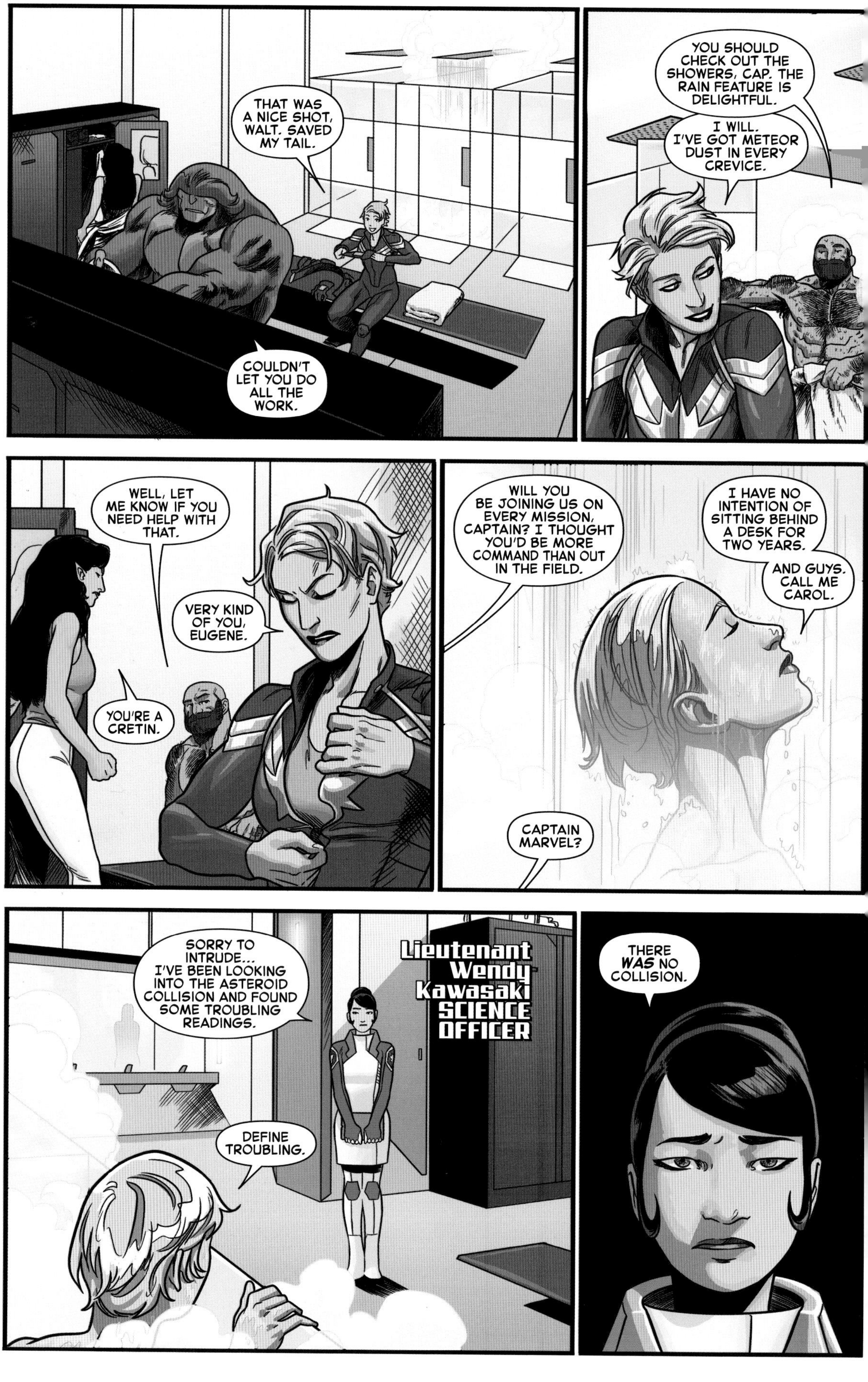
THAT WAS A NICE SHOT, WALT. SAVED MY TAIL.
COULDN'T LET YOU DO ALL THE WORK.
YOU SHOULD CHECK OUT THE SHOWERS, CAP. THE RAIN FEATURE IS DELIGHTFUL.
I WILL. I'VE GOT METEOR DUST IN EVERY CREVICE.
WELL, LET ME KNOW IF YOU NEED HELP WITH THAT.
VERY KIND OF YOU, EUGENE.
YOU'RE A CRETIN.
WILL YOU BE JOINING US ON EVERY MISSION, CAPTAIN? I THOUGHT YOU'D BE MORE COMMAND THAN OUT IN THE FIELD.
I HAVE NO INTENTION OF SITTING BEHIND A DESK FOR TWO YEARS.
AND GUYS. CALL ME CAROL.
CAPTAIN MARVEL?
SORRY TO INTRUDE... I'VE BEEN LOOKING INTO THE ASTEROID COLLISION AND FOUND SOME TROUBLING READINGS.
Lieutenant Wendy Kawasaki SCIENCE OFFICER
DEFINE TROUBLING.
THERE *WAS* NO COLLISION.

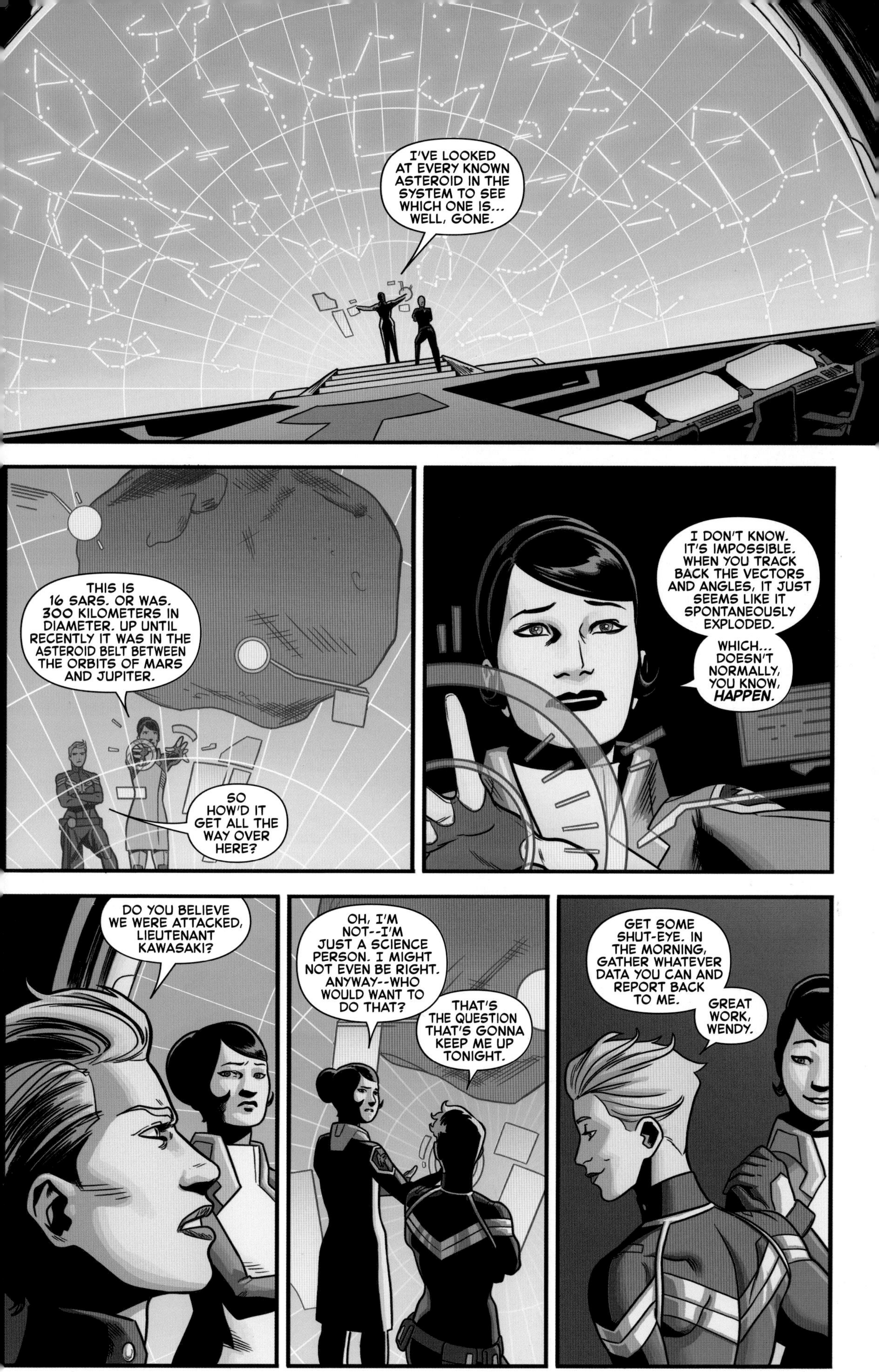
I'VE LOOKED AT EVERY KNOWN ASTEROID IN THE SYSTEM TO SEE WHICH ONE IS... WELL, GONE.
THIS IS 16 SARS. OR WAS. 300 KILOMETERS IN DIAMETER. UP UNTIL RECENTLY IT WAS IN THE ASTEROID BELT BETWEEN THE ORBITS OF MARS AND JUPITER.
SO HOW'D IT GET ALL THE WAY OVER HERE?
I DON'T KNOW. IT'S IMPOSSIBLE. WHEN YOU TRACK BACK THE VECTORS AND ANGLES, IT JUST SEEMS LIKE IT SPONTANEOUSLY EXPLODED.
WHICH... DOESN'T NORMALLY, YOU KNOW, ***HAPPEN***.
DO YOU BELIEVE WE WERE ATTACKED, LIEUTENANT KAWASAKI?
OH, I'M NOT--I'M JUST A SCIENCE PERSON. I MIGHT NOT EVEN BE RIGHT. ANYWAY--WHO WOULD WANT TO DO THAT?
THAT'S THE QUESTION THAT'S GONNA KEEP ME UP TONIGHT.
GET SOME SHUT-EYE. IN THE MORNING, GATHER WHATEVER DATA YOU CAN AND REPORT BACK TO ME.
GREAT WORK, WENDY.

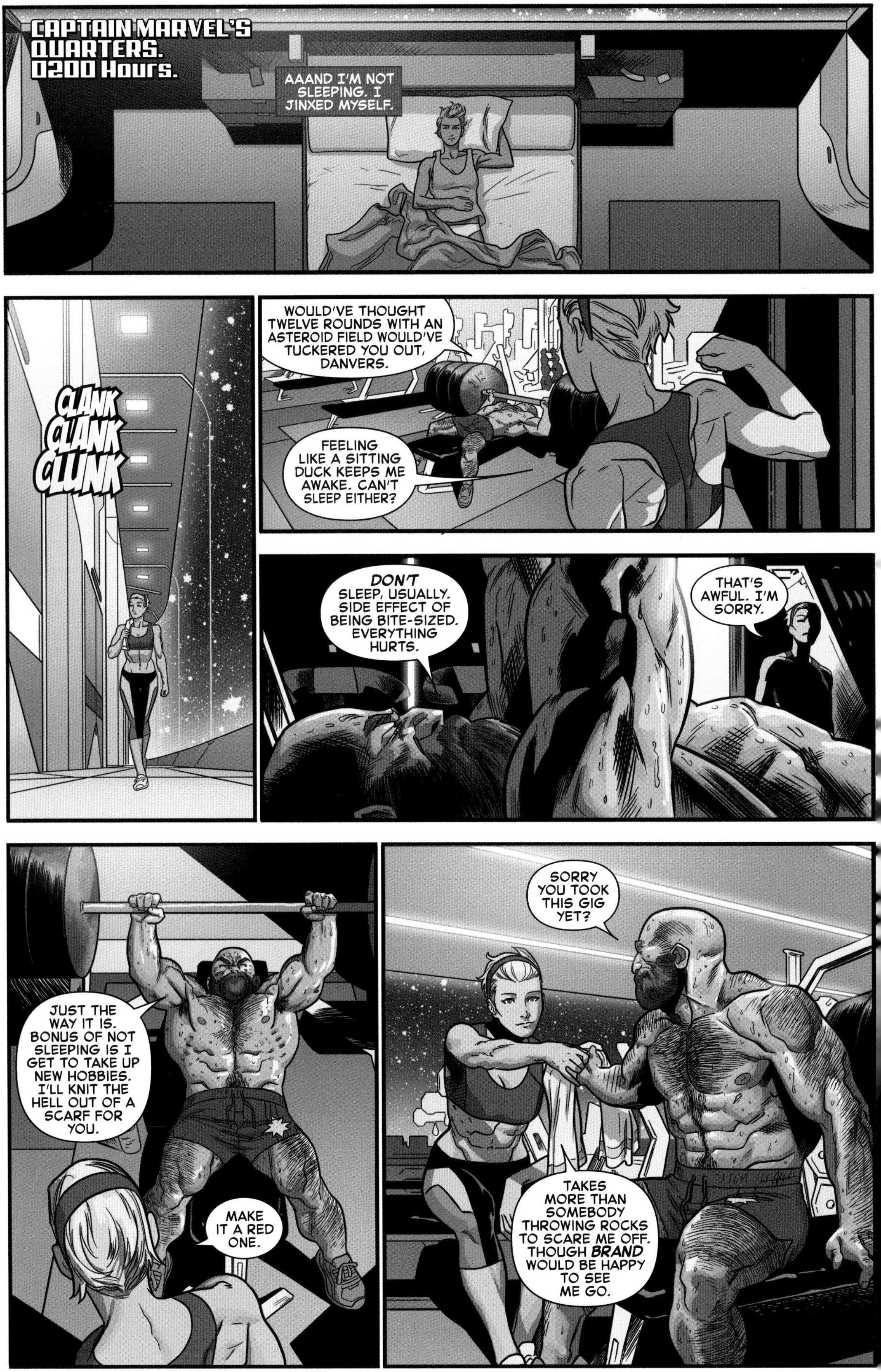
CAPTAIN MARVEL'S QUARTERS. 0200 Hours.
AAAND I'M NOT SLEEPING. I JINXED MYSELF.
CLANK CLANK CLUNK
WOULD'VE THOUGHT TWELVE ROUNDS WITH AN ASTEROID FIELD WOULD'VE TUCKERED YOU OUT, DANVERS.
FEELING LIKE A SITTING DUCK KEEPS ME AWAKE. CAN'T SLEEP EITHER?
DON'T SLEEP, USUALLY. SIDE EFFECT OF BEING BITE-SIZED. EVERYTHING HURTS.
THAT'S AWFUL. I'M SORRY.
JUST THE WAY IT IS. BONUS OF NOT SLEEPING IS I GET TO TAKE UP NEW HOBBIES. I'LL KNIT THE HELL OUT OF A SCARF FOR YOU.
MAKE IT A RED ONE.
SORRY YOU TOOK THIS GIG YET?
TAKES MORE THAN SOMEBODY THROWING ROCKS TO SCARE ME OFF. THOUGH BRAND WOULD BE HAPPY TO SEE ME GO.

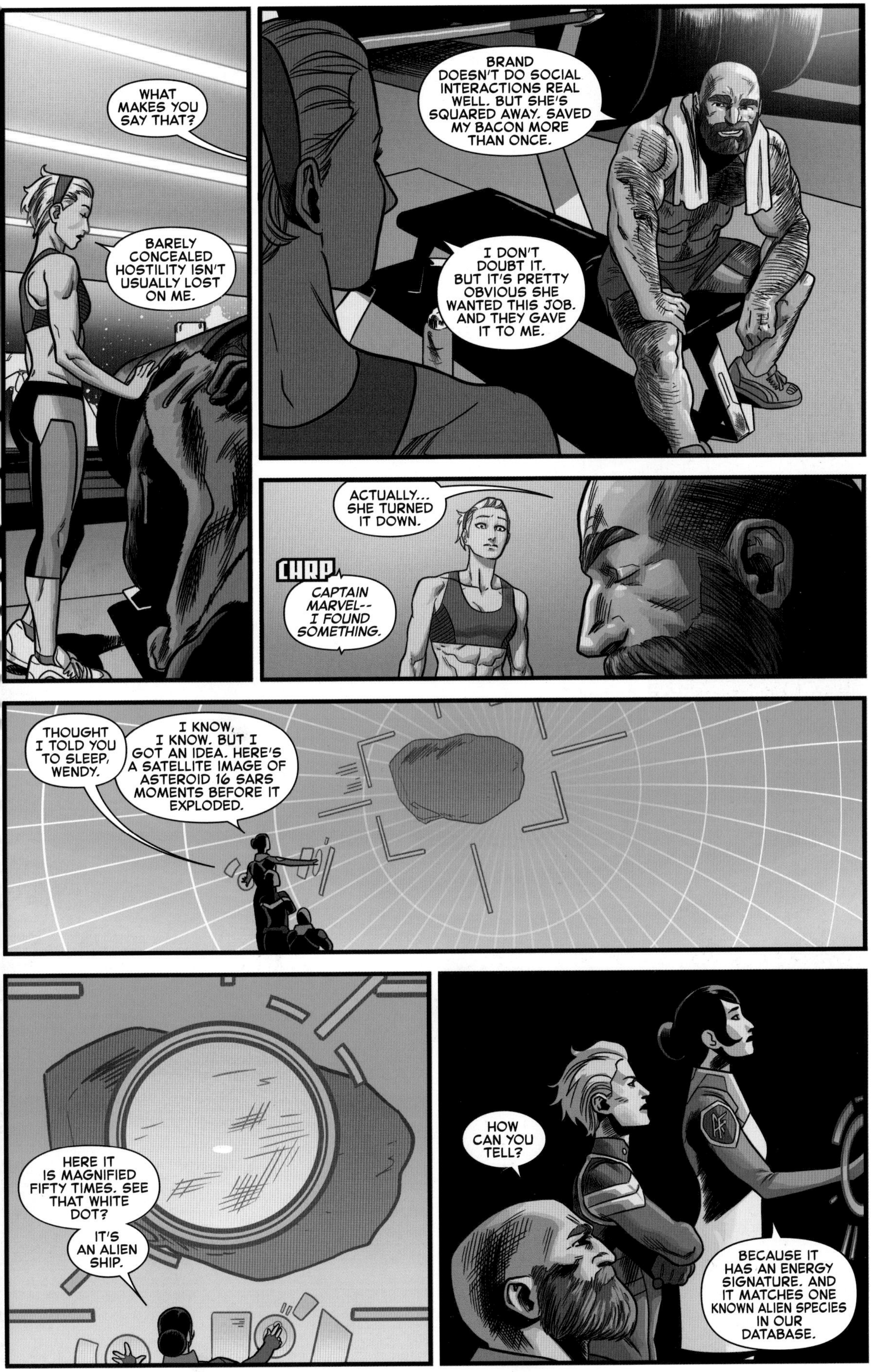
WHAT MAKES YOU SAY THAT?
BARELY CONCEALED HOSTILITY ISN'T USUALLY LOST ON ME.
BRAND DOESN'T DO SOCIAL INTERACTIONS REAL WELL. BUT SHE'S SQUARED AWAY. SAVED MY BACON MORE THAN ONCE.
I DON'T DOUBT IT. BUT IT'S PRETTY OBVIOUS SHE WANTED THIS JOB. AND THEY GAVE IT TO ME.
ACTUALLY... SHE TURNED IT DOWN.
CHRP
CAPTAIN MARVEL-- I FOUND SOMETHING.
THOUGHT I TOLD YOU TO SLEEP, WENDY.
I KNOW, I KNOW. BUT I GOT AN IDEA. HERE'S A SATELLITE IMAGE OF ASTEROID 16 SARS MOMENTS BEFORE IT EXPLODED.
HERE IT IS MAGNIFIED FIFTY TIMES. SEE THAT WHITE DOT?
IT'S AN ALIEN SHIP.
HOW CAN YOU TELL?
BECAUSE IT HAS AN ENERGY SIGNATURE. AND IT MATCHES ONE KNOWN ALIEN SPECIES IN OUR DATABASE.

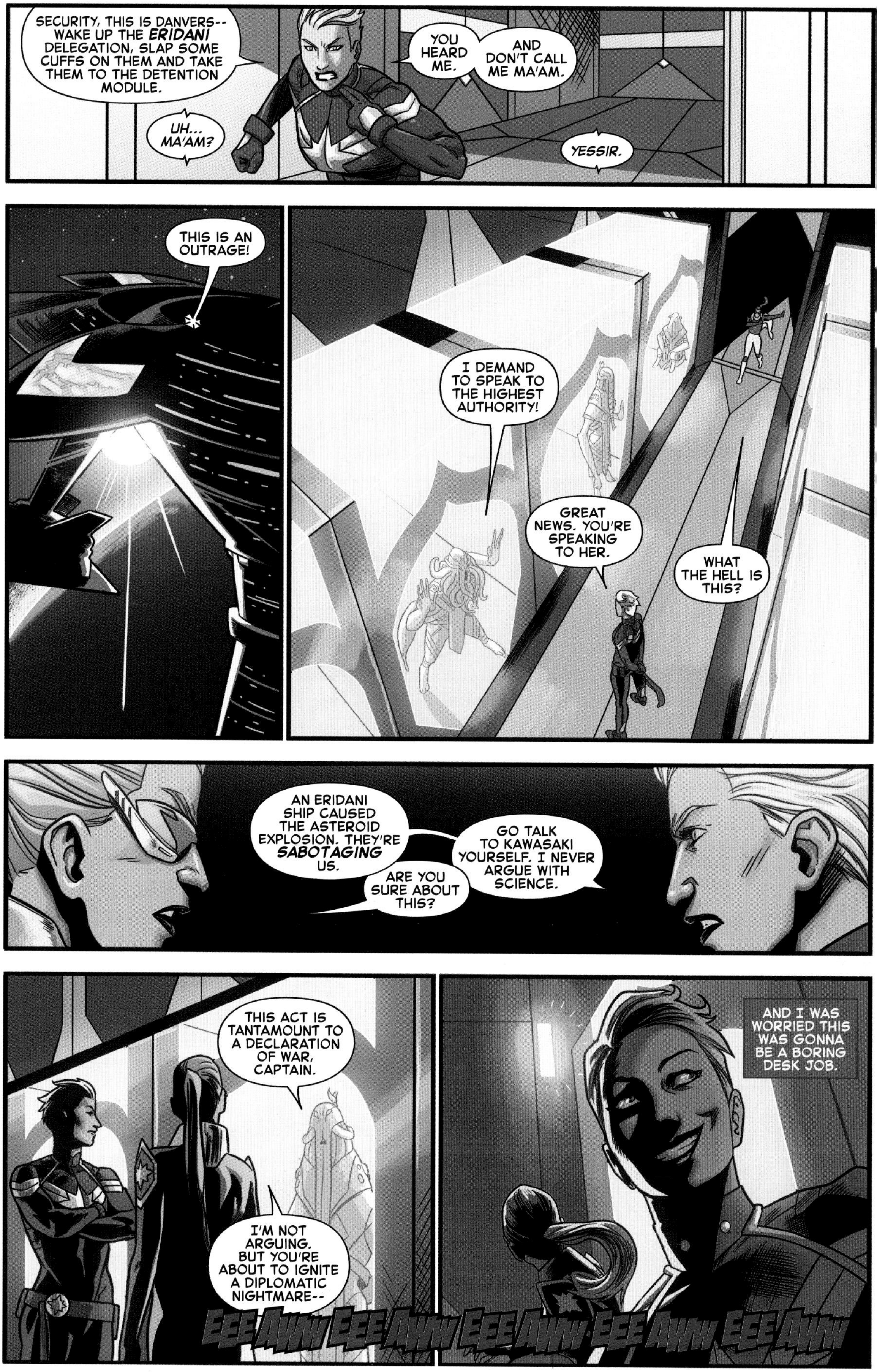
SECURITY, THIS IS DANVERS-- WAKE UP THE *ERIDANI* DELEGATION, SLAP SOME CUFFS ON THEM AND TAKE THEM TO THE DETENTION MODULE.
UH... MA'AM?
YOU HEARD ME.
AND DON'T CALL ME MA'AM.
YESSIR.
THIS IS AN OUTRAGE!
I DEMAND TO SPEAK TO THE HIGHEST AUTHORITY!
GREAT NEWS. YOU'RE SPEAKING TO HER.
WHAT THE HELL IS THIS?
AN ERIDANI SHIP CAUSED THE ASTEROID EXPLOSION. THEY'RE *SABOTAGING* US.
ARE YOU SURE ABOUT THIS?
GO TALK TO KAWASAKI YOURSELF. I NEVER ARGUE WITH SCIENCE.
THIS ACT IS TANTAMOUNT TO A DECLARATION OF WAR, CAPTAIN.
I'M NOT ARGUING. BUT YOU'RE ABOUT TO IGNITE A DIPLOMATIC NIGHTMARE--
EEE AWW EEE AWW EEE AWW EEE AWW EEE AWW
AND I WAS WORRIED THIS WAS GONNA BE A BORING DESK JOB.

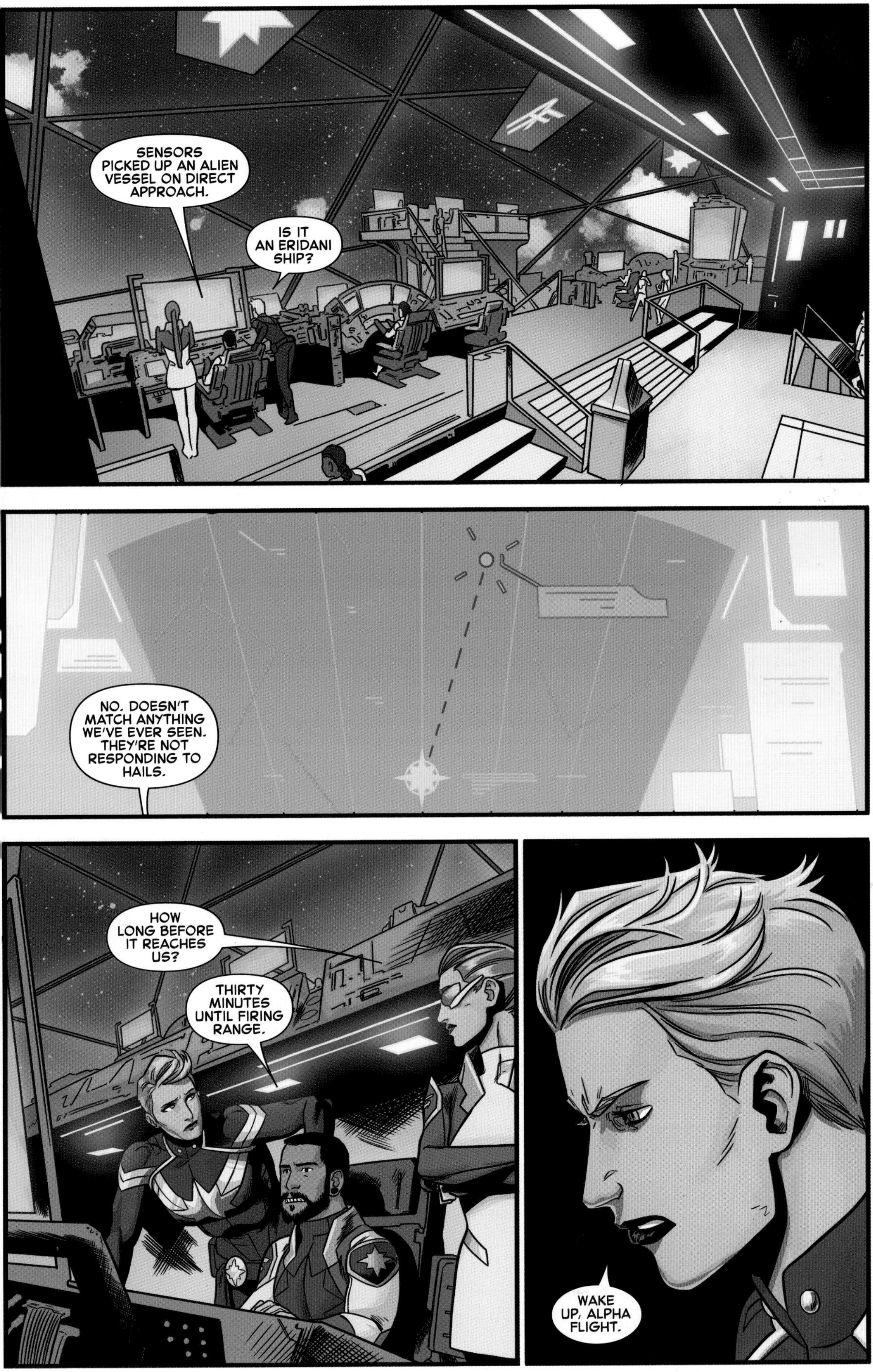
SENSORS PICKED UP AN ALIEN VESSEL ON DIRECT APPROACH.
IS IT AN ERIDANI SHIP?
NO. DOESN'T MATCH ANYTHING WE'VE EVER SEEN. THEY'RE NOT RESPONDING TO HAILS.
HOW LONG BEFORE IT REACHES US?
THIRTY MINUTES UNTIL FIRING RANGE.
WAKE UP, ALPHA FLIGHT.

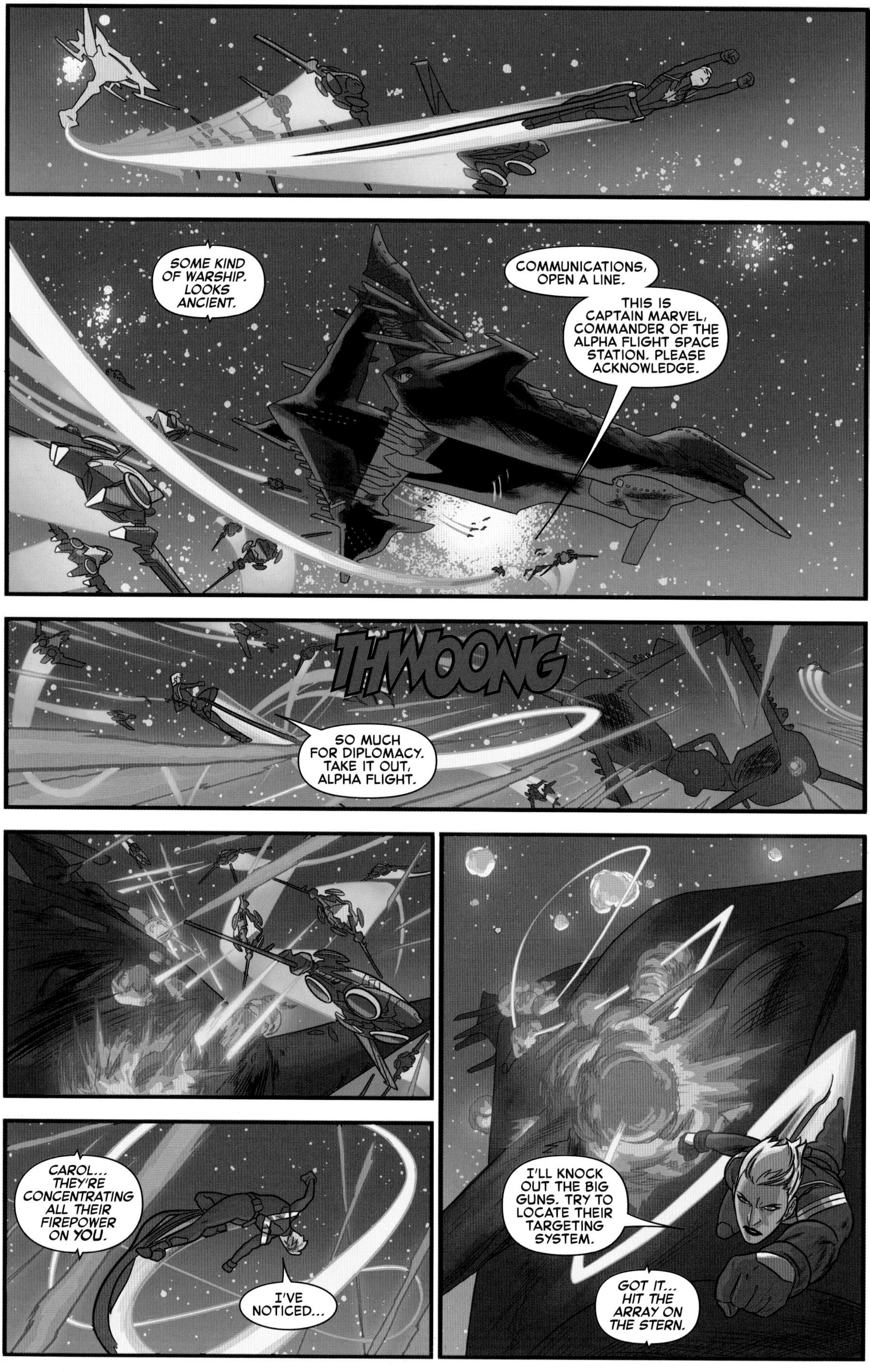
SOME KIND OF WARSHIP. LOOKS ANCIENT.
COMMUNICATIONS, OPEN A LINE.
THIS IS CAPTAIN MARVEL, COMMANDER OF THE ALPHA FLIGHT SPACE STATION. PLEASE ACKNOWLEDGE.
THWOONG
SO MUCH FOR DIPLOMACY. TAKE IT OUT, ALPHA FLIGHT.
CAROL... THEY'RE CONCENTRATING ALL THEIR FIREPOWER ON YOU.
I'VE NOTICED...
I'LL KNOCK OUT THE BIG GUNS. TRY TO LOCATE THEIR TARGETING SYSTEM.
GOT IT... HIT THE ARRAY ON THE STERN.

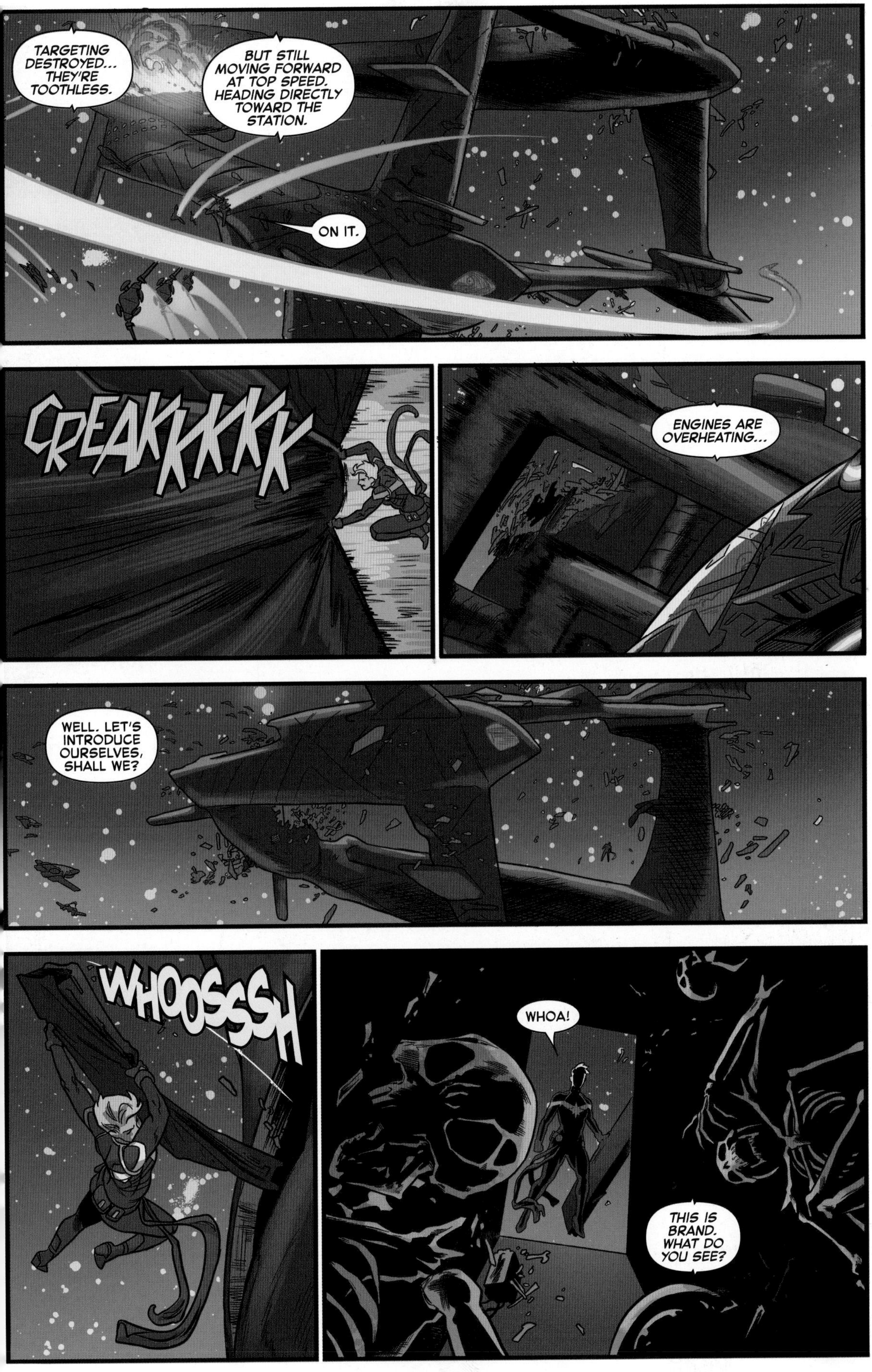
TARGETING DESTROYED... THEY'RE TOOTHLESS.
BUT STILL MOVING FORWARD AT TOP SPEED. HEADING DIRECTLY TOWARD THE STATION.
ON IT.
CREAKKKKK
ENGINES ARE OVERHEATING...
WELL. LET'S INTRODUCE OURSELVES, SHALL WE?
WHOOSSSH
WHOA!
THIS IS BRAND. WHAT DO YOU SEE?

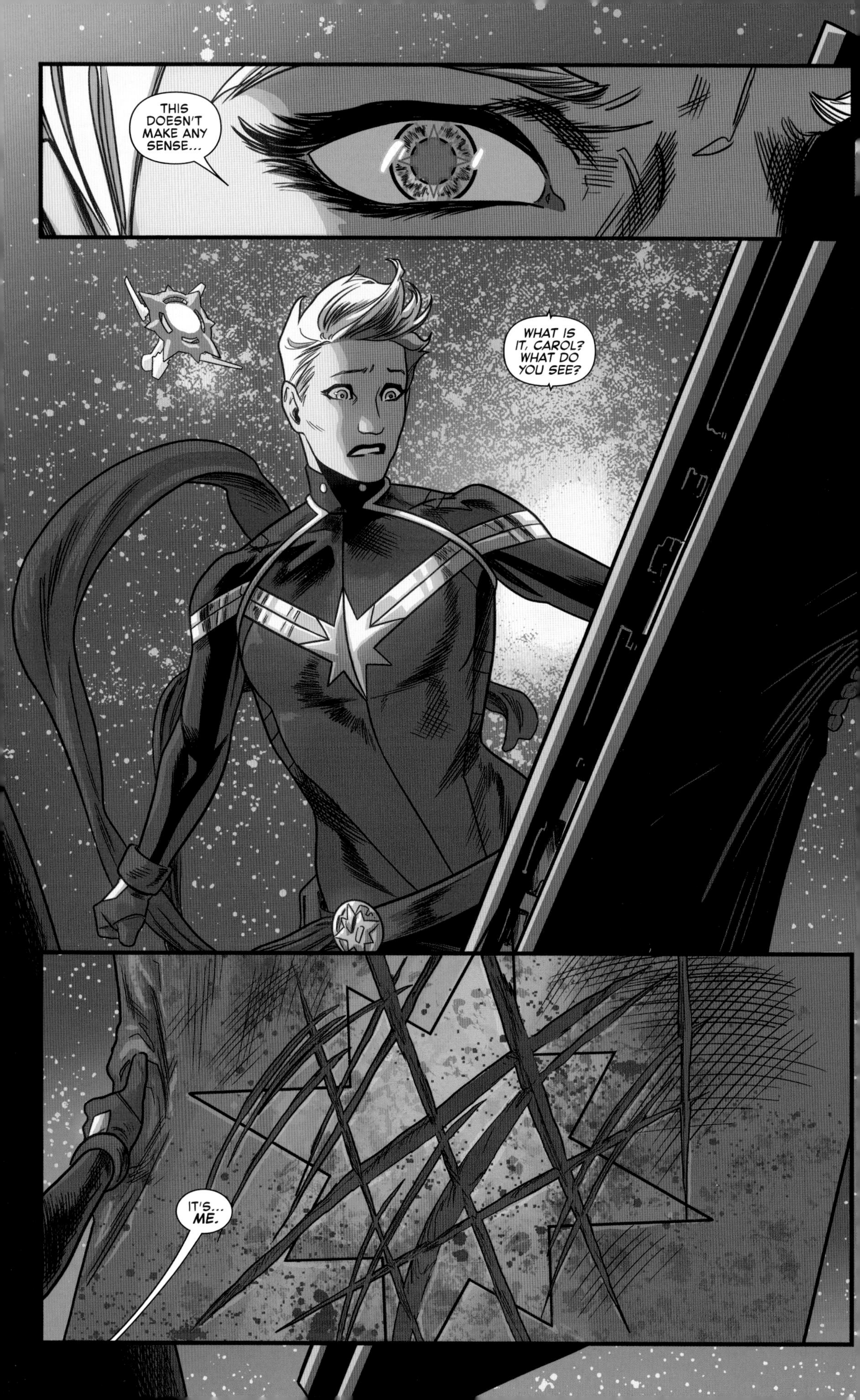
THIS DOESN'T MAKE ANY SENSE...
WHAT IS IT, CAROL? WHAT DO YOU SEE?
IT'S... ME.

MARVEL GRAPHIC NOVEL

CAPTAIN MARVEL #2

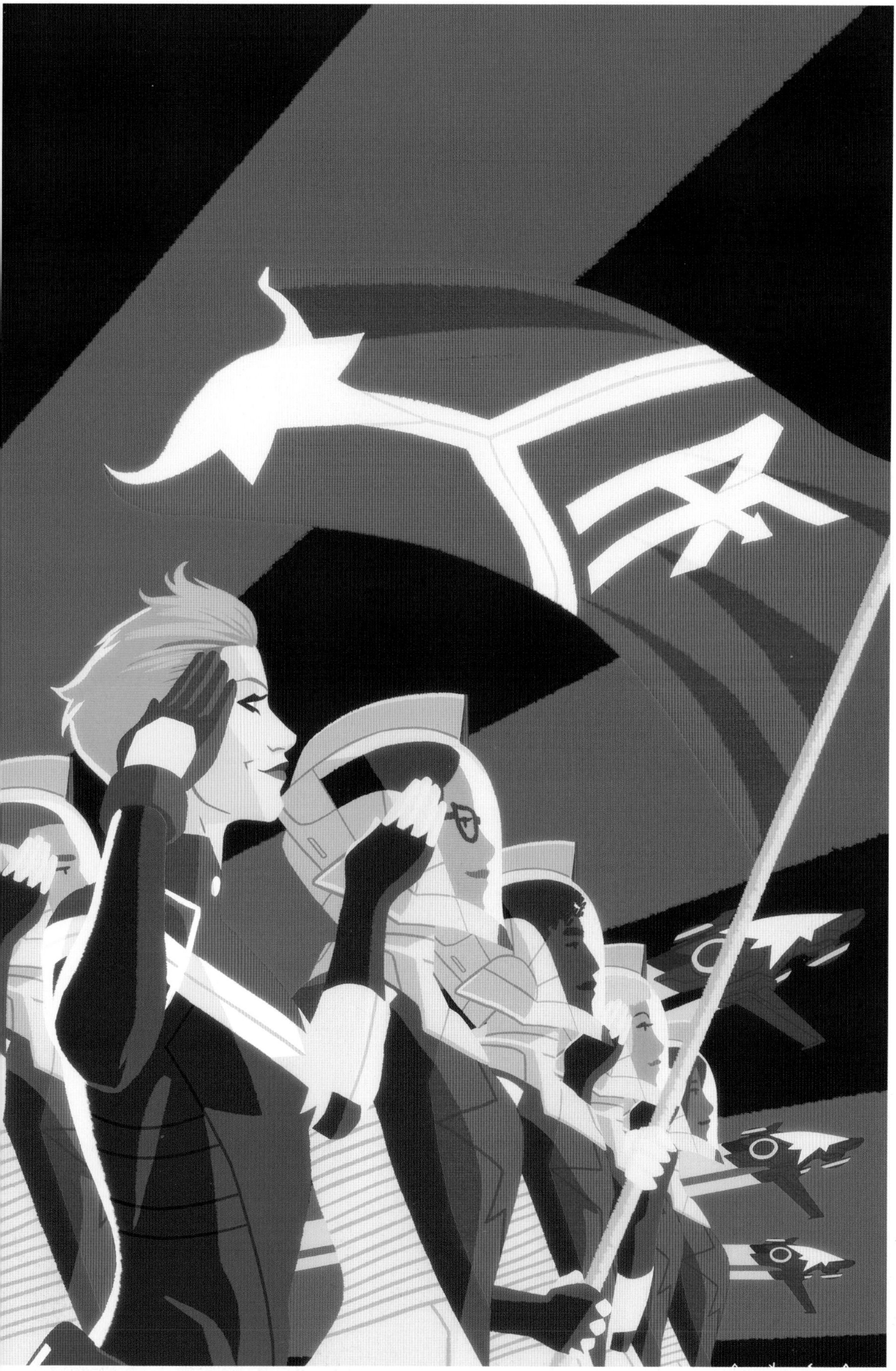

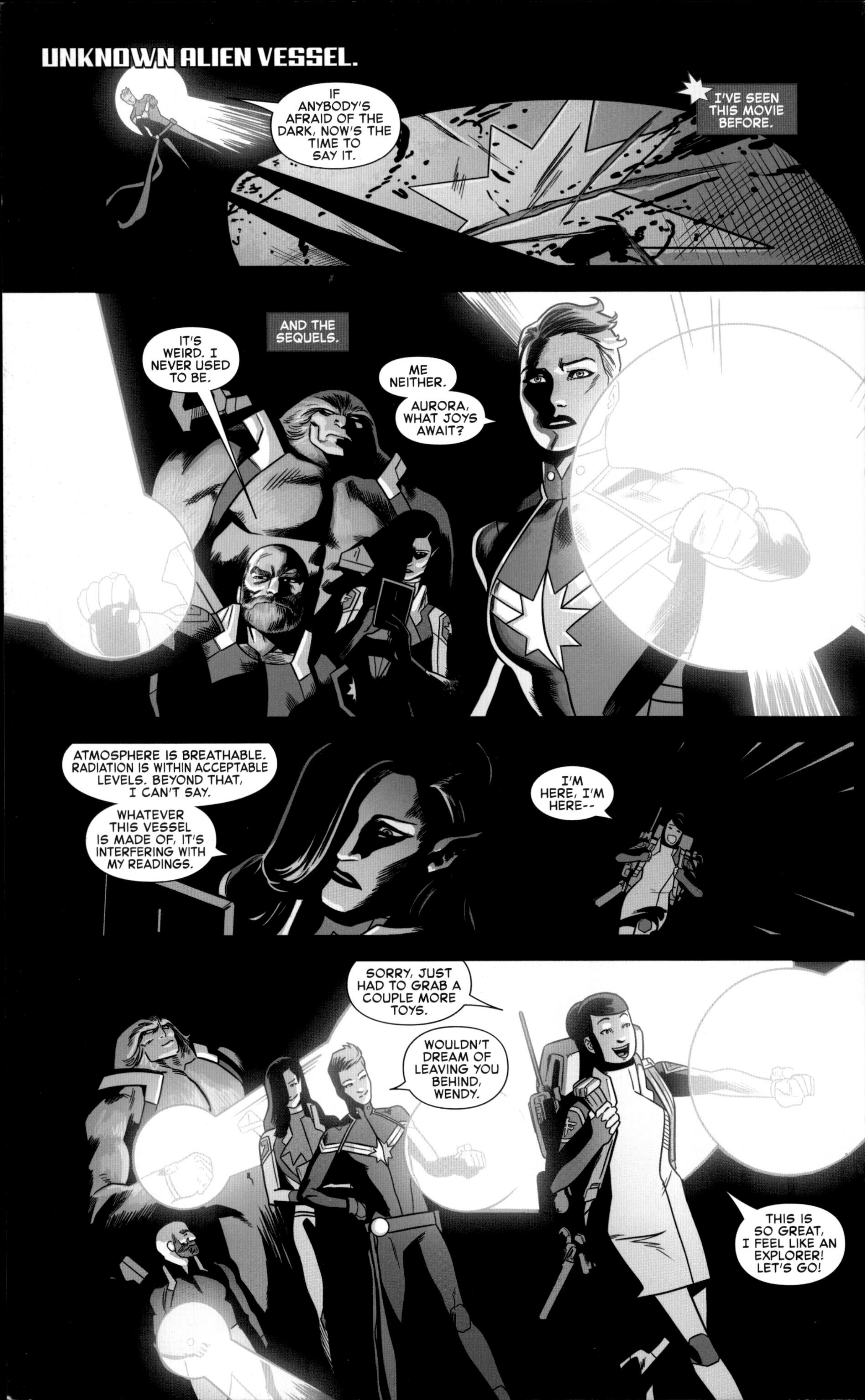
UNKNOWN ALIEN VESSEL.
IF ANYBODY'S AFRAID OF THE DARK, NOW'S THE TIME TO SAY IT.
I'VE SEEN THIS MOVIE BEFORE.
AND THE SEQUELS.
IT'S WEIRD. I NEVER USED TO BE.
ME NEITHER.
AURORA, WHAT JOYS AWAIT?
ATMOSPHERE IS BREATHABLE. RADIATION IS WITHIN ACCEPTABLE LEVELS. BEYOND THAT, I CAN'T SAY.
WHATEVER THIS VESSEL IS MADE OF, IT'S INTERFERING WITH MY READINGS.
I'M HERE, I'M HERE--
SORRY, JUST HAD TO GRAB A COUPLE MORE TOYS.
WOULDN'T DREAM OF LEAVING YOU BEHIND, WENDY.
THIS IS SO GREAT, I FEEL LIKE AN EXPLORER! LET'S GO!

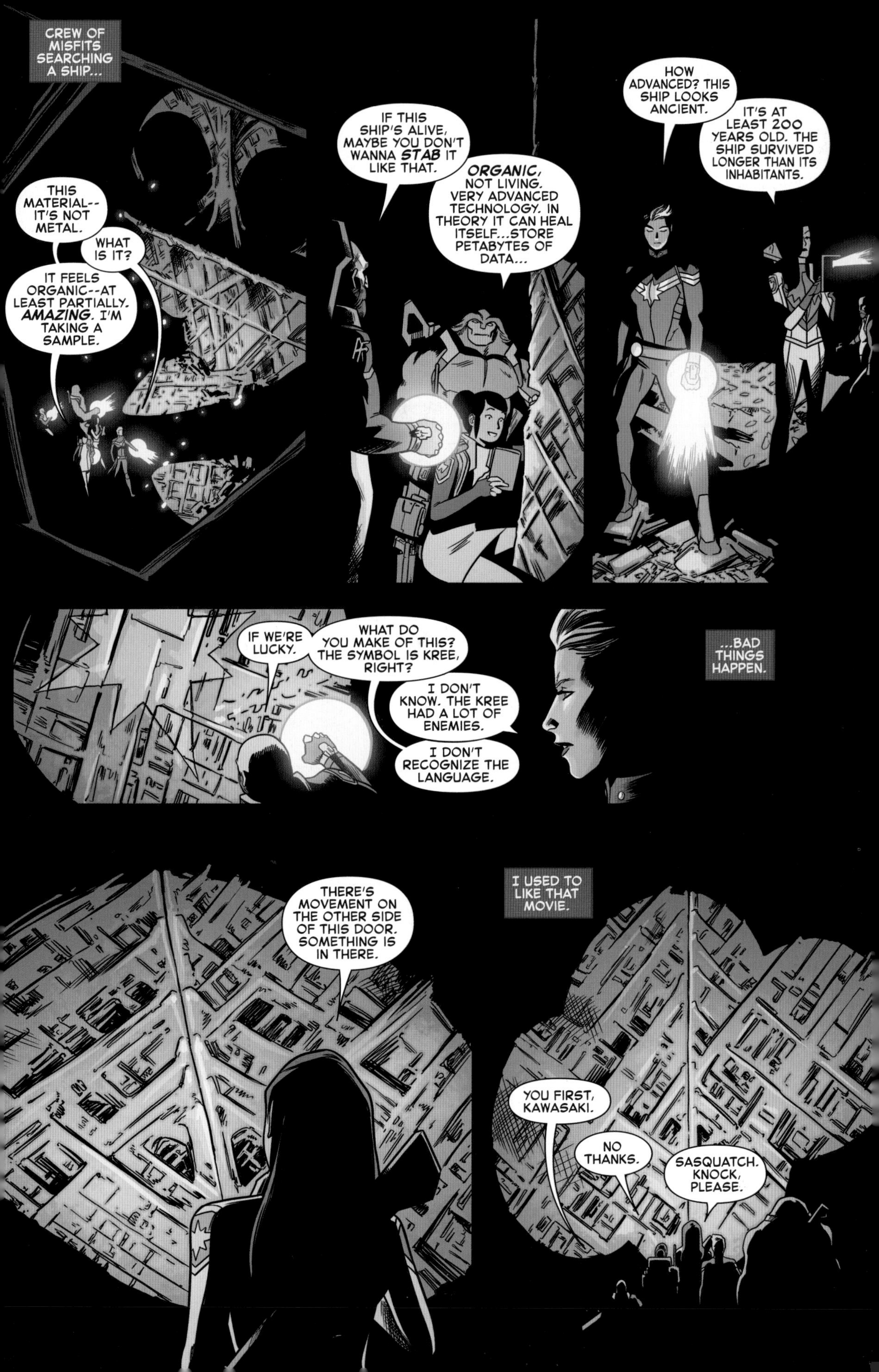
CREW OF MISFITS SEARCHING A SHIP...
THIS MATERIAL-- IT'S NOT METAL.
WHAT IS IT?
IT FEELS ORGANIC--AT LEAST PARTIALLY. AMAZING. I'M TAKING A SAMPLE.
IF THIS SHIP'S ALIVE, MAYBE YOU DON'T WANNA STAB IT LIKE THAT.
ORGANIC, NOT LIVING. VERY ADVANCED TECHNOLOGY. IN THEORY IT CAN HEAL ITSELF...STORE PETABYTES OF DATA...
HOW ADVANCED? THIS SHIP LOOKS ANCIENT.
IT'S AT LEAST 200 YEARS OLD. THE SHIP SURVIVED LONGER THAN ITS INHABITANTS.
IF WE'RE LUCKY.
WHAT DO YOU MAKE OF THIS? THE SYMBOL IS KREE, RIGHT?
I DON'T KNOW. THE KREE HAD A LOT OF ENEMIES.
I DON'T RECOGNIZE THE LANGUAGE.
...BAD THINGS HAPPEN.
THERE'S MOVEMENT ON THE OTHER SIDE OF THIS DOOR. SOMETHING IS IN THERE.
I USED TO LIKE THAT MOVIE.
YOU FIRST, KAWASAKI.
NO THANKS.
SASQUATCH. KNOCK, PLEASE.

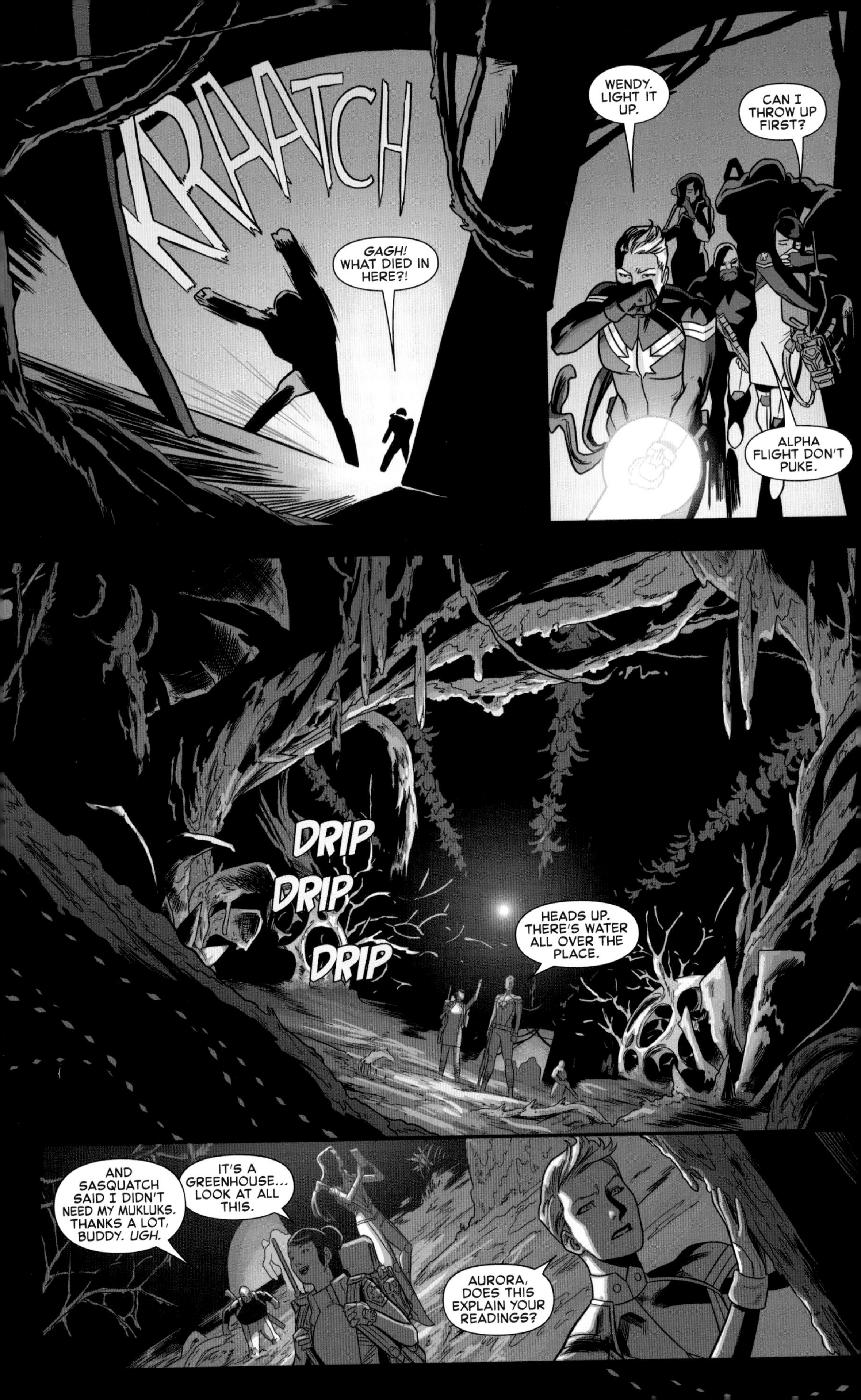
KRAATCH
GAGH! WHAT DIED IN HERE?!
WENDY. LIGHT IT UP.
CAN I THROW UP FIRST?
ALPHA FLIGHT DON'T PUKE.
DRIP
DRIP
DRIP
HEADS UP. THERE'S WATER ALL OVER THE PLACE.
AND SASQUATCH SAID I DIDN'T NEED MY MUKLUKS. THANKS A LOT, BUDDY. *UGH.*
IT'S A GREENHOUSE... LOOK AT ALL THIS.
AURORA, DOES THIS EXPLAIN YOUR READINGS?

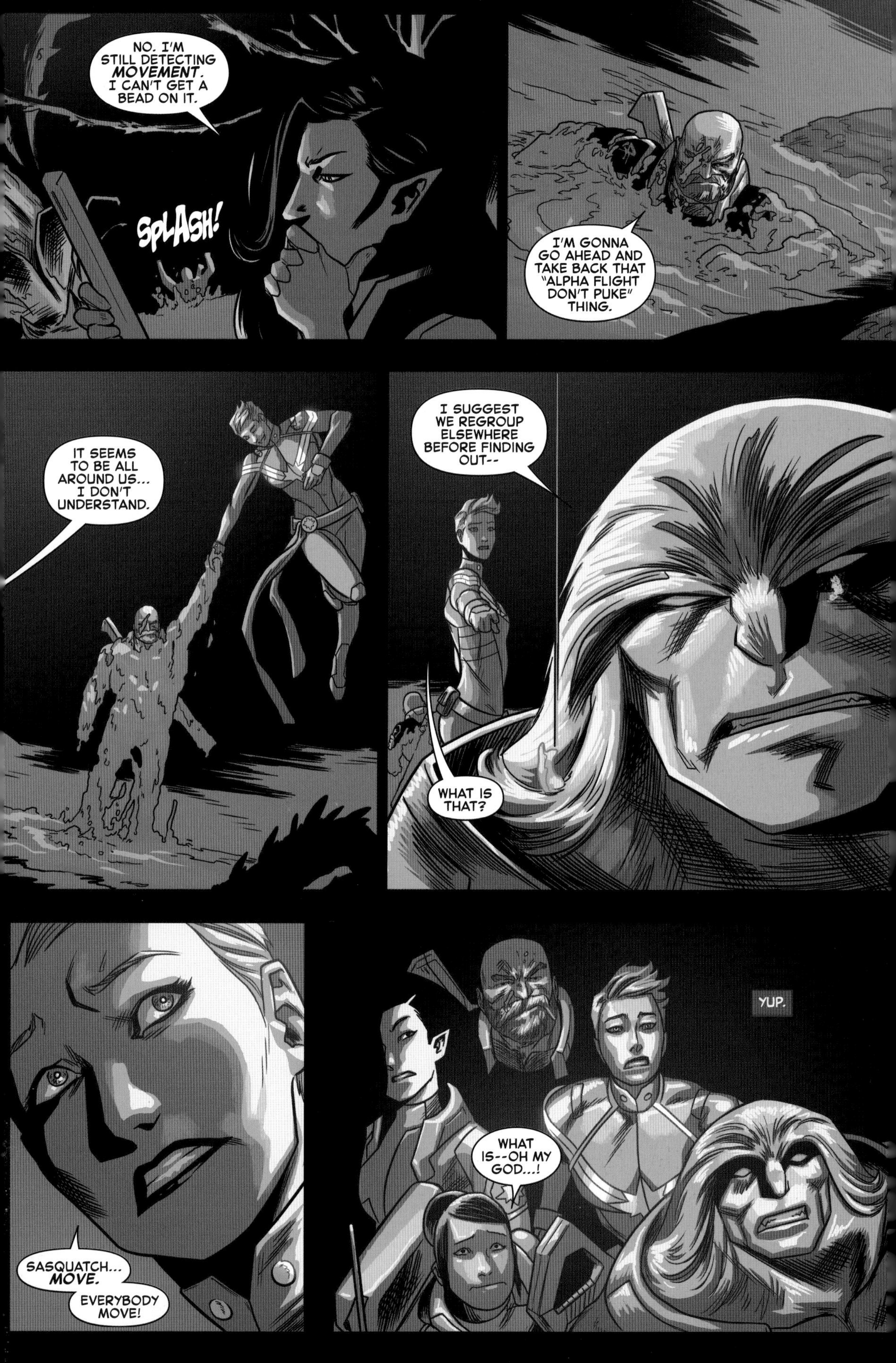
NO. I'M STILL DETECTING MOVEMENT. I CAN'T GET A BEAD ON IT.
SPLASH!
I'M GONNA GO AHEAD AND TAKE BACK THAT "ALPHA FLIGHT DON'T PUKE" THING.
IT SEEMS TO BE ALL AROUND US... I DON'T UNDERSTAND.
I SUGGEST WE REGROUP ELSEWHERE BEFORE FINDING OUT--
WHAT IS THAT?
SASQUATCH... MOVE.
EVERYBODY MOVE!
WHAT IS--OH MY GOD...!
YUP.

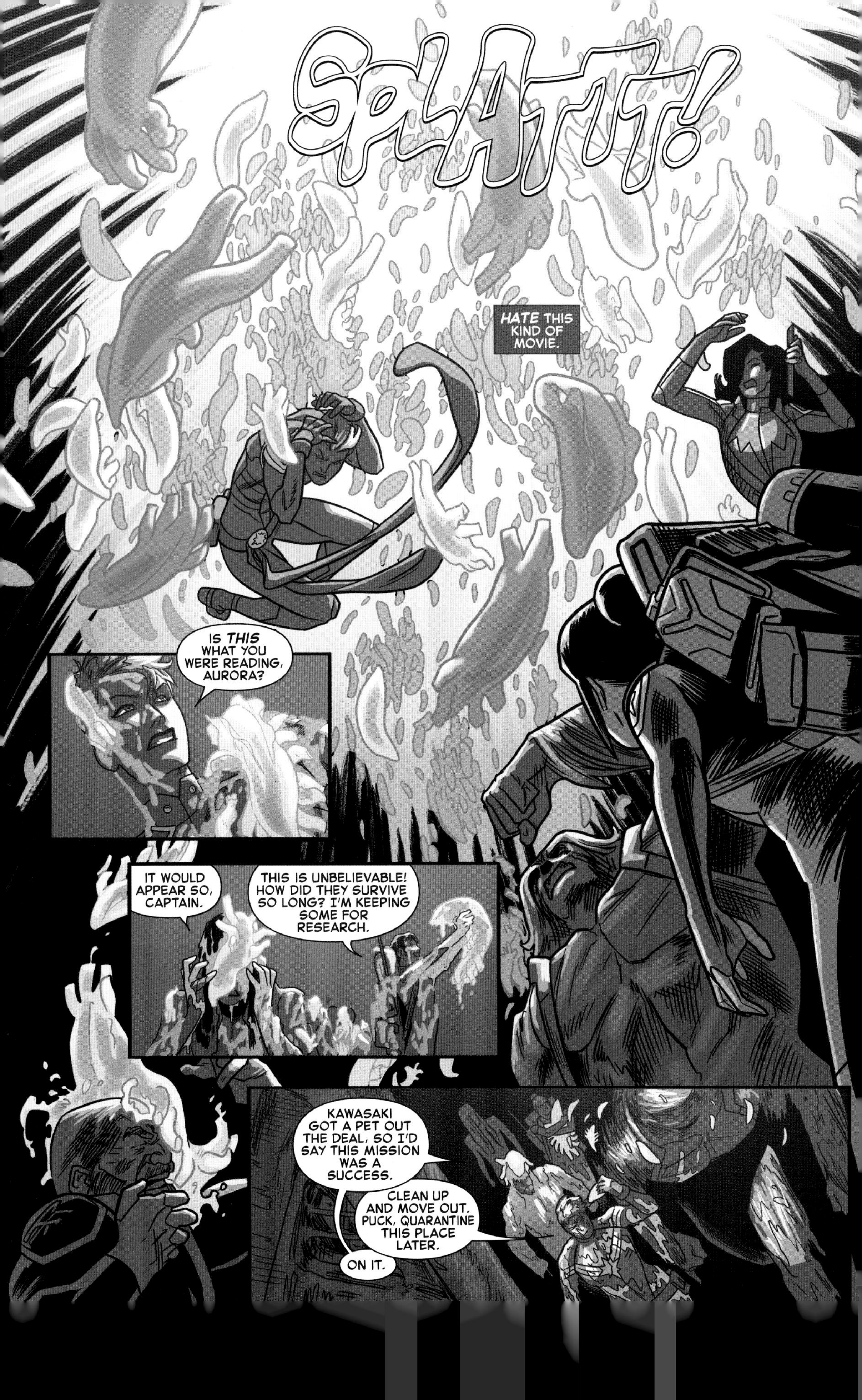
SPLATTT!
HATE THIS KIND OF MOVIE.
IS THIS WHAT YOU WERE READING, AURORA?
IT WOULD APPEAR SO, CAPTAIN.
THIS IS UNBELIEVABLE! HOW DID THEY SURVIVE SO LONG? I'M KEEPING SOME FOR RESEARCH.
KAWASAKI GOT A PET OUT THE DEAL, SO I'D SAY THIS MISSION WAS A SUCCESS.
CLEAN UP AND MOVE OUT. PUCK, QUARANTINE THIS PLACE LATER.
ON IT.

ALPHA FLIGHT SPACE STATION.
CARGO HOLD 7.

UH, COMMANDER BRAND...DID YOU HEAR ME?

YEP. BUT TELL ME AGAIN JUST TO BE SURE.

THE ERIDANI DELEGATION IS DEMANDING TO BE RELEASED. AND TO BE APPOINTED COUNSEL.

AND... THEY DON'T LIKE OUR FOOD.

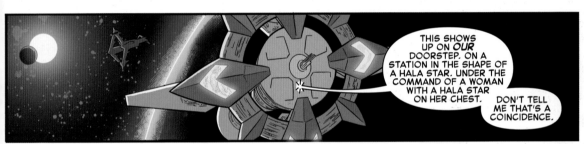

THIS SHOWS UP ON *OUR* DOORSTEP. ON A STATION IN THE SHAPE OF A HALA STAR. UNDER THE COMMAND OF A WOMAN WITH A HALA STAR ON HER CHEST.

DON'T TELL ME THAT'S A COINCIDENCE.

THE ERIDANI AMBASSADOR IS DEMANDING A MEETING. THEY'RE CONVENING AN EMERGENCY SESSION OF THE INTERGALACTIC COUNCIL. AND THE PRESIDENT CALLED.

TWICE.

TAKE A MESSAGE.

WITH CAPTAIN MARVEL ON A MISSION, THEY'RE ALL DEMANDING TO TALK TO *YOU*, COMMANDER. WE CAN'T HOLD THEM OFF FOREVER.

I SUPPOSE YOU'RE RIGHT, ENSIGN.

CONGRATULATIONS. YOU'VE BEEN APPOINTED ACTING COUNSEL TO THE ERIDANI. LET'S SEE IF THEY CAN GIVE US SOME ANSWERS.

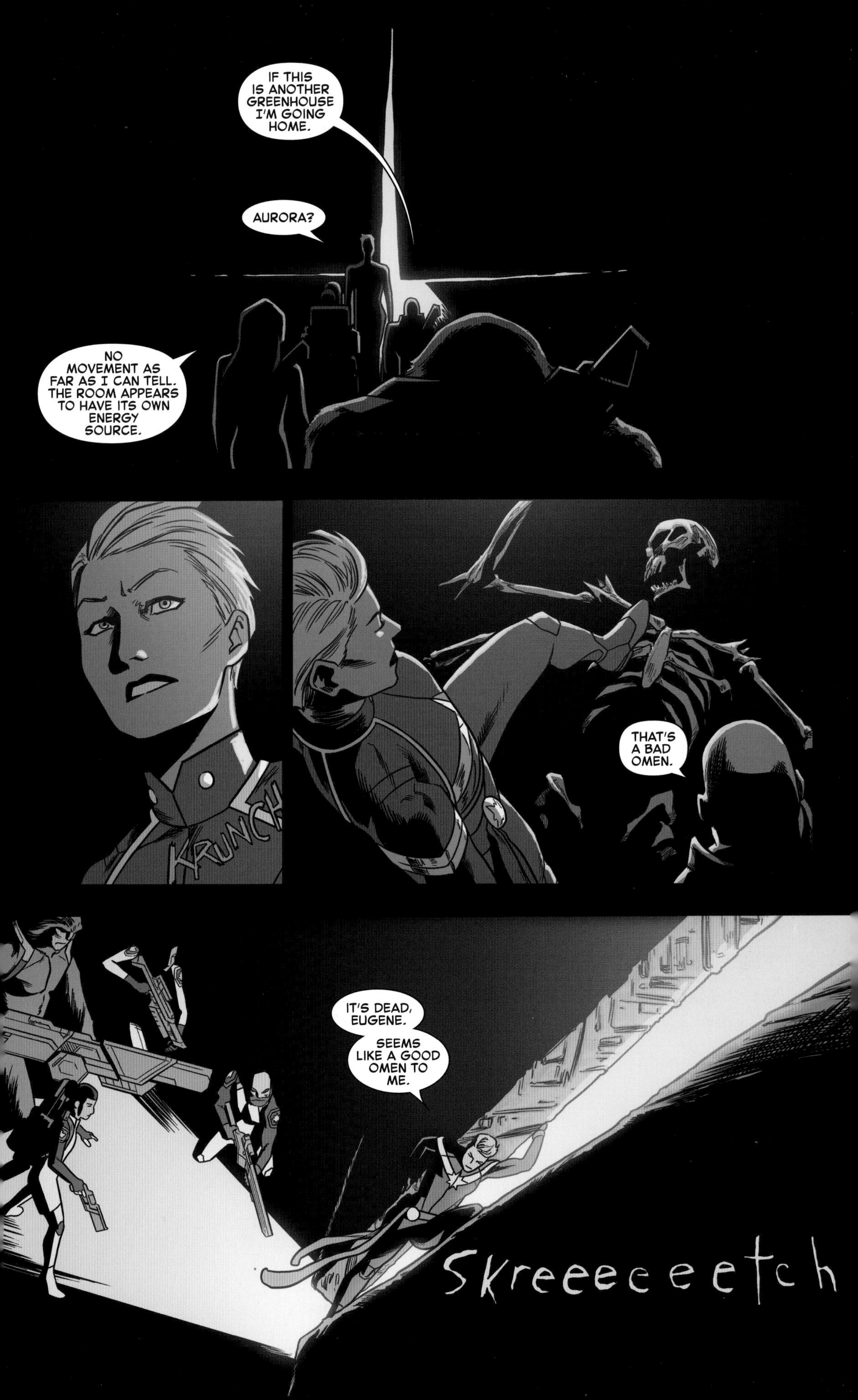
IF THIS IS ANOTHER GREENHOUSE I'M GOING HOME.
AURORA?
NO MOVEMENT AS FAR AS I CAN TELL. THE ROOM APPEARS TO HAVE ITS OWN ENERGY SOURCE.
KRUNCH
THAT'S A BAD OMEN.
IT'S DEAD, EUGENE.
SEEMS LIKE A GOOD OMEN TO ME.
Skreeeeeetch

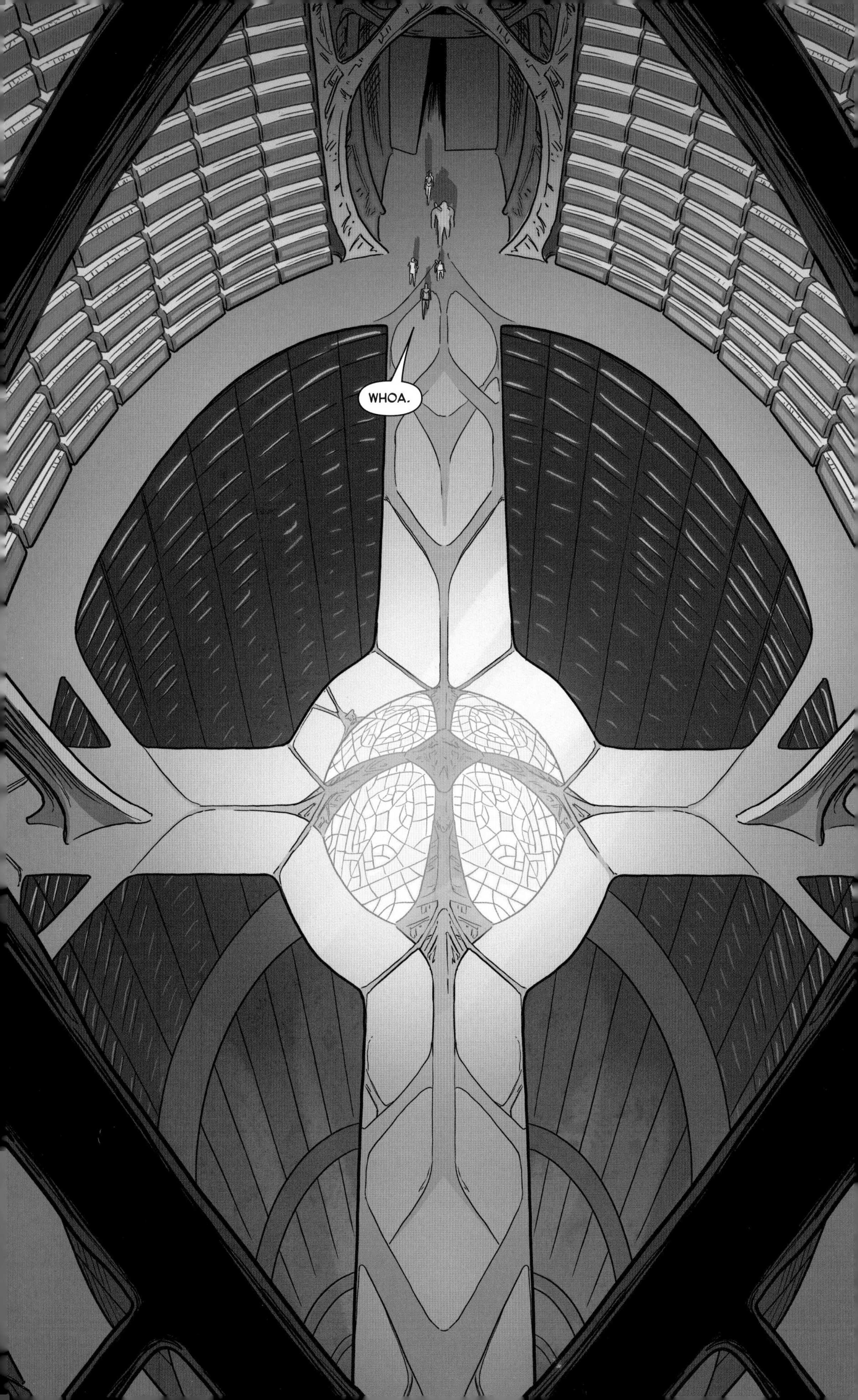
WHOA.

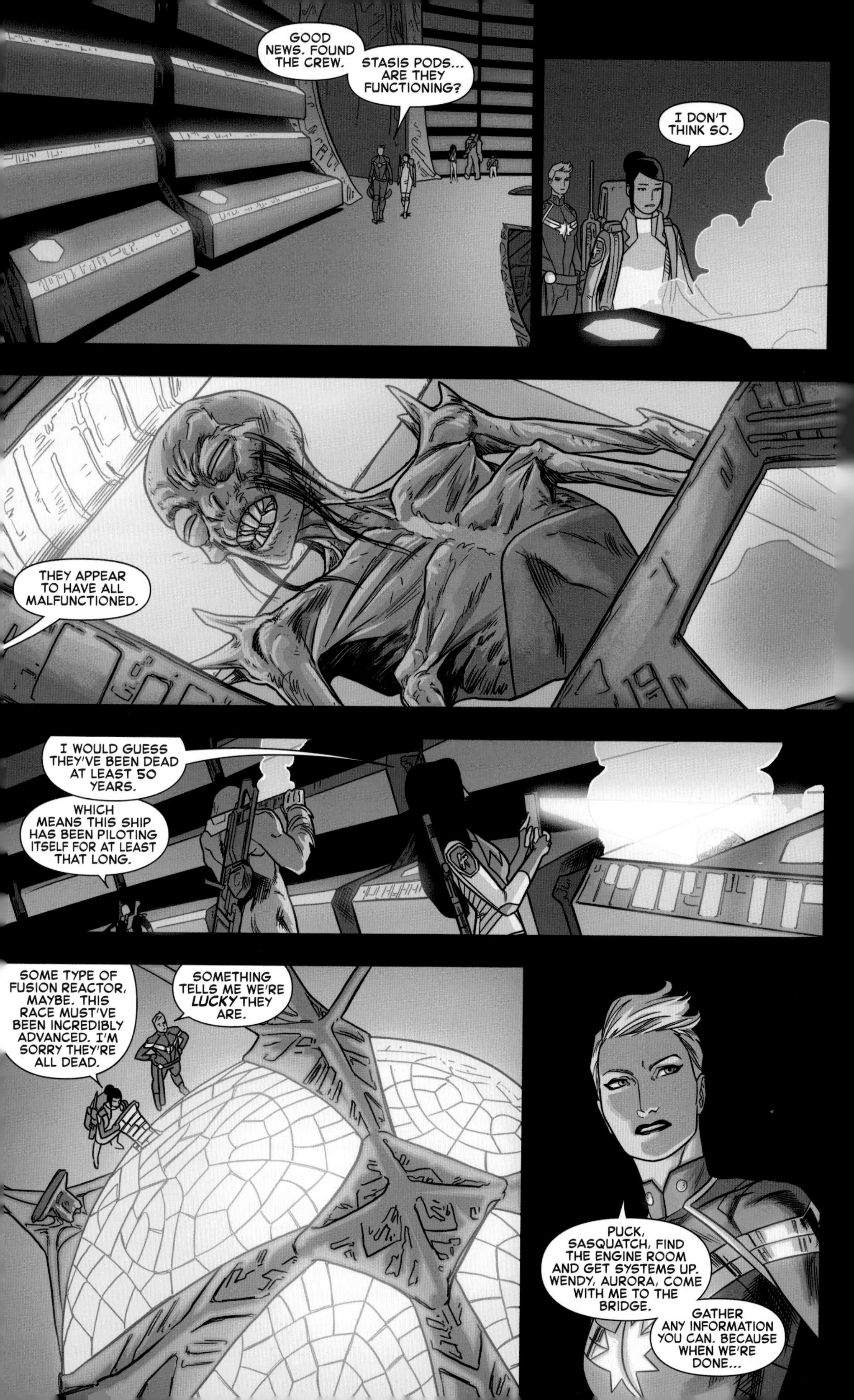
GOOD NEWS. FOUND THE CREW.
STASIS PODS... ARE THEY FUNCTIONING?
I DON'T THINK SO.
THEY APPEAR TO HAVE ALL MALFUNCTIONED.
I WOULD GUESS THEY'VE BEEN DEAD AT LEAST 50 YEARS.
WHICH MEANS THIS SHIP HAS BEEN PILOTING ITSELF FOR AT LEAST THAT LONG.
SOME TYPE OF FUSION REACTOR, MAYBE. THIS RACE MUST'VE BEEN INCREDIBLY ADVANCED. I'M SORRY THEY'RE ALL DEAD.
SOMETHING TELLS ME WE'RE *LUCKY* THEY ARE.
PUCK, SASQUATCH, FIND THE ENGINE ROOM AND GET SYSTEMS UP. WENDY, AURORA, COME WITH ME TO THE BRIDGE.
GATHER ANY INFORMATION YOU CAN. BECAUSE WHEN WE'RE DONE...

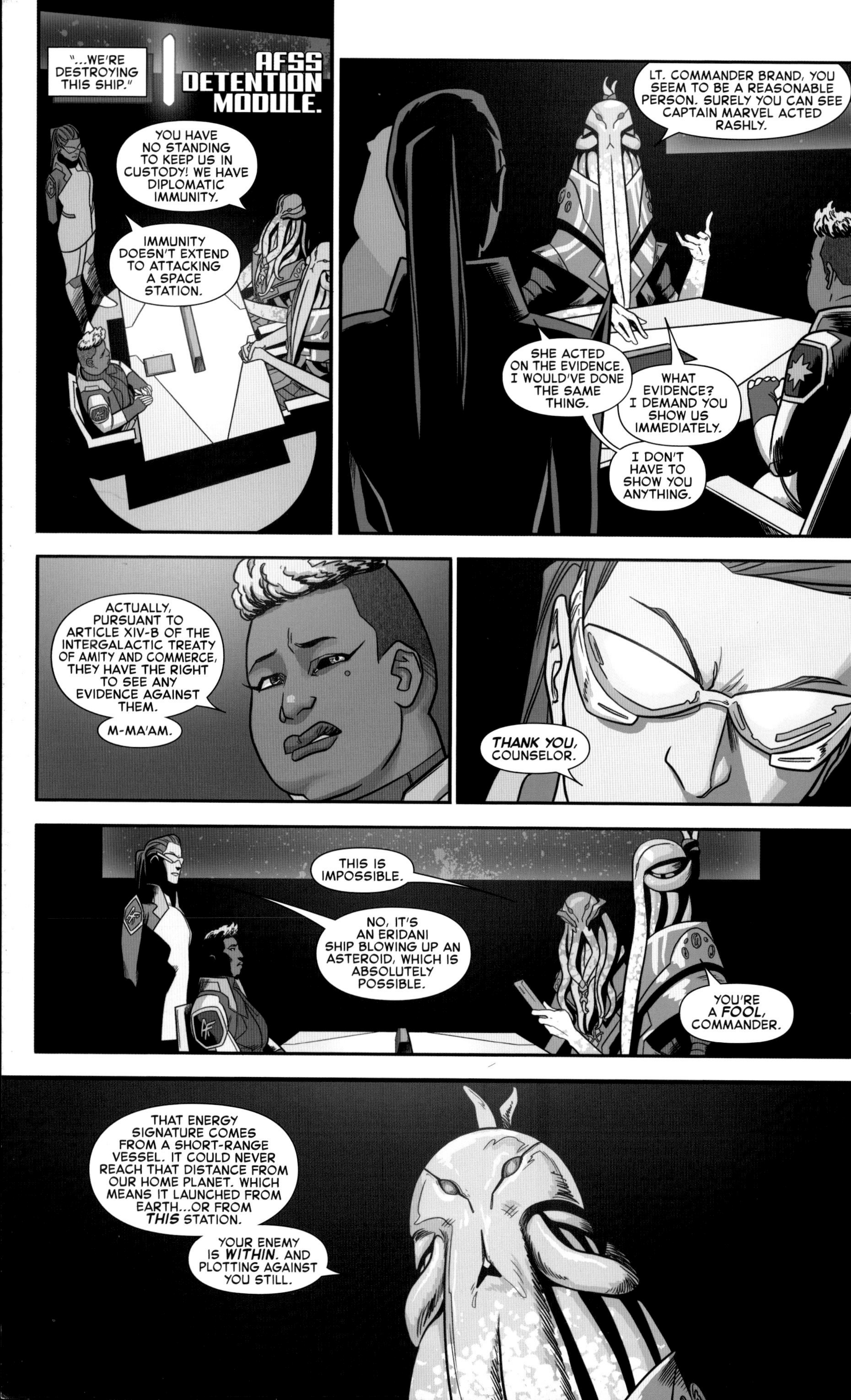
"...WE'RE DESTROYING THIS SHIP."
AFSS DETENTION MODULE.
YOU HAVE NO STANDING TO KEEP US IN CUSTODY! WE HAVE DIPLOMATIC IMMUNITY.
IMMUNITY DOESN'T EXTEND TO ATTACKING A SPACE STATION.
LT. COMMANDER BRAND, YOU SEEM TO BE A REASONABLE PERSON. SURELY YOU CAN SEE CAPTAIN MARVEL ACTED RASHLY.
SHE ACTED ON THE EVIDENCE. I WOULD'VE DONE THE SAME THING.
WHAT EVIDENCE? I DEMAND YOU SHOW US IMMEDIATELY.
I DON'T HAVE TO SHOW YOU ANYTHING.
ACTUALLY, PURSUANT TO ARTICLE XIV-B OF THE INTERGALACTIC TREATY OF AMITY AND COMMERCE, THEY HAVE THE RIGHT TO SEE ANY EVIDENCE AGAINST THEM.
M-MA'AM.
THANK YOU, COUNSELOR.
THIS IS IMPOSSIBLE.
NO, IT'S AN ERIDANI SHIP BLOWING UP AN ASTEROID, WHICH IS ABSOLUTELY POSSIBLE.
YOU'RE A *FOOL,* COMMANDER.
THAT ENERGY SIGNATURE COMES FROM A SHORT-RANGE VESSEL. IT COULD NEVER REACH THAT DISTANCE FROM OUR HOME PLANET. WHICH MEANS IT LAUNCHED FROM EARTH...OR FROM *THIS* STATION.
YOUR ENEMY IS *WITHIN.* AND PLOTTING AGAINST YOU STILL.

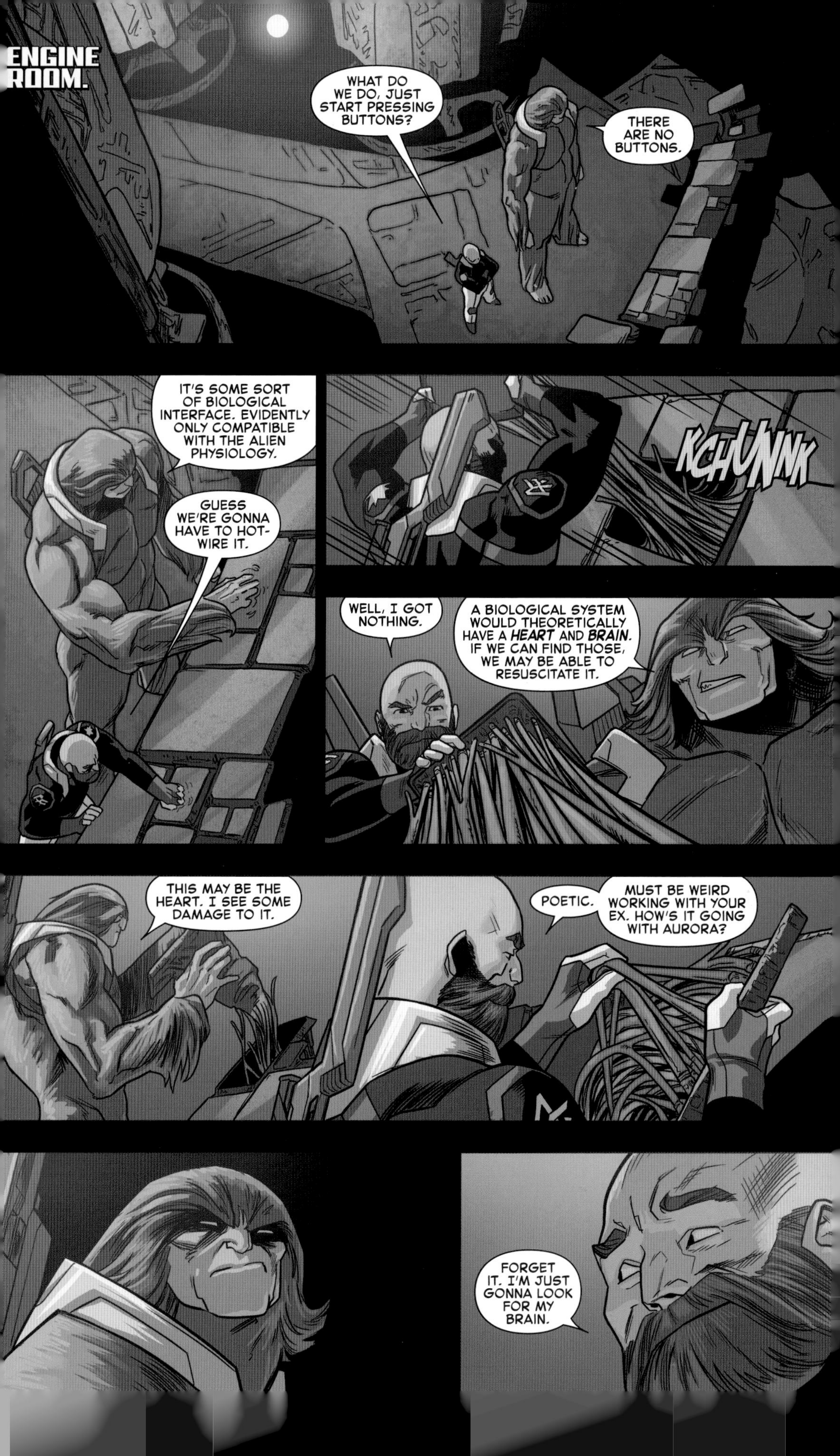
ENGINE ROOM.
WHAT DO WE DO, JUST START PRESSING BUTTONS?
THERE ARE NO BUTTONS.
IT'S SOME SORT OF BIOLOGICAL INTERFACE. EVIDENTLY ONLY COMPATIBLE WITH THE ALIEN PHYSIOLOGY.
GUESS WE'RE GONNA HAVE TO HOT-WIRE IT.
KCHUNNK
WELL, I GOT NOTHING.
A BIOLOGICAL SYSTEM WOULD THEORETICALLY HAVE A HEART AND BRAIN. IF WE CAN FIND THOSE, WE MAY BE ABLE TO RESUSCITATE IT.
THIS MAY BE THE HEART. I SEE SOME DAMAGE TO IT.
POETIC.
MUST BE WEIRD WORKING WITH YOUR EX. HOW'S IT GOING WITH AURORA?
FORGET IT. I'M JUST GONNA LOOK FOR MY BRAIN.

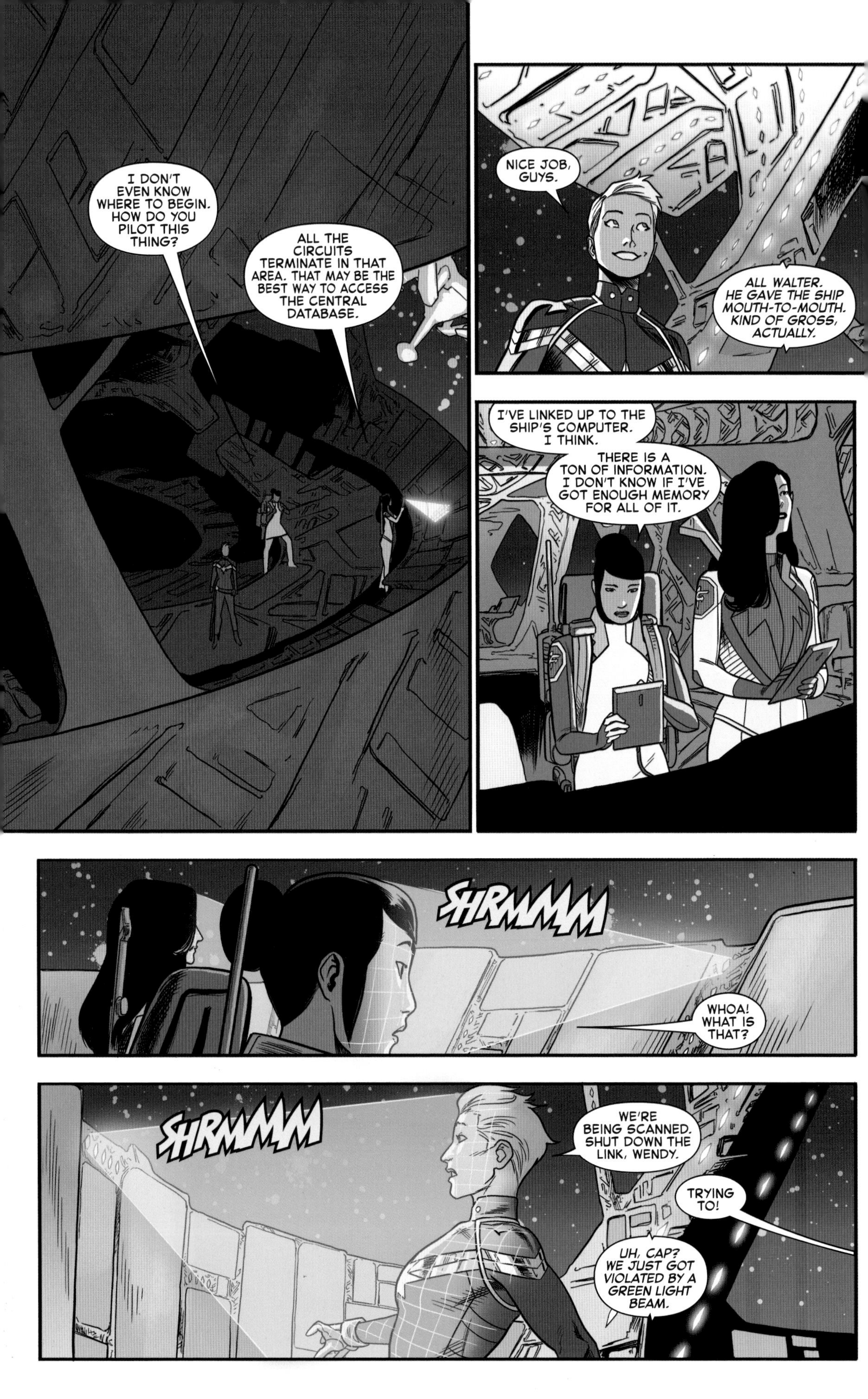
I DON'T EVEN KNOW WHERE TO BEGIN. HOW DO YOU PILOT THIS THING?
ALL THE CIRCUITS TERMINATE IN THAT AREA. THAT MAY BE THE BEST WAY TO ACCESS THE CENTRAL DATABASE.
NICE JOB, GUYS.
ALL WALTER. HE GAVE THE SHIP MOUTH-TO-MOUTH. KIND OF GROSS, ACTUALLY.
I'VE LINKED UP TO THE SHIP'S COMPUTER. I THINK.
THERE IS A TON OF INFORMATION. I DON'T KNOW IF I'VE GOT ENOUGH MEMORY FOR ALL OF IT.
SHRMMM
WHOA! WHAT IS THAT?
SHRMMM
WE'RE BEING SCANNED. SHUT DOWN THE LINK, WENDY.
TRYING TO!
UH, CAP? WE JUST GOT VIOLATED BY A GREEN LIGHT BEAM.

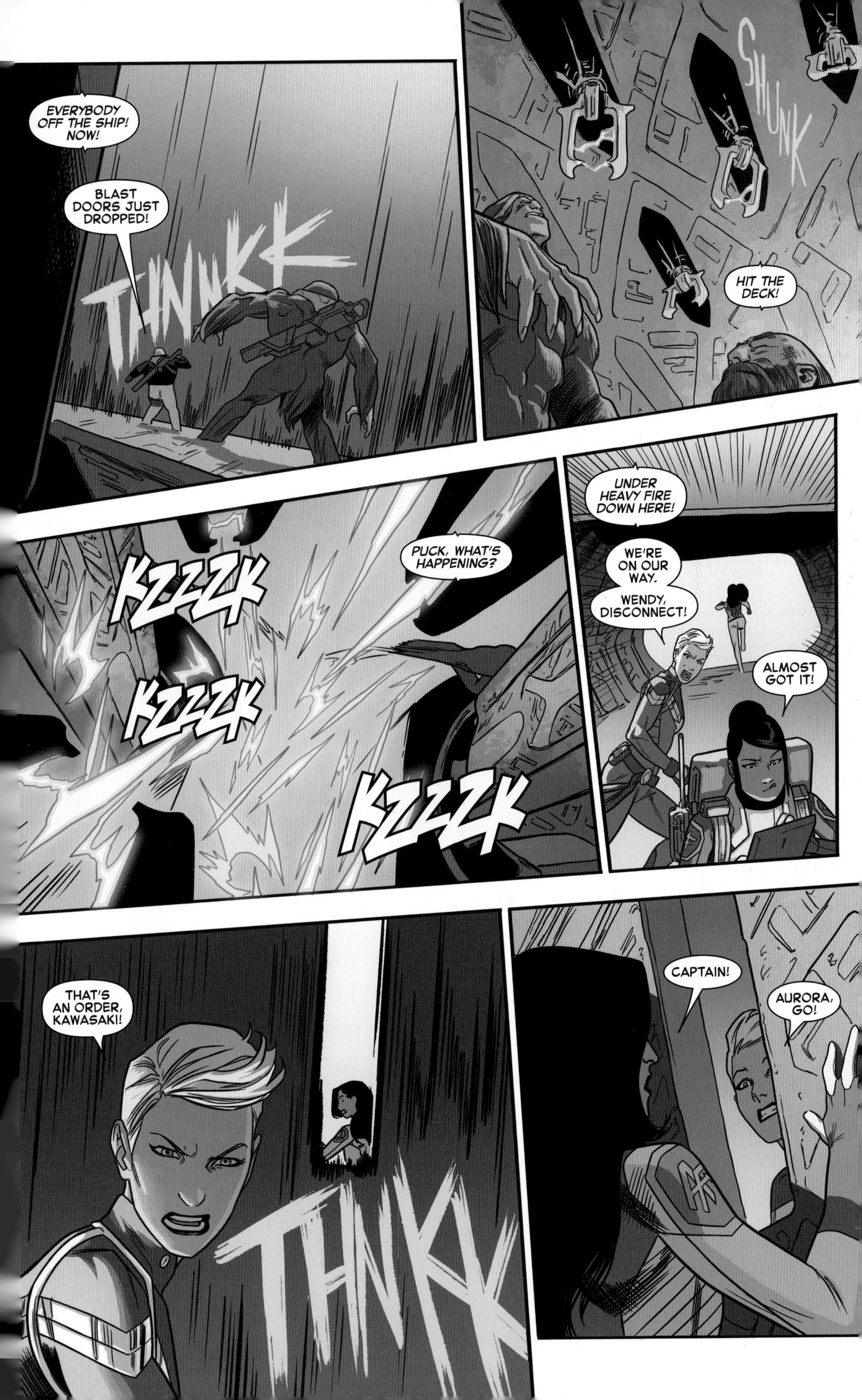
EVERYBODY OFF THE SHIP! NOW!
BLAST DOORS JUST DROPPED!
THNKK
SHUNK
HIT THE DECK!
KZZZK
KZZZK
PUCK, WHAT'S HAPPENING?
KZZZK
UNDER HEAVY FIRE DOWN HERE!
WE'RE ON OUR WAY.
WENDY, DISCONNECT!
ALMOST GOT IT!
THAT'S AN ORDER, KAWASAKI!
THNK
CAPTAIN!
AURORA, GO!

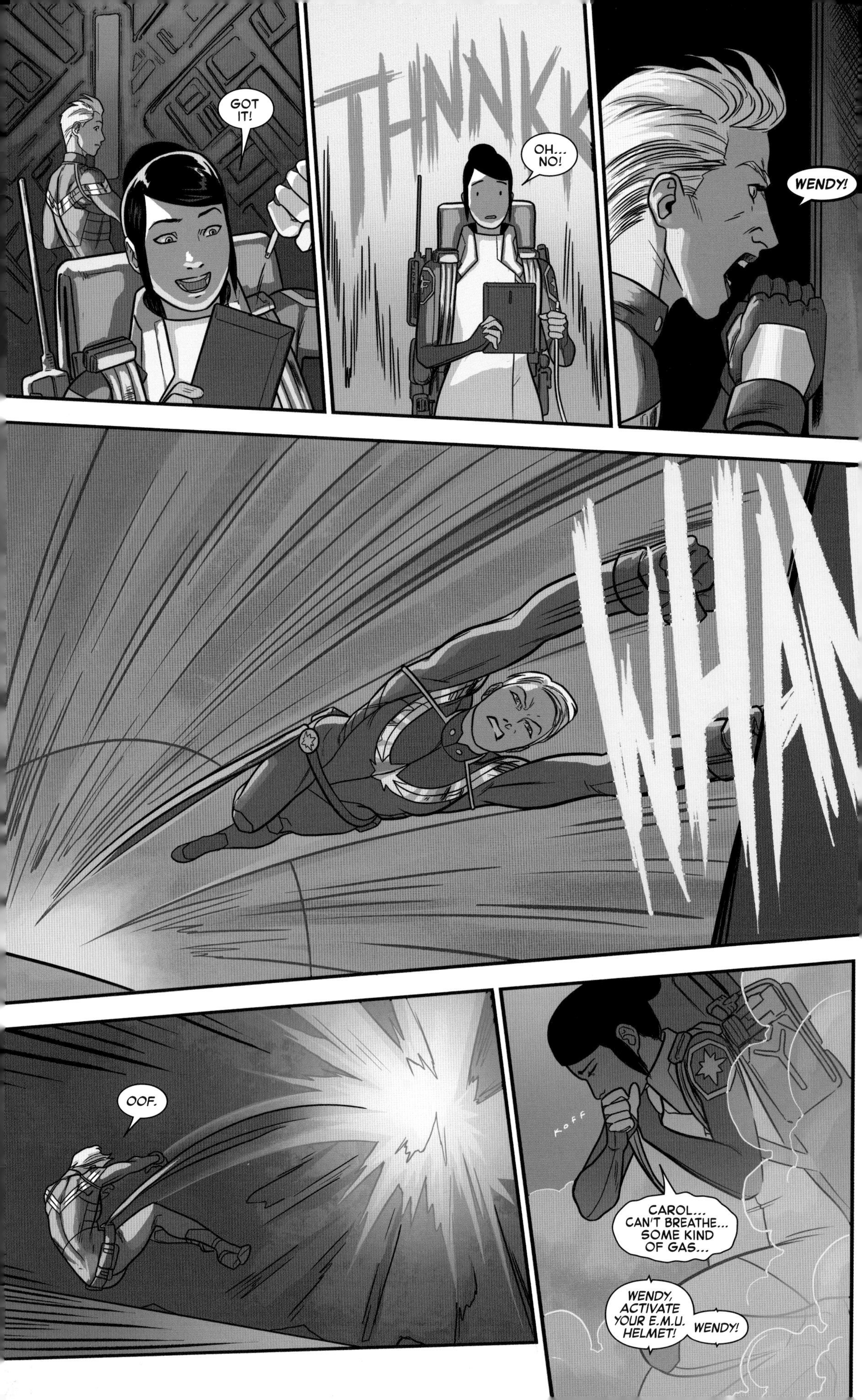
GOT IT!
THNNKK
OH... NO!
WENDY!
OOF.
KOFF
CAROL... CAN'T BREATHE... SOME KIND OF GAS...
WENDY, ACTIVATE YOUR E.M.U. HELMET!
WENDY!

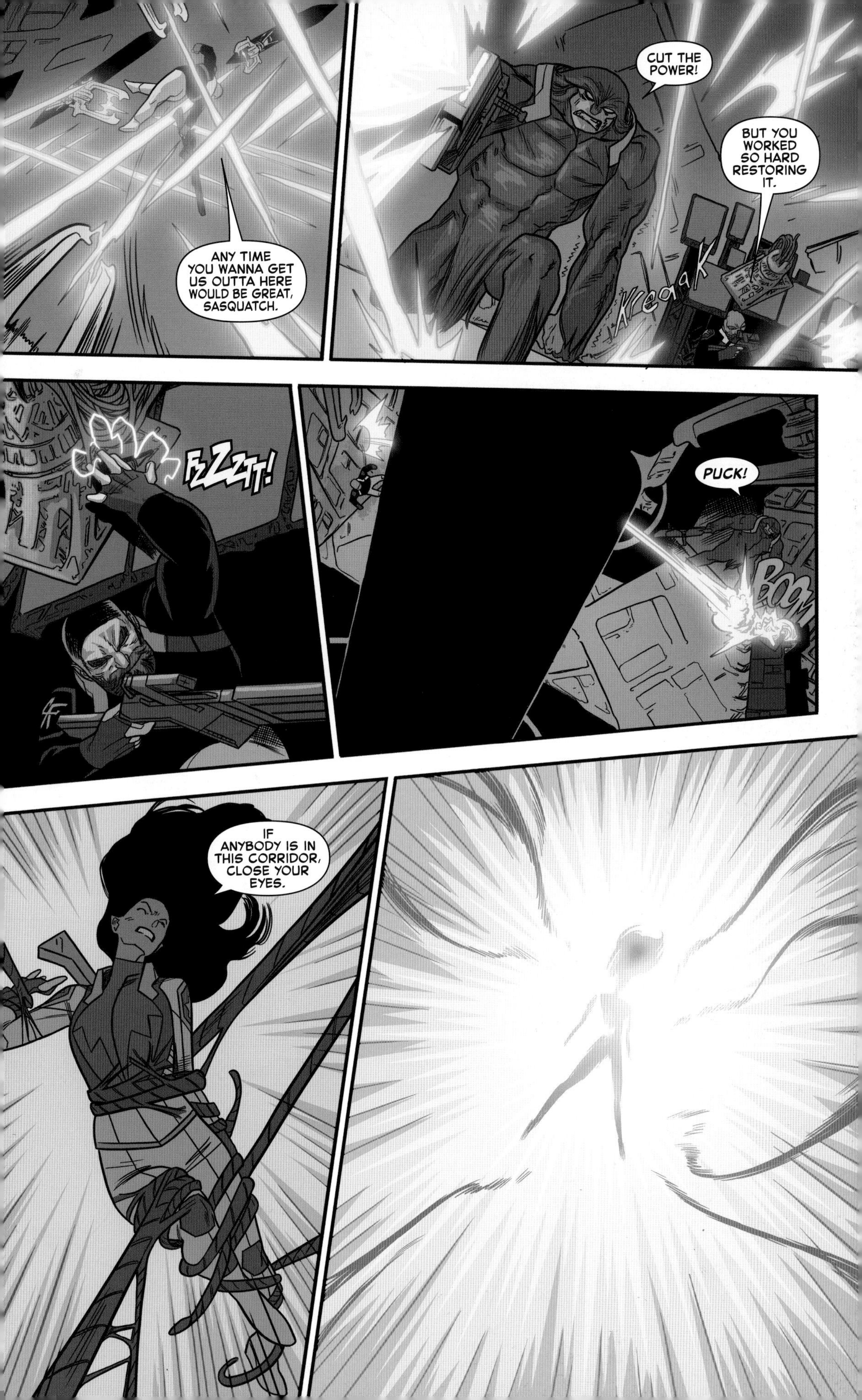
ANY TIME YOU WANNA GET US OUTTA HERE WOULD BE GREAT, SASQUATCH.
CUT THE POWER!
BUT YOU WORKED SO HARD RESTORING IT.
Kreaak
FZZZTT!
PUCK!
BOOM
IF ANYBODY IS IN THIS CORRIDOR, CLOSE YOUR EYES.

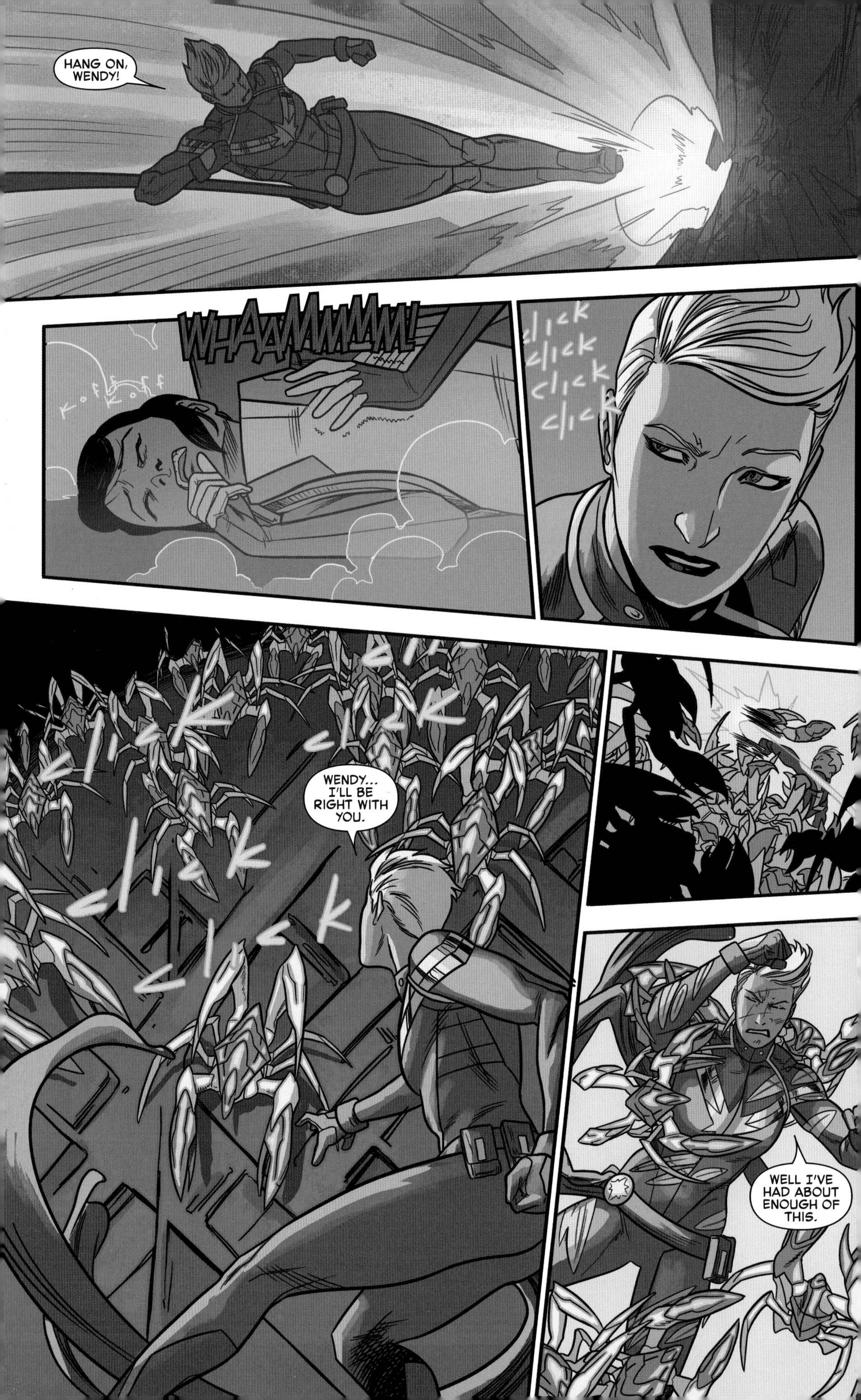
HANG ON, WENDY!
WHAAMMMM!
koff koff
click click click click
click click click click
WENDY... I'LL BE RIGHT WITH YOU.
WELL I'VE HAD ABOUT ENOUGH OF THIS.

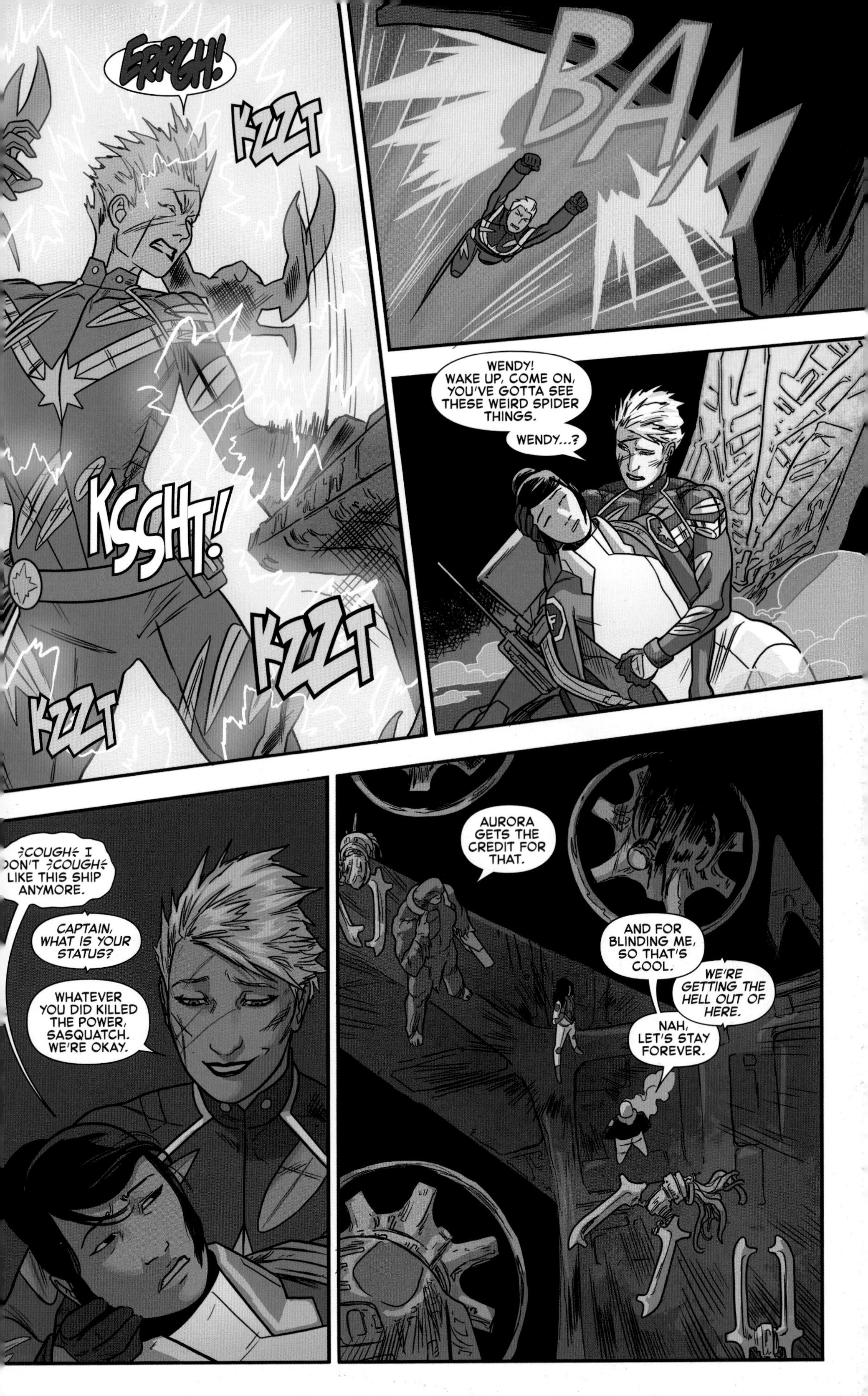
ERRGH!
KZZT
KSSHT!
KZZT
KZZT
BAM
WENDY! WAKE UP, COME ON, YOU'VE GOTTA SEE THESE WEIRD SPIDER THINGS.
WENDY...?
≠COUGH≠ I DON'T ≠COUGH≠ LIKE THIS SHIP ANYMORE.
CAPTAIN, WHAT IS YOUR STATUS?
WHATEVER YOU DID KILLED THE POWER, SASQUATCH. WE'RE OKAY.
AURORA GETS THE CREDIT FOR THAT.
AND FOR BLINDING ME, SO THAT'S COOL.
WE'RE GETTING THE HELL OUT OF HERE.
NAH, LET'S STAY FOREVER.

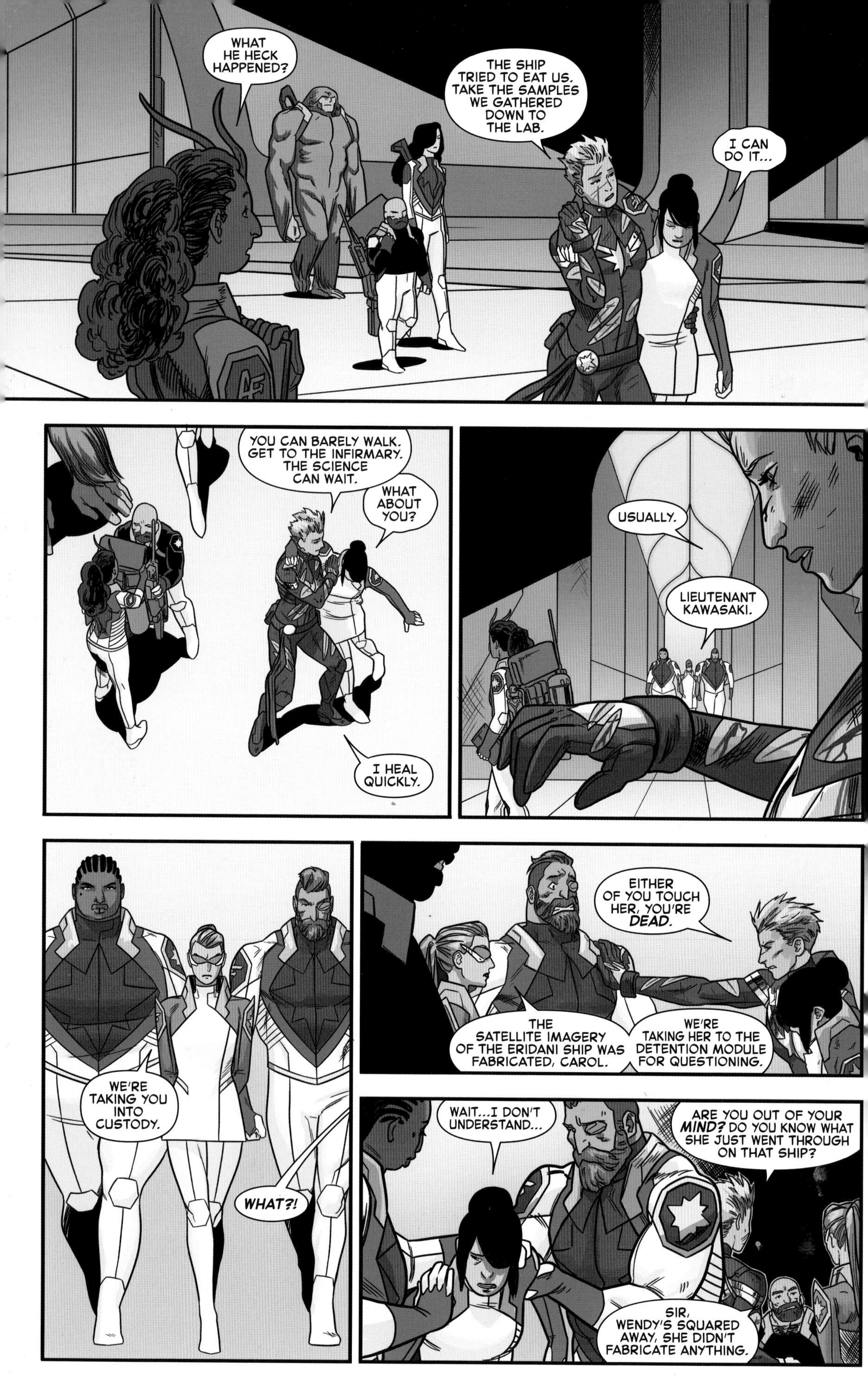
WHAT HE HECK HAPPENED?
THE SHIP TRIED TO EAT US. TAKE THE SAMPLES WE GATHERED DOWN TO THE LAB.
I CAN DO IT...
YOU CAN BARELY WALK. GET TO THE INFIRMARY. THE SCIENCE CAN WAIT.
WHAT ABOUT YOU?
I HEAL QUICKLY.
USUALLY.
LIEUTENANT KAWASAKI.
WE'RE TAKING YOU INTO CUSTODY.
WHAT?!
EITHER OF YOU TOUCH HER, YOU'RE DEAD.
THE SATELLITE IMAGERY OF THE ERIDANI SHIP WAS FABRICATED, CAROL.
WE'RE TAKING HER TO THE DETENTION MODULE FOR QUESTIONING.
WAIT...I DON'T UNDERSTAND...
ARE YOU OUT OF YOUR MIND? DO YOU KNOW WHAT SHE JUST WENT THROUGH ON THAT SHIP?
SIR, WENDY'S SQUARED AWAY, SHE DIDN'T FABRICATE ANYTHING.

THIS ISN'T YOUR CALL. I'M OVERRIDING YOUR ORDER.

THIS *IS* MY CALL--

DANVERS. YOU'RE BLEEDING.

ARE YOU ALL RIGHT?

"WHAT THE HELL DID YOU FIND ON THAT SHIP?"

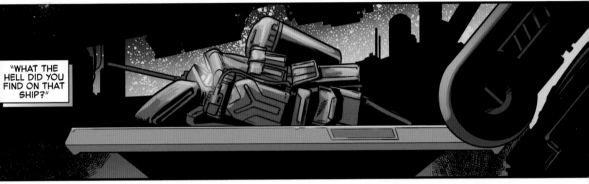

GET A MEDIC! NOW!

CAPTAIN MARVEL
Variant Covers

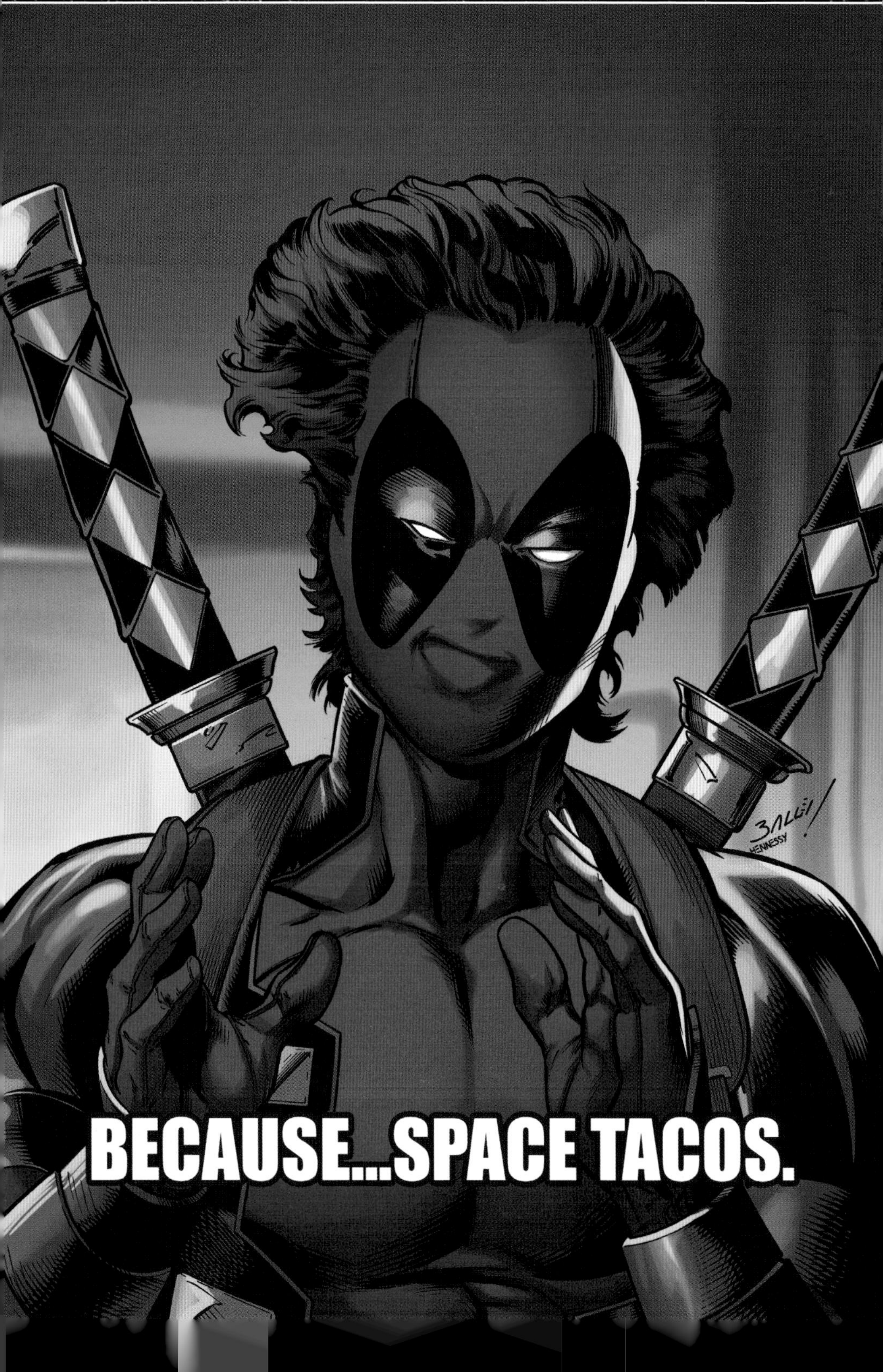
BECAUSE...SPACE TACOS.

MARVEL GRAPHIC NOVEL

CAPTAIN MARVEL #3

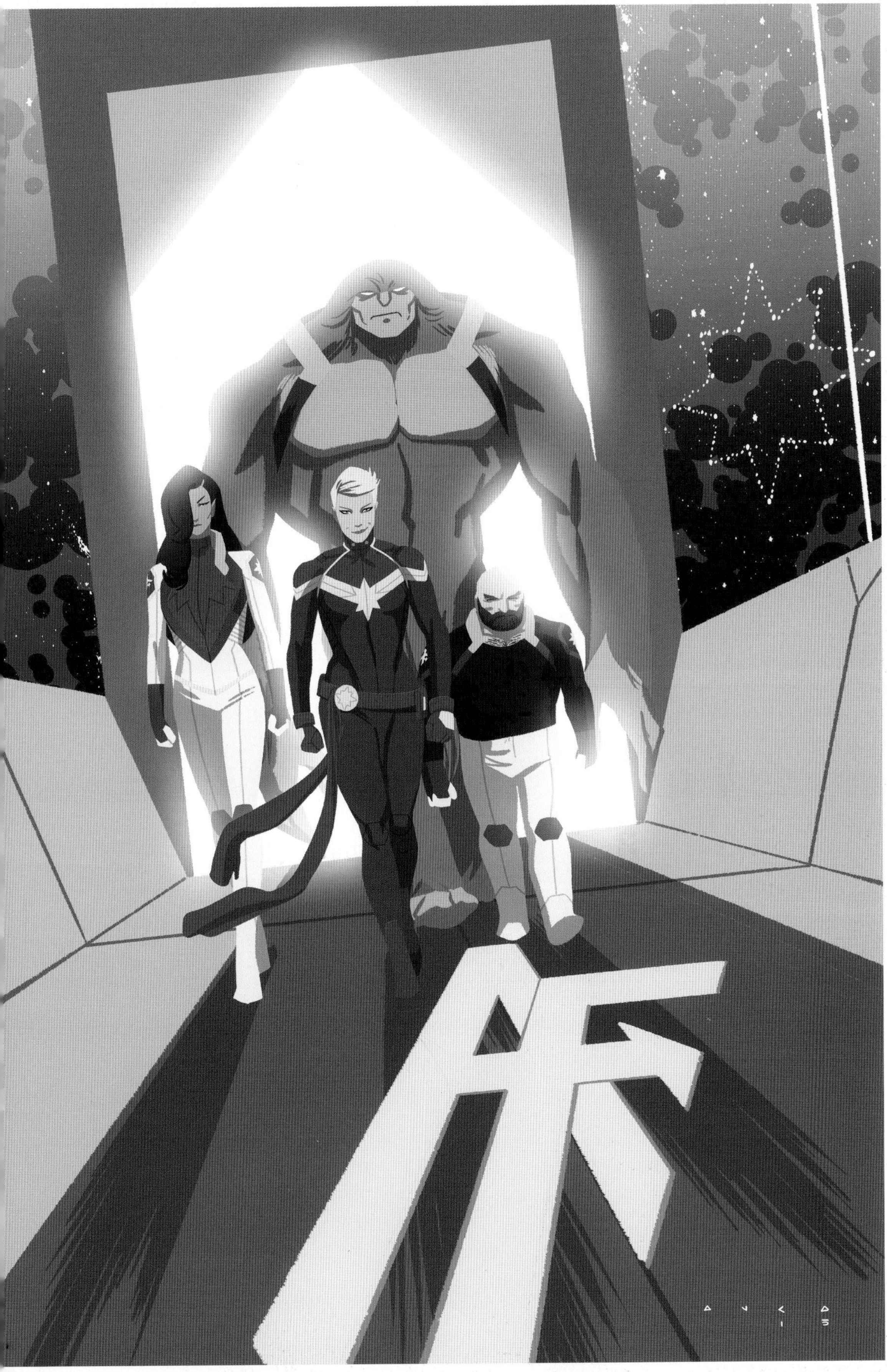

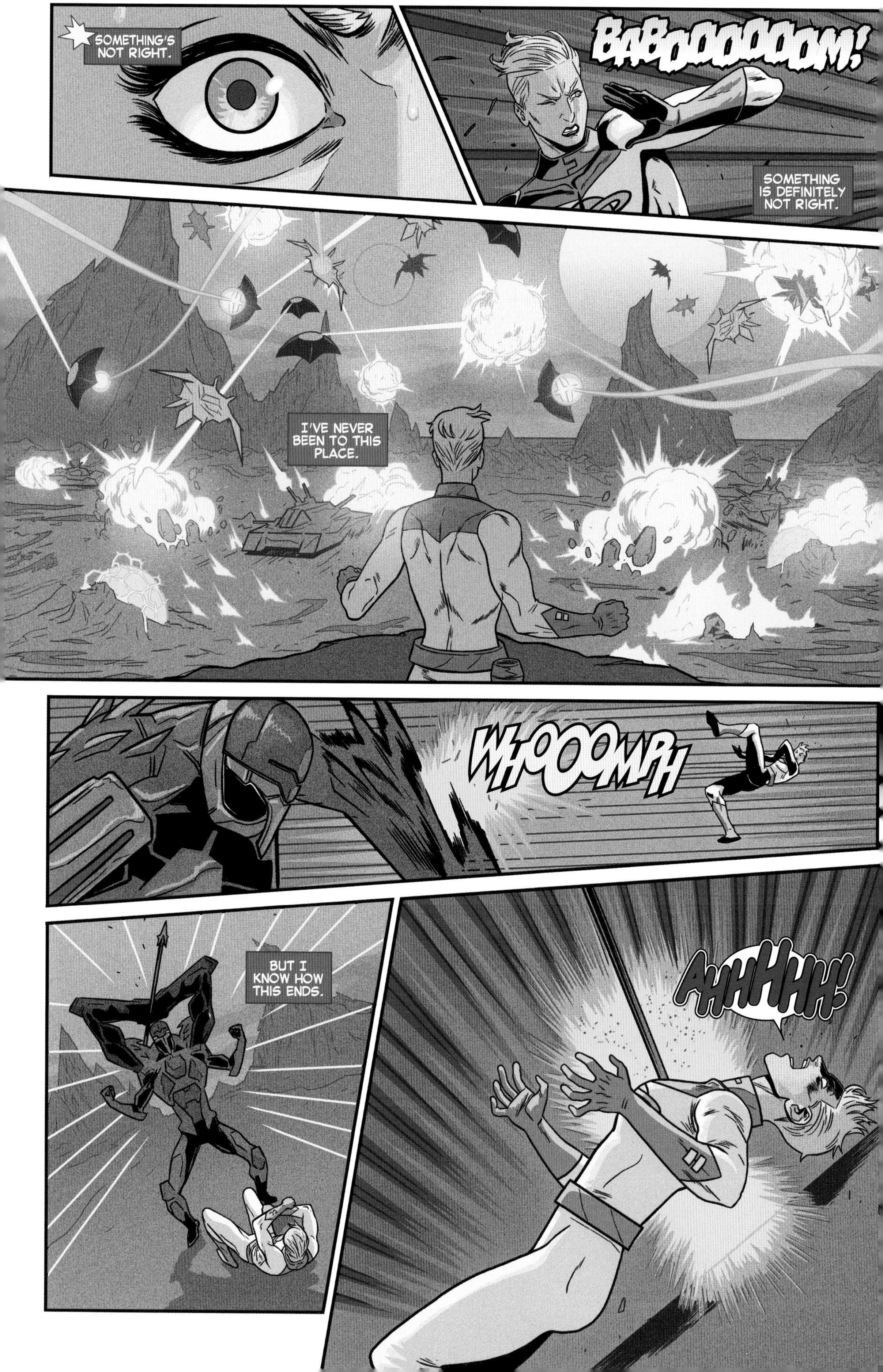
SOMETHING'S NOT RIGHT.
BABOOOOOOOM!
SOMETHING IS DEFINITELY NOT RIGHT.
I'VE NEVER BEEN TO THIS PLACE.
WHOOOMPH
BUT I KNOW HOW THIS ENDS.
AHHHHH!

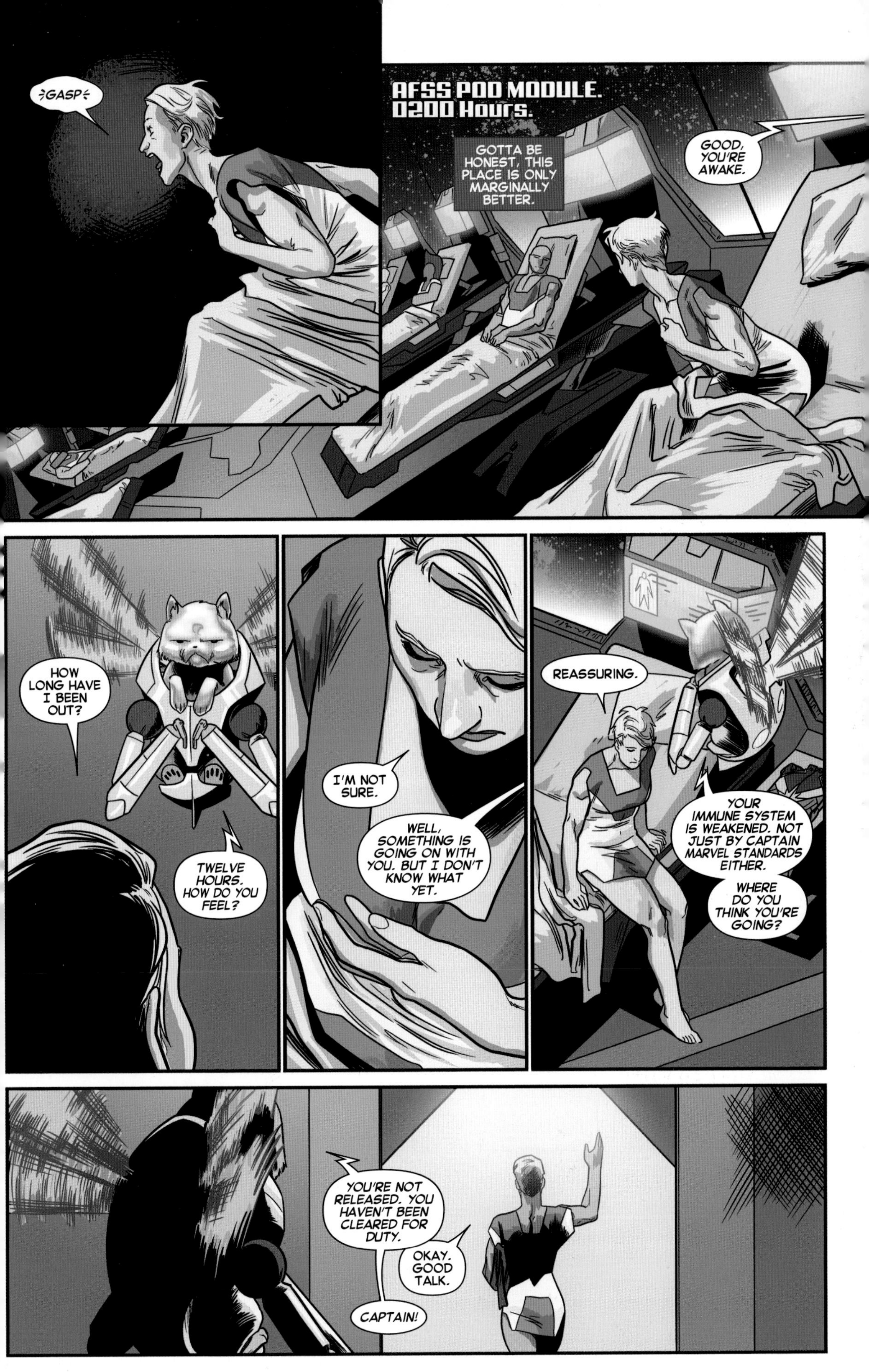
GASP
AFSS POD MODULE. 0200 Hours.
GOTTA BE HONEST, THIS PLACE IS ONLY MARGINALLY BETTER.
GOOD, YOU'RE AWAKE.
HOW LONG HAVE I BEEN OUT?
TWELVE HOURS. HOW DO YOU FEEL?
I'M NOT SURE.
WELL, SOMETHING IS GOING ON WITH YOU. BUT I DON'T KNOW WHAT YET.
REASSURING.
YOUR IMMUNE SYSTEM IS WEAKENED. NOT JUST BY CAPTAIN MARVEL STANDARDS EITHER.
WHERE DO YOU THINK YOU'RE GOING?
YOU'RE NOT RELEASED. YOU HAVEN'T BEEN CLEARED FOR DUTY.
OKAY. GOOD TALK.
CAPTAIN!

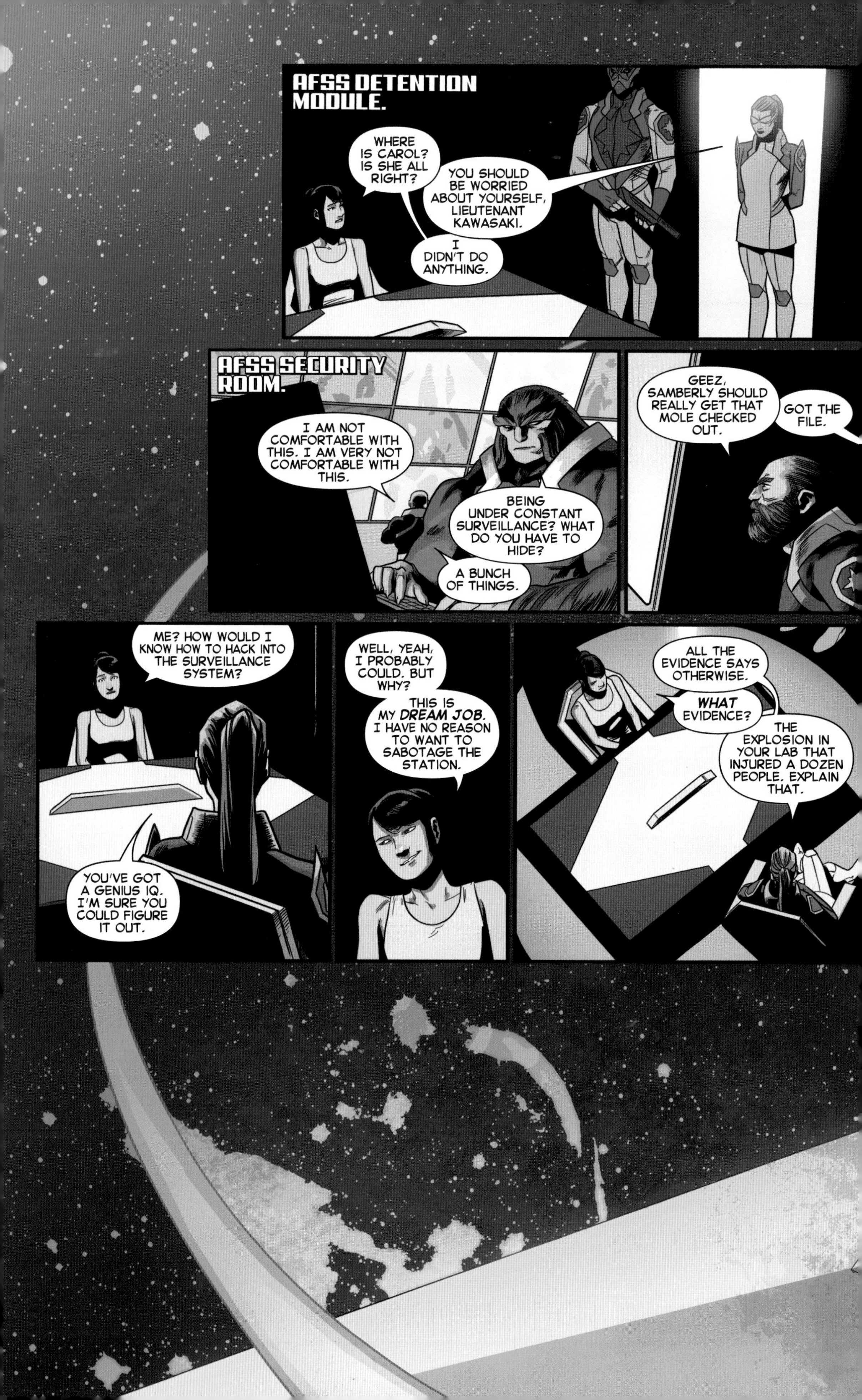
AFSS DETENTION MODULE.
WHERE IS CAROL? IS SHE ALL RIGHT?
YOU SHOULD BE WORRIED ABOUT YOURSELF, LIEUTENANT KAWASAKI.
I DIDN'T DO ANYTHING.
AFSS SECURITY ROOM.
I AM NOT COMFORTABLE WITH THIS. I AM VERY NOT COMFORTABLE WITH THIS.
BEING UNDER CONSTANT SURVEILLANCE? WHAT DO YOU HAVE TO HIDE?
A BUNCH OF THINGS.
GEEZ, SAMBERLY SHOULD REALLY GET THAT MOLE CHECKED OUT.
GOT THE FILE.
ME? HOW WOULD I KNOW HOW TO HACK INTO THE SURVEILLANCE SYSTEM?
YOU'VE GOT A GENIUS IQ. I'M SURE YOU COULD FIGURE IT OUT.
WELL, YEAH, I PROBABLY COULD. BUT WHY?
THIS IS MY *DREAM JOB*. I HAVE NO REASON TO WANT TO SABOTAGE THE STATION.
ALL THE EVIDENCE SAYS OTHERWISE.
WHAT EVIDENCE?
THE EXPLOSION IN YOUR LAB THAT INJURED A DOZEN PEOPLE. EXPLAIN THAT.

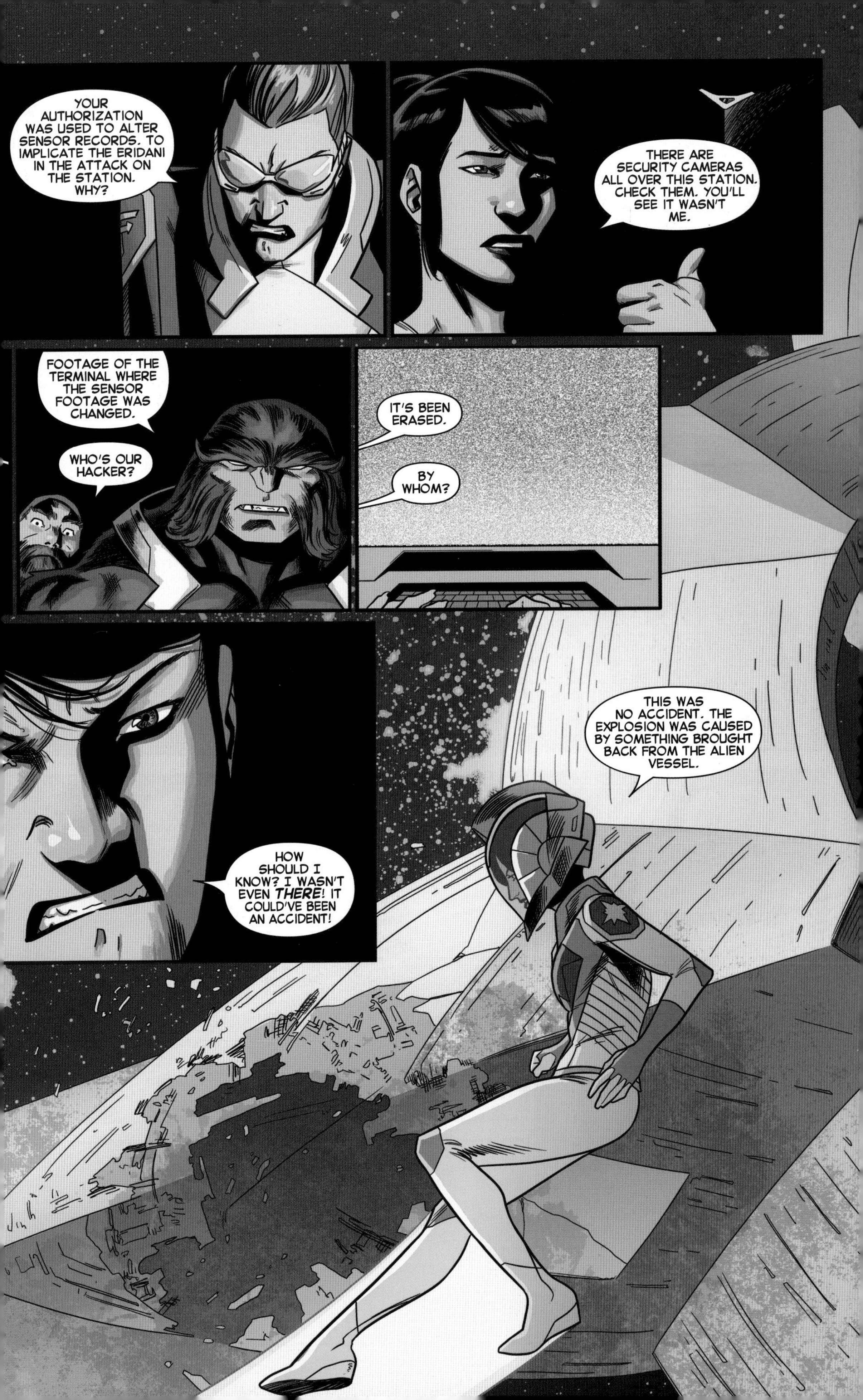
YOUR AUTHORIZATION WAS USED TO ALTER SENSOR RECORDS. TO IMPLICATE THE ERIDANI IN THE ATTACK ON THE STATION. WHY?
THERE ARE SECURITY CAMERAS ALL OVER THIS STATION. CHECK THEM. YOU'LL SEE IT WASN'T ME.
FOOTAGE OF THE TERMINAL WHERE THE SENSOR FOOTAGE WAS CHANGED.
WHO'S OUR HACKER?
IT'S BEEN ERASED.
BY WHOM?
HOW SHOULD I KNOW? I WASN'T EVEN *THERE*! IT COULD'VE BEEN AN ACCIDENT!
THIS WAS NO ACCIDENT. THE EXPLOSION WAS CAUSED BY SOMETHING BROUGHT BACK FROM THE ALIEN VESSEL.

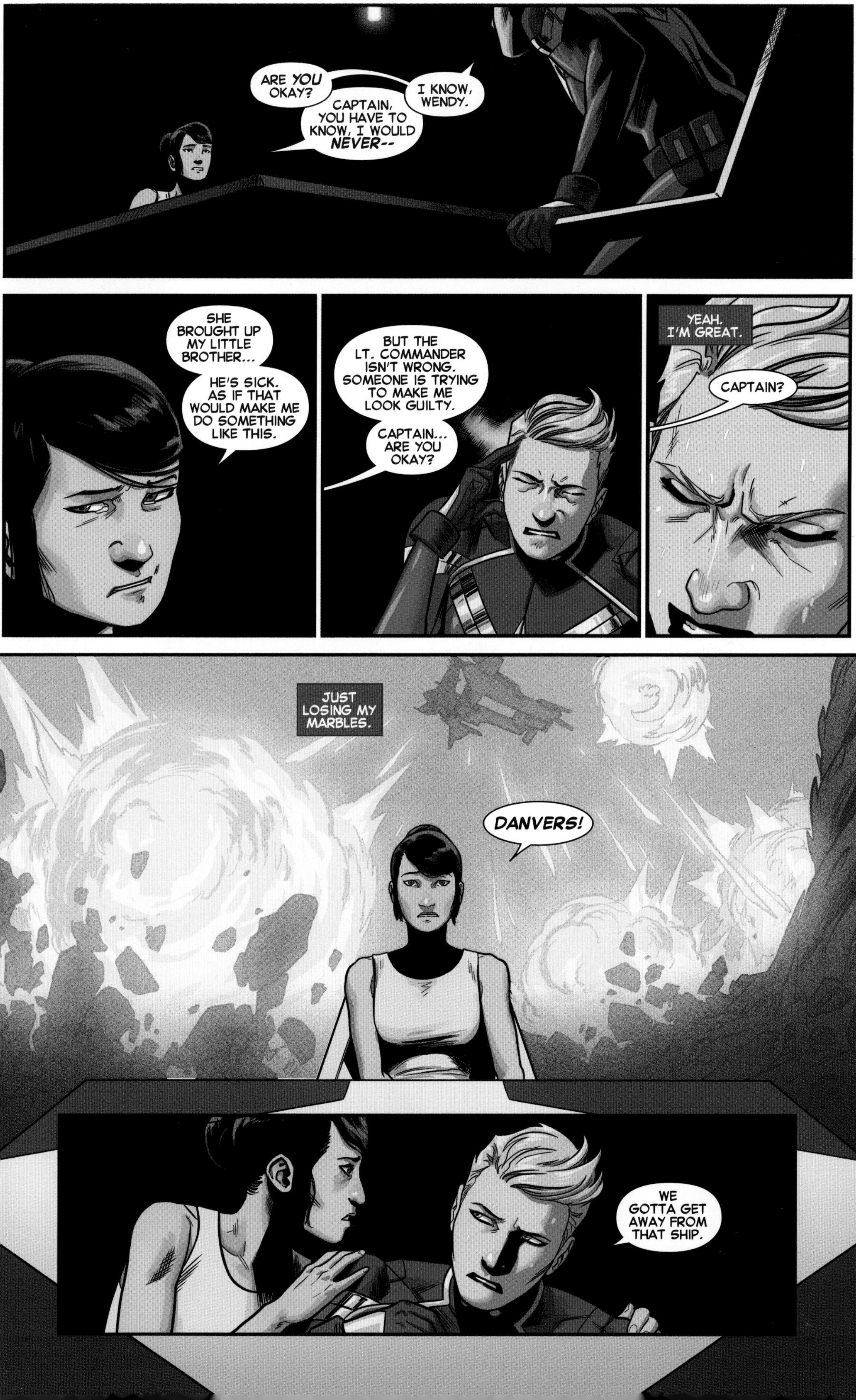
ARE *YOU* OKAY?
CAPTAIN, YOU HAVE TO KNOW, I WOULD ***NEVER--***
I KNOW, WENDY.
SHE BROUGHT UP MY LITTLE BROTHER...
HE'S SICK. AS IF THAT WOULD MAKE ME DO SOMETHING LIKE THIS.
BUT THE LT. COMMANDER ISN'T WRONG. SOMEONE IS TRYING TO MAKE ME LOOK GUILTY.
CAPTAIN... ARE YOU OKAY?
YEAH. I'M GREAT.
CAPTAIN?
JUST LOSING MY MARBLES.
DANVERS!
WE GOTTA GET AWAY FROM THAT SHIP.

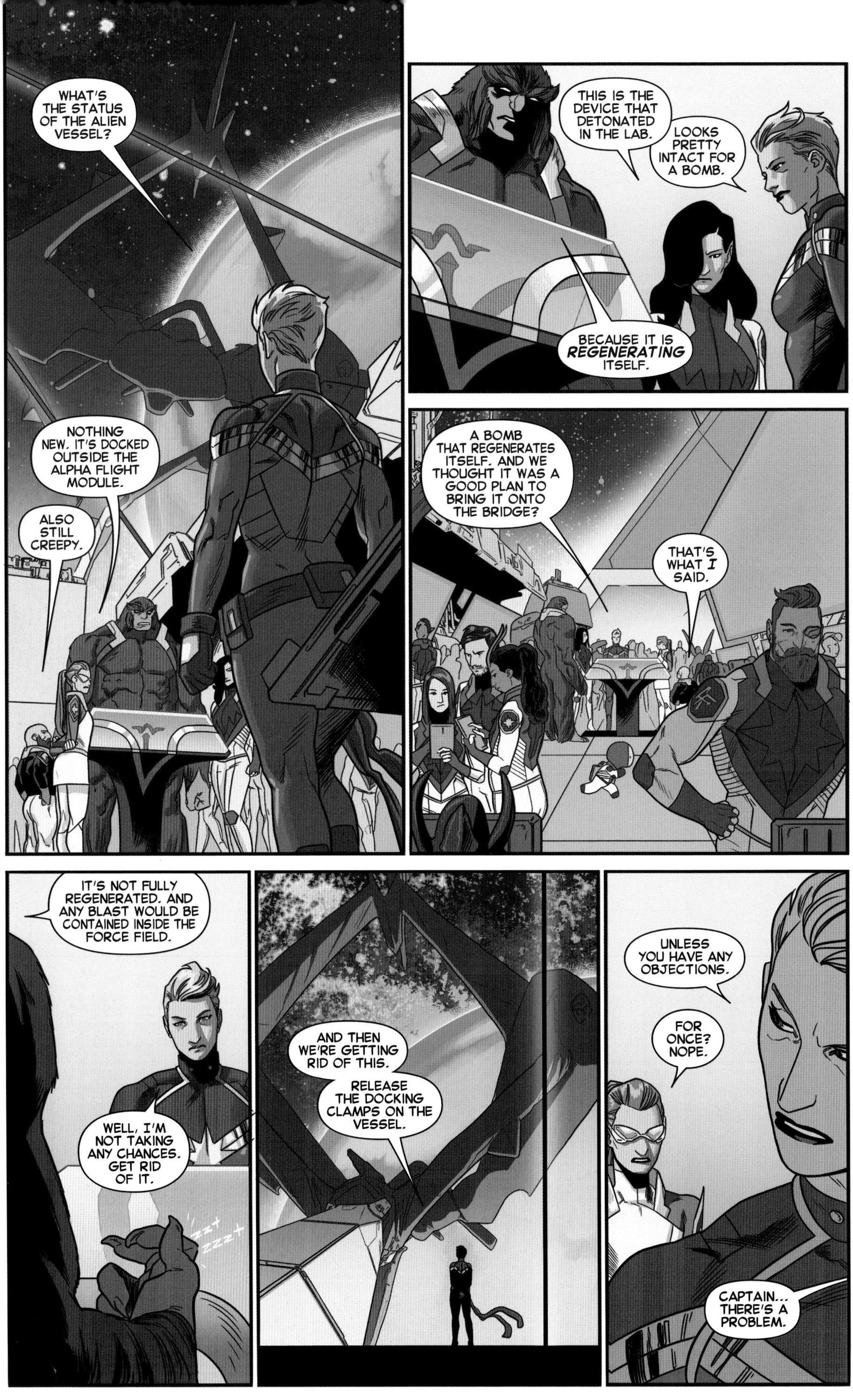
WHAT'S THE STATUS OF THE ALIEN VESSEL?
NOTHING NEW. IT'S DOCKED OUTSIDE THE ALPHA FLIGHT MODULE.
ALSO STILL CREEPY.
THIS IS THE DEVICE THAT DETONATED IN THE LAB.
LOOKS PRETTY INTACT FOR A BOMB.
BECAUSE IT IS *REGENERATING* ITSELF.
A BOMB THAT REGENERATES ITSELF. AND WE THOUGHT IT WAS A GOOD PLAN TO BRING IT ONTO THE BRIDGE?
THAT'S WHAT *I* SAID.
IT'S NOT FULLY REGENERATED. AND ANY BLAST WOULD BE CONTAINED INSIDE THE FORCE FIELD.
WELL, I'M NOT TAKING ANY CHANCES. GET RID OF IT.
AND THEN WE'RE GETTING RID OF THIS.
RELEASE THE DOCKING CLAMPS ON THE VESSEL.
UNLESS YOU HAVE ANY OBJECTIONS.
FOR ONCE? NOPE.
CAPTAIN... THERE'S A PROBLEM.

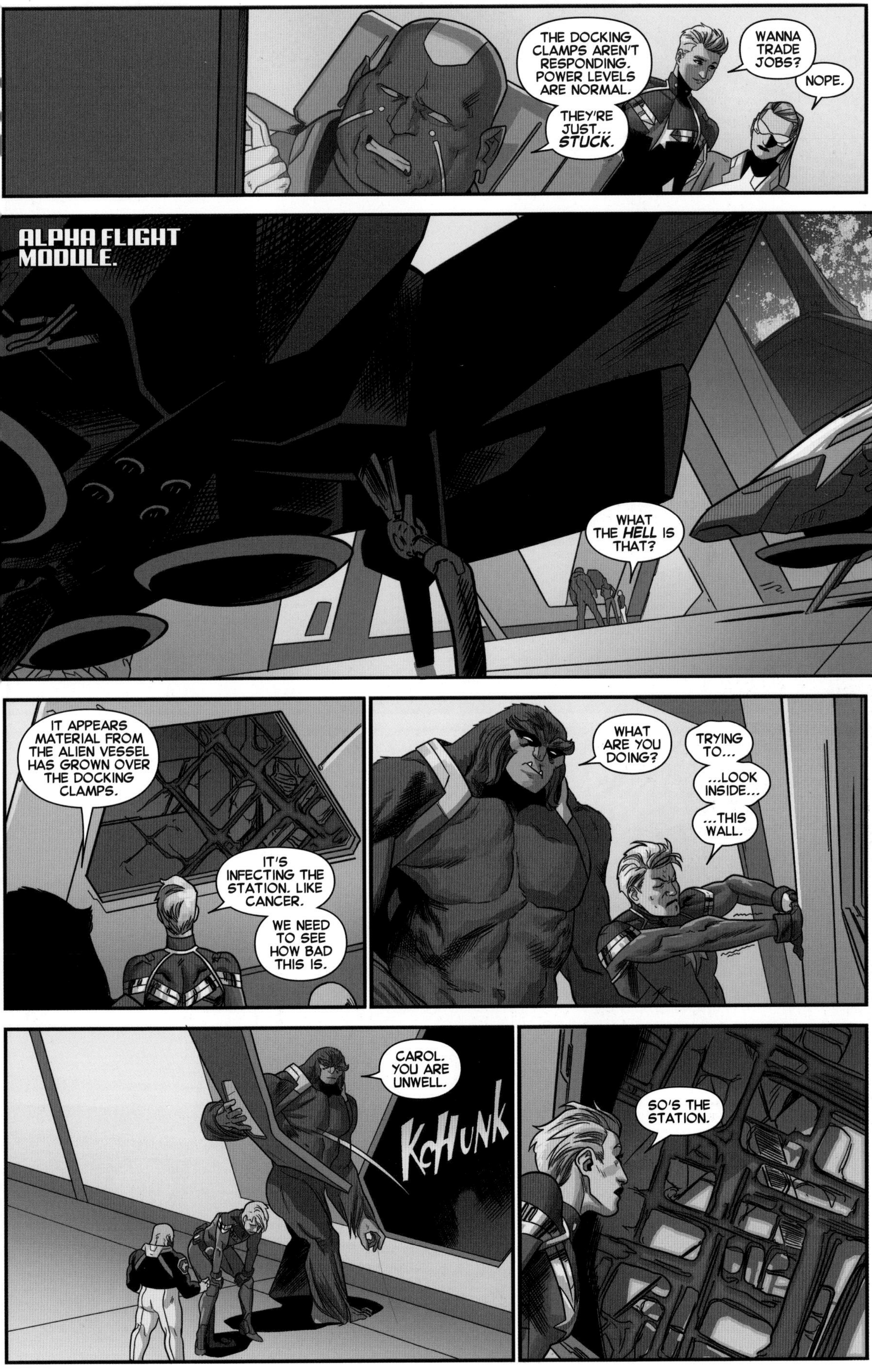
THE DOCKING CLAMPS AREN'T RESPONDING. POWER LEVELS ARE NORMAL.
THEY'RE JUST... STUCK.
WANNA TRADE JOBS?
NOPE.
ALPHA FLIGHT MODULE.
WHAT THE HELL IS THAT?
IT APPEARS MATERIAL FROM THE ALIEN VESSEL HAS GROWN OVER THE DOCKING CLAMPS.
IT'S INFECTING THE STATION. LIKE CANCER.
WE NEED TO SEE HOW BAD THIS IS.
WHAT ARE YOU DOING?
TRYING TO...
...LOOK INSIDE...
...THIS WALL.
CAROL. YOU ARE UNWELL.
KCHUNK
SO'S THE STATION.

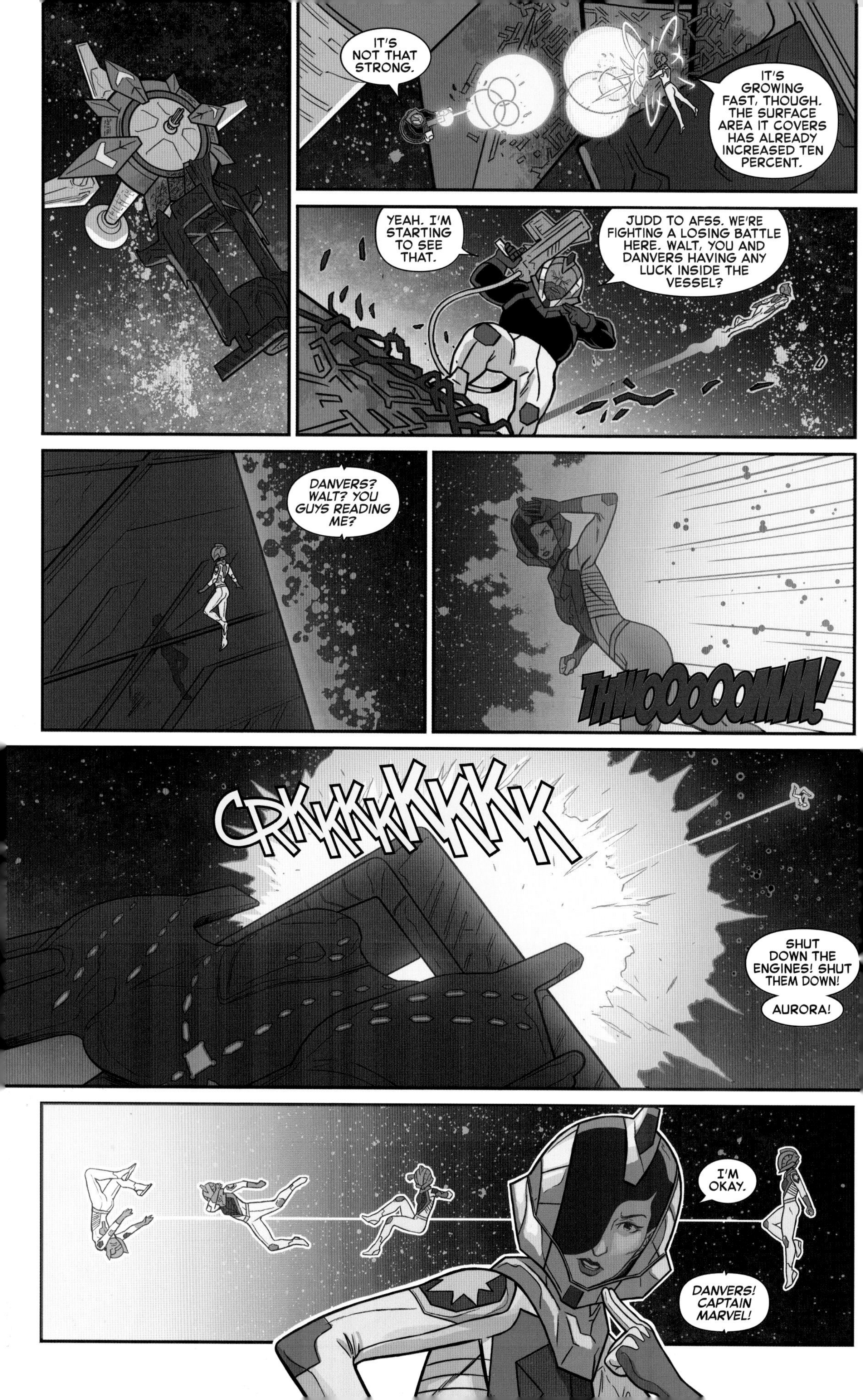
IT'S NOT THAT STRONG.
IT'S GROWING FAST, THOUGH. THE SURFACE AREA IT COVERS HAS ALREADY INCREASED TEN PERCENT.
YEAH. I'M STARTING TO SEE THAT.
JUDD TO AFSS. WE'RE FIGHTING A LOSING BATTLE HERE. WALT, YOU AND DANVERS HAVING ANY LUCK INSIDE THE VESSEL?
DANVERS? WALT? YOU GUYS READING ME?
THMOOOOOMM!
CRKKKKKKKKK
SHUT DOWN THE ENGINES! SHUT THEM DOWN!
AURORA!
I'M OKAY.
DANVERS! CAPTAIN MARVEL!

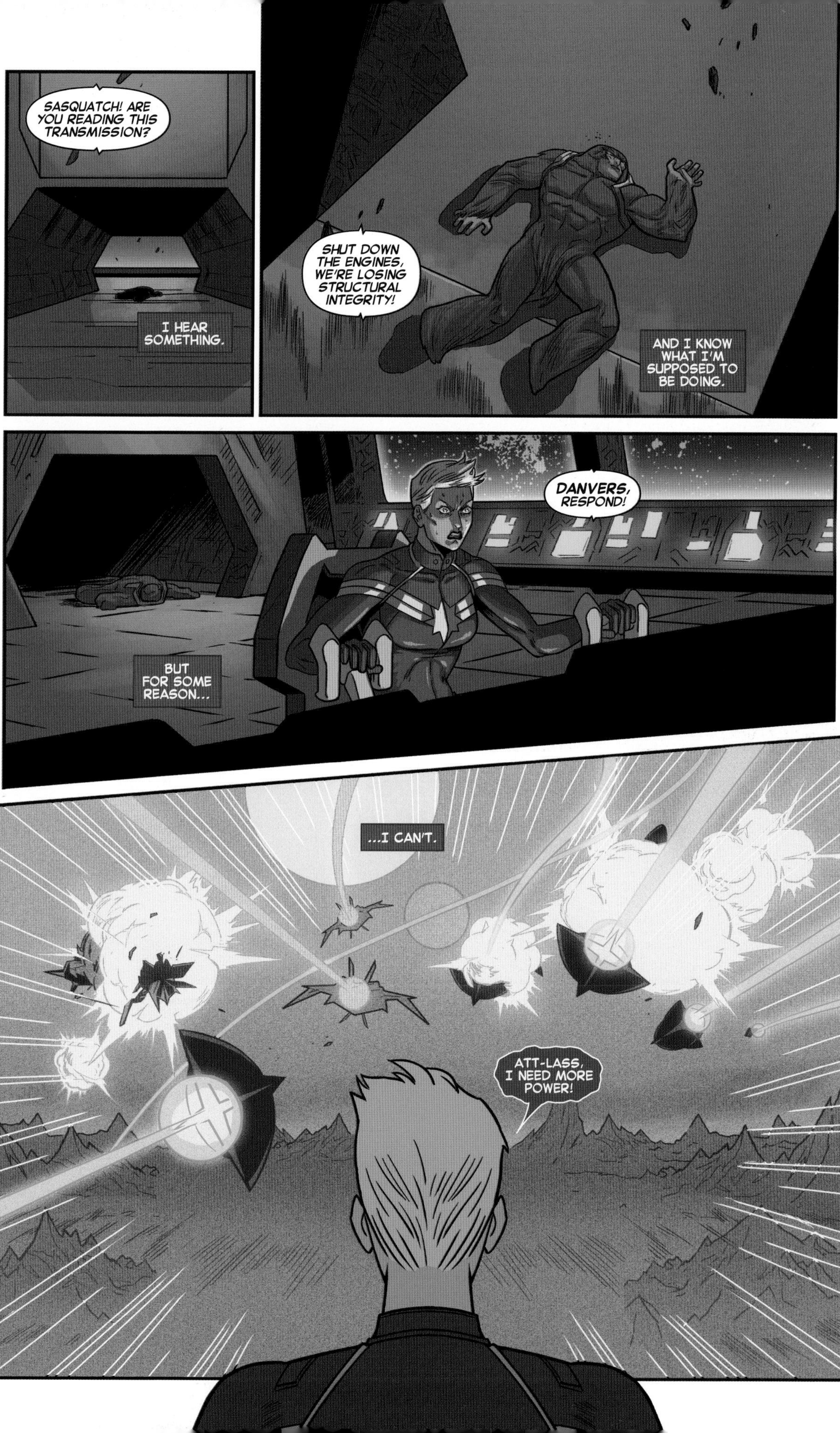
SASQUATCH! ARE YOU READING THIS TRANSMISSION?
I HEAR SOMETHING.
SHUT DOWN THE ENGINES, WE'RE LOSING STRUCTURAL INTEGRITY!
AND I KNOW WHAT I'M SUPPOSED TO BE DOING.
DANVERS, RESPOND!
BUT FOR SOME REASON...
...I CAN'T.
ATT-LASS, I NEED MORE POWER!

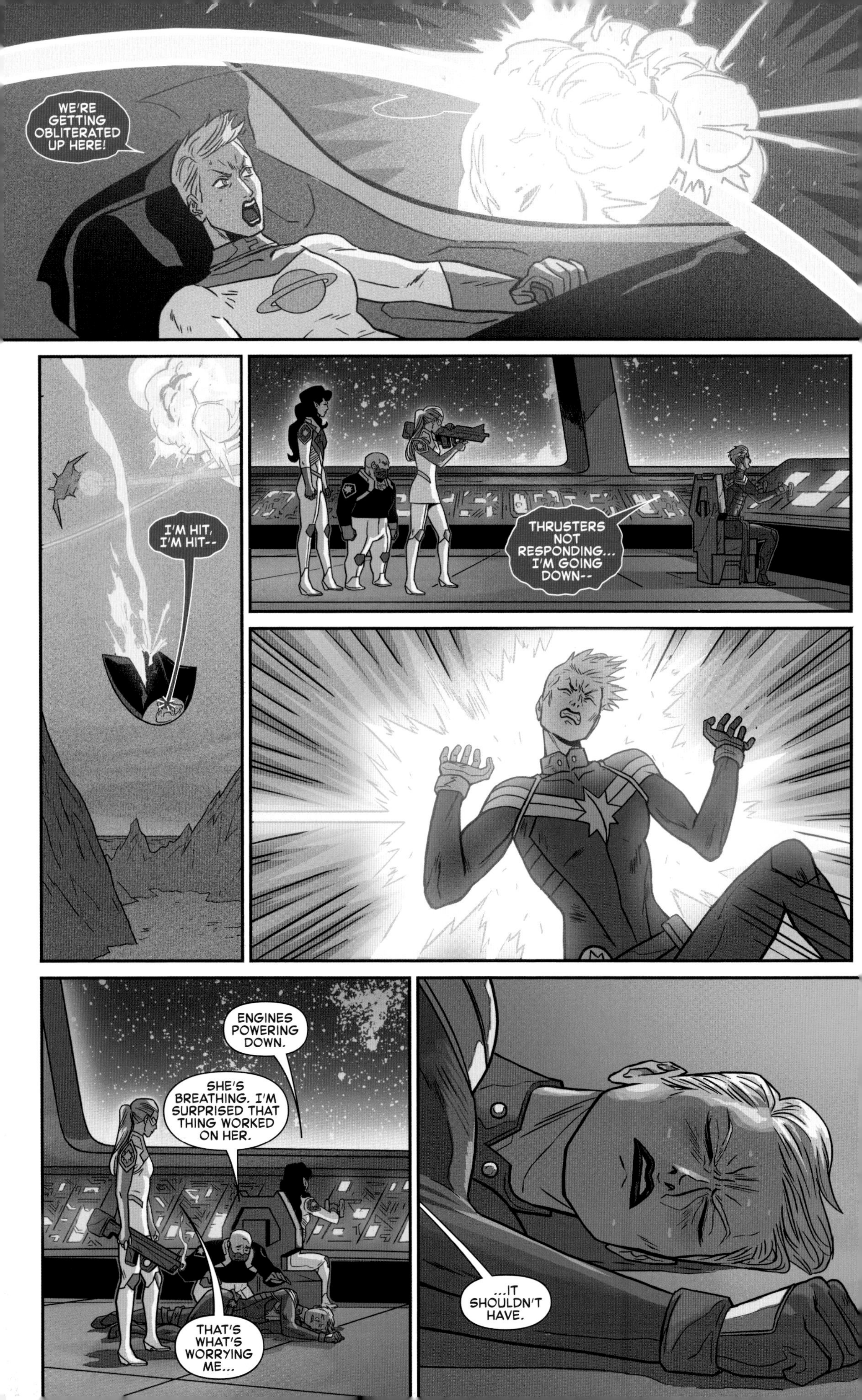
WE'RE GETTING OBLITERATED UP HERE!
I'M HIT, I'M HIT--
THRUSTERS NOT RESPONDING... I'M GOING DOWN--
ENGINES POWERING DOWN.
SHE'S BREATHING. I'M SURPRISED THAT THING WORKED ON HER.
THAT'S WHAT'S WORRYING ME...
...IT SHOULDN'T HAVE.

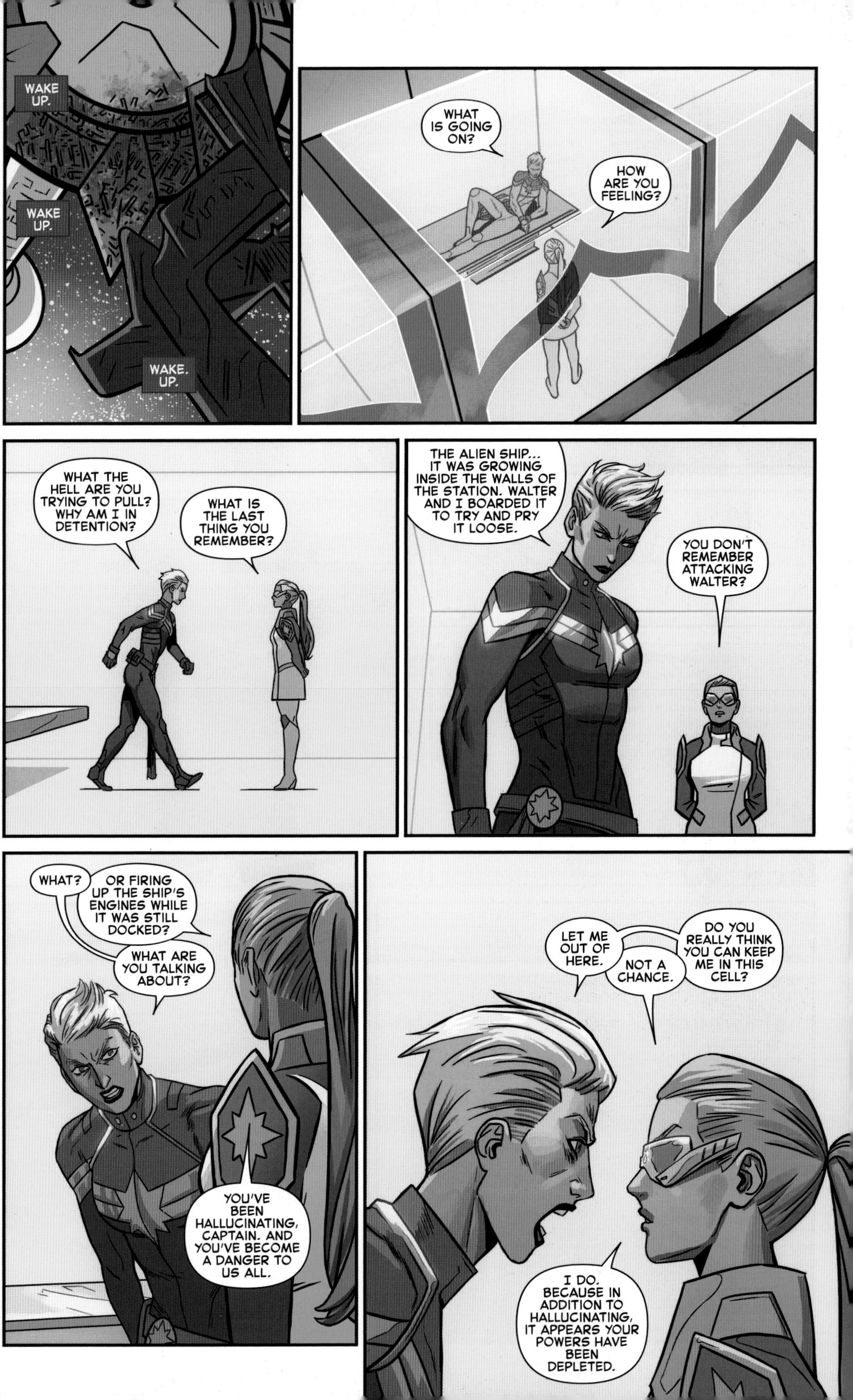
WAKE UP.
WAKE UP.
WAKE. UP.
WHAT IS GOING ON?
HOW ARE YOU FEELING?
WHAT THE HELL ARE YOU TRYING TO PULL? WHY AM I IN DETENTION?
WHAT IS THE LAST THING YOU REMEMBER?
THE ALIEN SHIP... IT WAS GROWING INSIDE THE WALLS OF THE STATION. WALTER AND I BOARDED IT TO TRY AND PRY IT LOOSE.
YOU DON'T REMEMBER ATTACKING WALTER?
WHAT?
OR FIRING UP THE SHIP'S ENGINES WHILE IT WAS STILL DOCKED?
WHAT ARE YOU TALKING ABOUT?
YOU'VE BEEN HALLUCINATING, CAPTAIN. AND YOU'VE BECOME A DANGER TO US ALL.
LET ME OUT OF HERE.
NOT A CHANCE.
DO YOU REALLY THINK YOU CAN KEEP ME IN THIS CELL?
I DO. BECAUSE IN ADDITION TO HALLUCINATING, IT APPEARS YOUR POWERS HAVE BEEN DEPLETED.

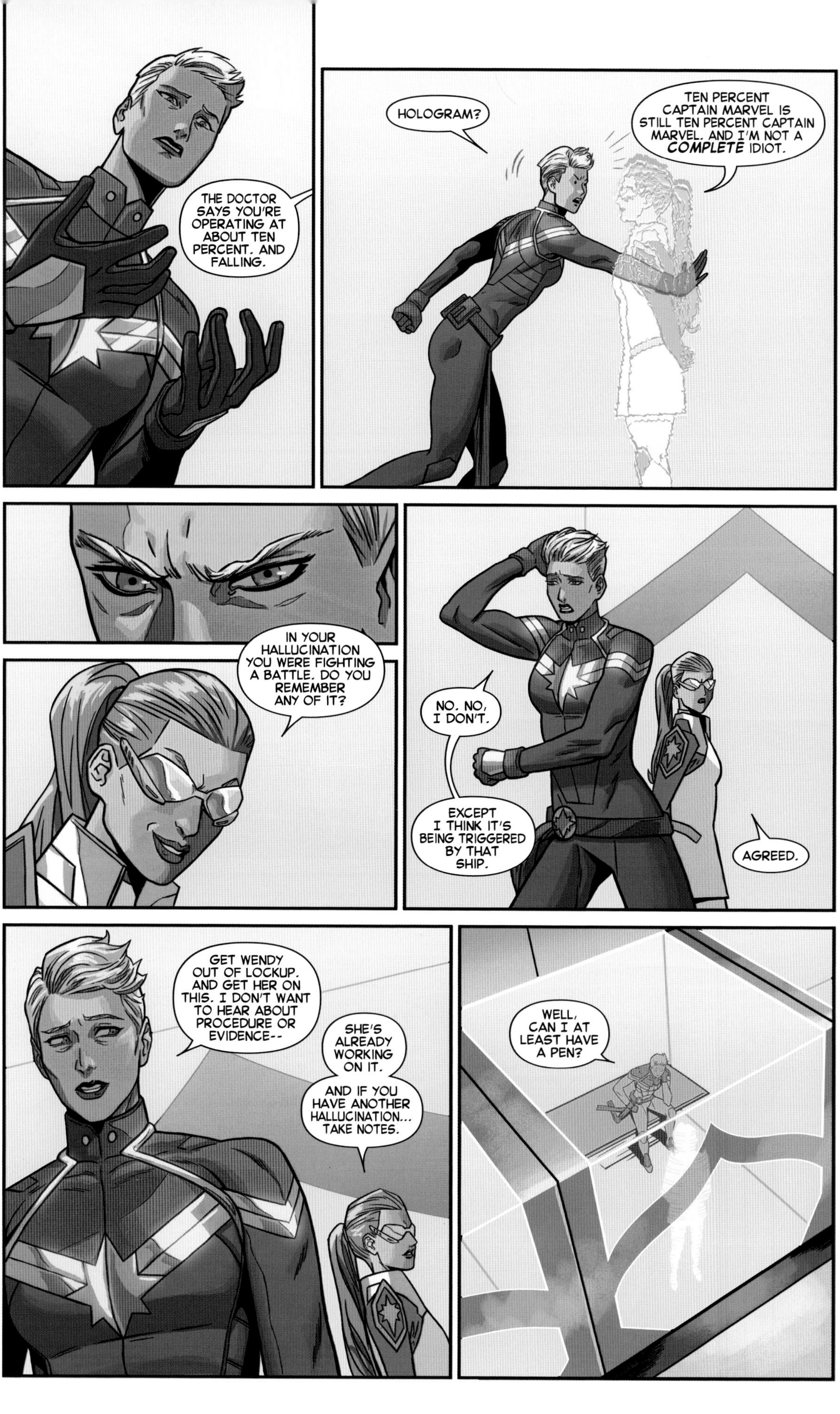
THE DOCTOR SAYS YOU'RE OPERATING AT ABOUT TEN PERCENT. AND FALLING.
HOLOGRAM?
TEN PERCENT CAPTAIN MARVEL IS STILL TEN PERCENT CAPTAIN MARVEL. AND I'M NOT A *COMPLETE* IDIOT.
IN YOUR HALLUCINATION YOU WERE FIGHTING A BATTLE. DO YOU REMEMBER ANY OF IT?
NO. NO, I DON'T.
EXCEPT I THINK IT'S BEING TRIGGERED BY THAT SHIP.
AGREED.
GET WENDY OUT OF LOCKUP. AND GET HER ON THIS. I DON'T WANT TO HEAR ABOUT PROCEDURE OR EVIDENCE--
SHE'S ALREADY WORKING ON IT.
AND IF YOU HAVE ANOTHER HALLUCINATION... TAKE NOTES.
WELL, CAN I AT LEAST HAVE A PEN?

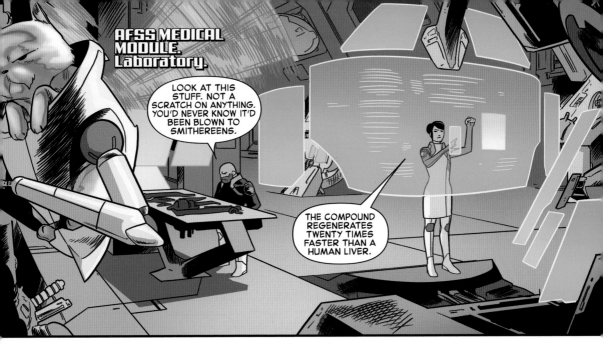

AFSS MEDICAL MODULE. Laboratory.
LOOK AT THIS STUFF. NOT A SCRATCH ON ANYTHING. YOU'D NEVER KNOW IT'D BEEN BLOWN TO SMITHEREENS.
THE COMPOUND REGENERATES TWENTY TIMES FASTER THAN A HUMAN LIVER.
I'M SORRY YOUR SLUG DIDN'T REGENERATE.
UH-HUH.
I'D OFFER TO GET YOU ANOTHER ONE, BUT I CAN'T.
BECAUSE SLUGS.
I'M NOT HELPING, AM I?
LOOK AT THAT PATTERN. IT'S ALL OVER THEIR MAIN COMPUTER. THIS MEANS SOMETHING. I JUST DON'T KNOW WHAT.
AND THERE ARE TWENTY-TWO OTHER PATTERNS THAT ARE SIMILAR. ALL REPEATING TOGETHER.
CHROMOSOMES.
HUMANOIDS HAVE TWENTY-THREE CHROMOSOMES.
THE COMPUTER CAN GIVE US A GRAPHIC REPRESENTATION OF THE CODE.
IT'S DNA.
WHOSE?

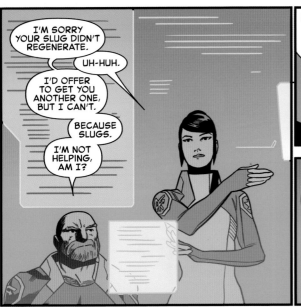

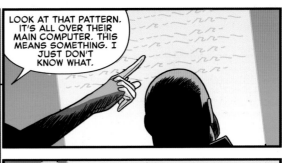

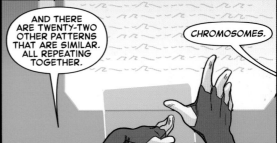

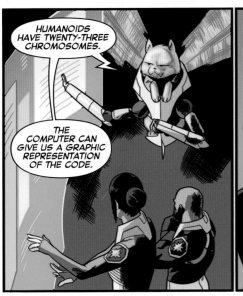

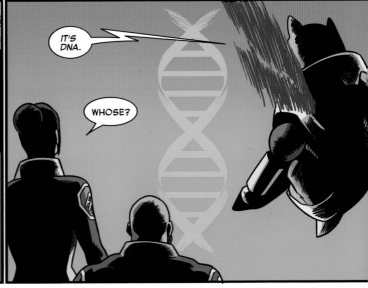

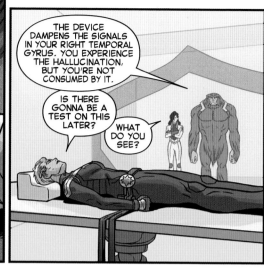

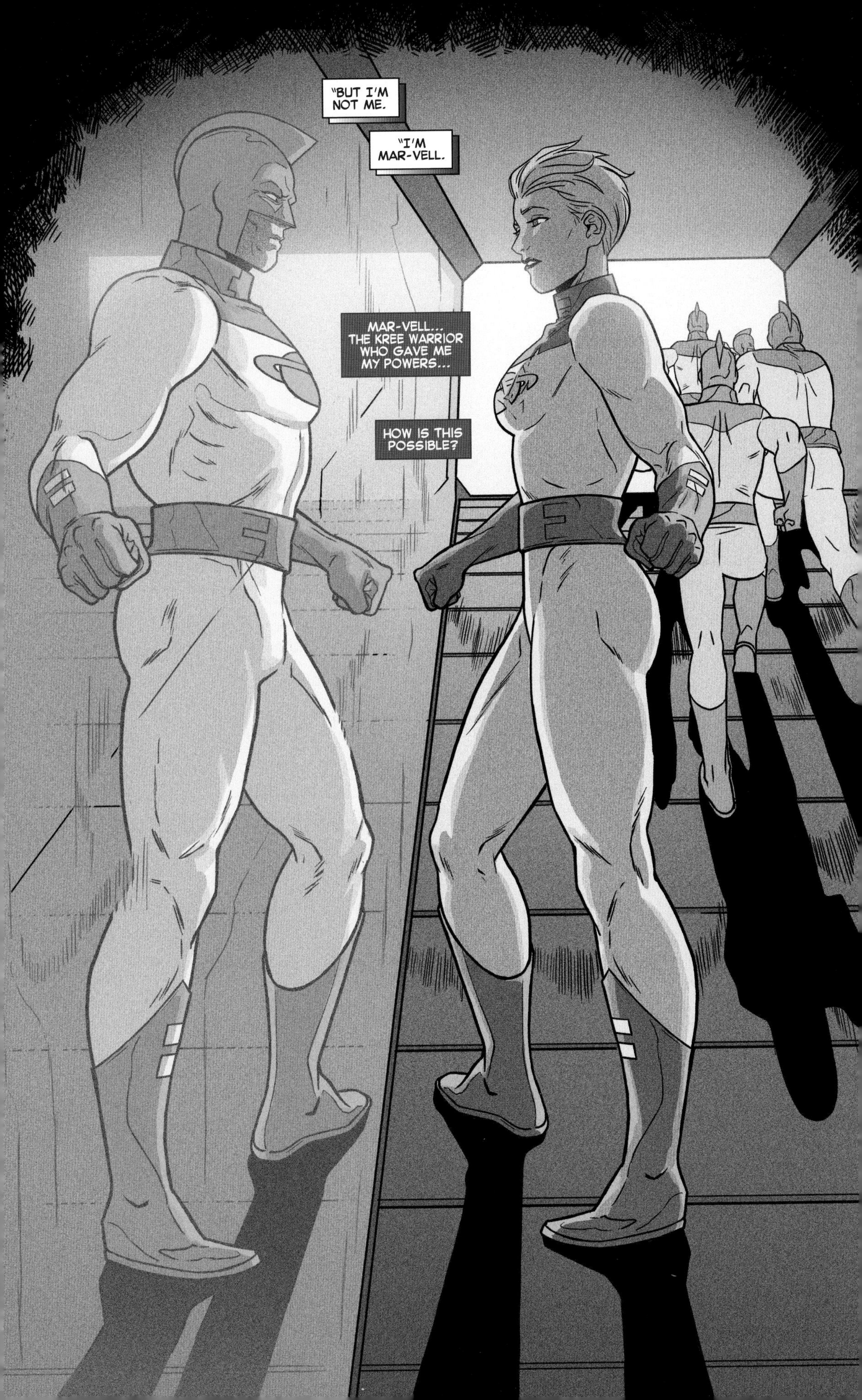
"BUT I'M NOT ME.
"I'M MAR-VELL.
MAR-VELL... THE KREE WARRIOR WHO GAVE ME MY POWERS...
HOW IS THIS POSSIBLE?

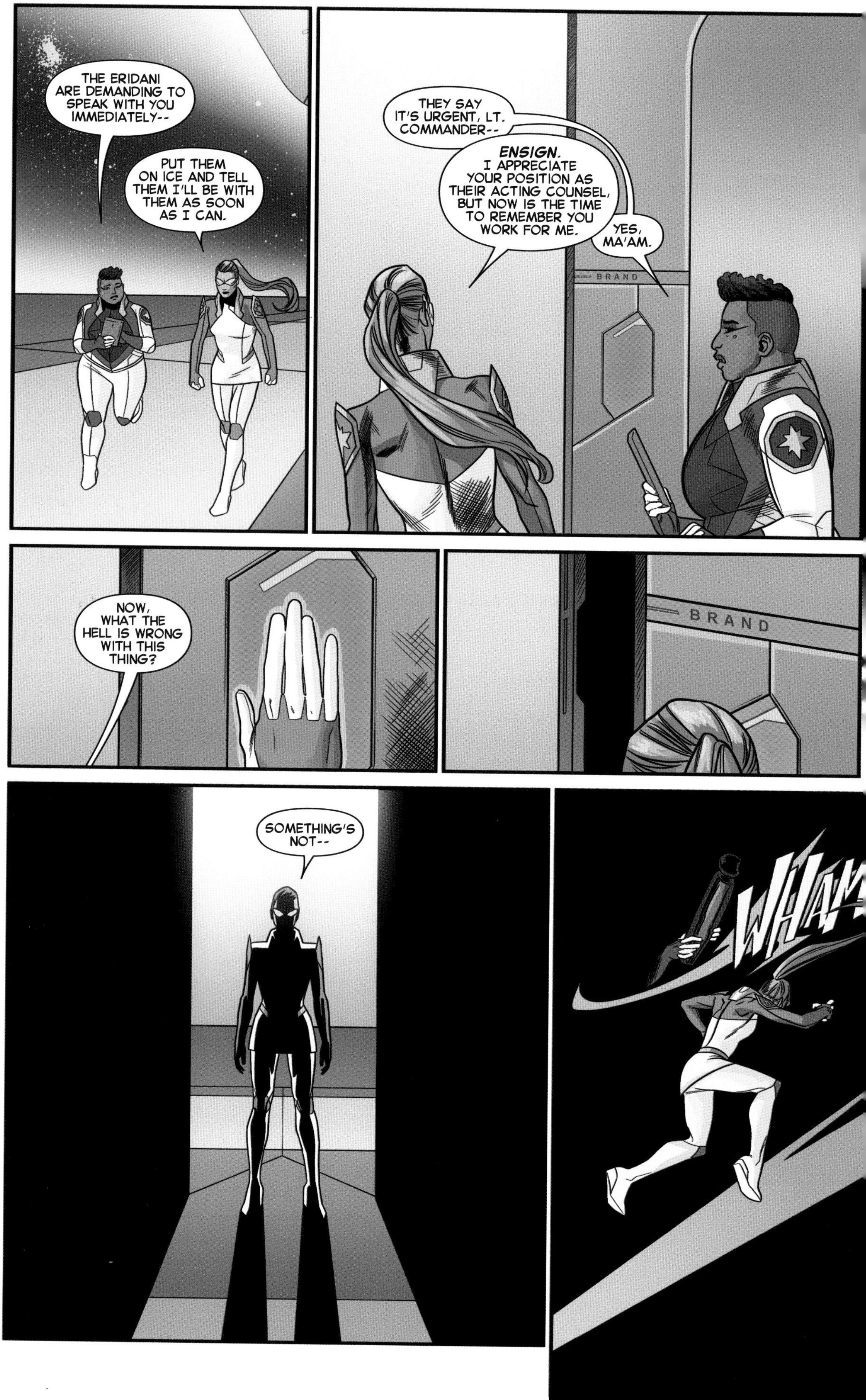
THE ERIDANI ARE DEMANDING TO SPEAK WITH YOU IMMEDIATELY--
PUT THEM ON ICE AND TELL THEM I'LL BE WITH THEM AS SOON AS I CAN.
THEY SAY IT'S URGENT, LT. COMMANDER--
ENSIGN. I APPRECIATE YOUR POSITION AS THEIR ACTING COUNSEL, BUT NOW IS THE TIME TO REMEMBER YOU WORK FOR ME.
YES, MA'AM.
BRAND
NOW, WHAT THE HELL IS WRONG WITH THIS THING?
BRAND
SOMETHING'S NOT--
WHAM

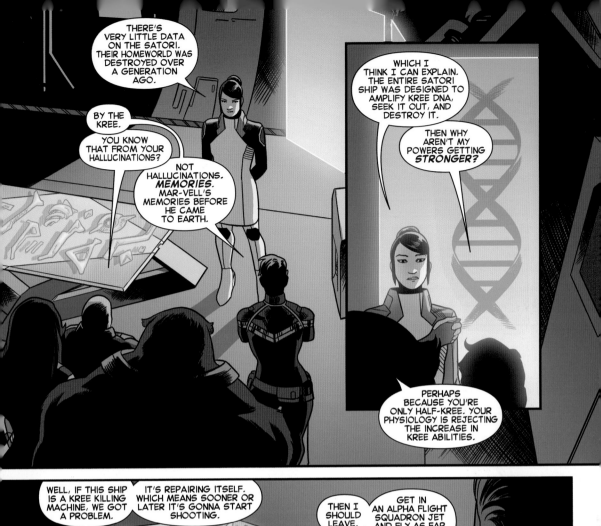

THERE'S VERY LITTLE DATA ON THE SATORI. THEIR HOMEWORLD WAS DESTROYED OVER A GENERATION AGO.

BY THE KREE.

YOU KNOW THAT FROM YOUR HALLUCINATIONS?

NOT HALLUCINATIONS. *MEMORIES.* MAR-VELL'S MEMORIES BEFORE HE CAME TO EARTH.

WHICH I THINK I CAN EXPLAIN. THE ENTIRE SATORI SHIP WAS DESIGNED TO AMPLIFY KREE DNA, SEEK IT OUT, AND DESTROY IT.

THEN WHY AREN'T MY POWERS GETTING *STRONGER?*

PERHAPS BECAUSE YOU'RE ONLY HALF-KREE. YOUR PHYSIOLOGY IS REJECTING THE INCREASE IN KREE ABILITIES.

WELL, IF THIS SHIP IS A KREE KILLING MACHINE, WE GOT A PROBLEM.

IT'S REPAIRING ITSELF. WHICH MEANS SOONER OR LATER IT'S GONNA START SHOOTING.

THEN I SHOULD LEAVE.

GET IN AN ALPHA FLIGHT SQUADRON JET AND FLY AS FAR AWAY AS POSSIBLE.

THE SATORI SHIP IS STILL ENTANGLED WITH THE STATION. ONCE IT AWAKENS, IT WILL STILL TRY TO PURSUE YOU.

TEARING THE STATION APART IN THE PROCESS.

THEN LET'S PULL IT APART OURSELVES.

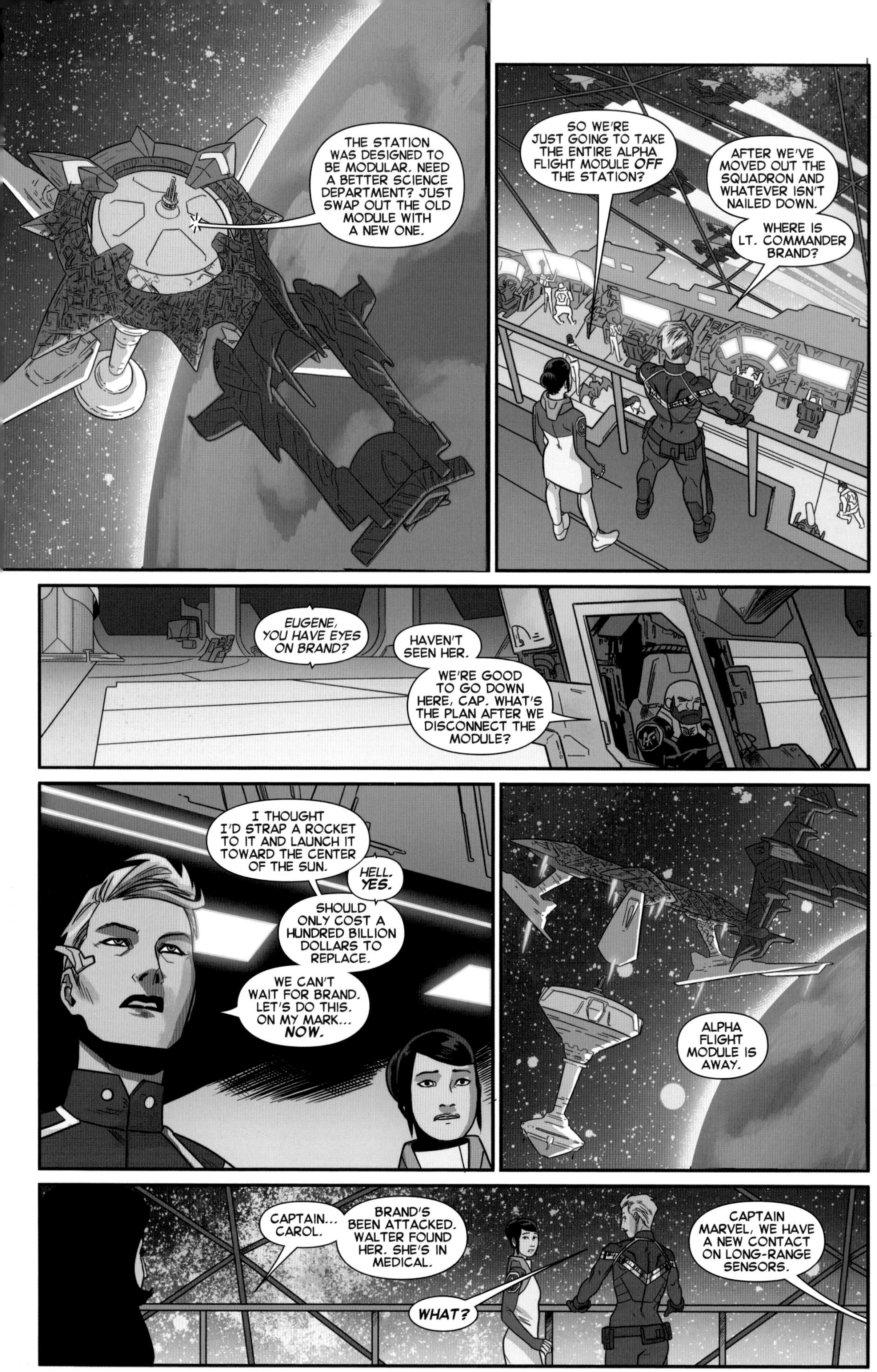
THE STATION WAS DESIGNED TO BE MODULAR. NEED A BETTER SCIENCE DEPARTMENT? JUST SWAP OUT THE OLD MODULE WITH A NEW ONE.
SO WE'RE JUST GOING TO TAKE THE ENTIRE ALPHA FLIGHT MODULE OFF THE STATION?
AFTER WE'VE MOVED OUT THE SQUADRON AND WHATEVER ISN'T NAILED DOWN.
WHERE IS LT. COMMANDER BRAND?
EUGENE, YOU HAVE EYES ON BRAND?
HAVEN'T SEEN HER.
WE'RE GOOD TO GO DOWN HERE, CAP. WHAT'S THE PLAN AFTER WE DISCONNECT THE MODULE?
I THOUGHT I'D STRAP A ROCKET TO IT AND LAUNCH IT TOWARD THE CENTER OF THE SUN.
HELL. YES.
SHOULD ONLY COST A HUNDRED BILLION DOLLARS TO REPLACE.
WE CAN'T WAIT FOR BRAND. LET'S DO THIS. ON MY MARK... NOW.
ALPHA FLIGHT MODULE IS AWAY.
CAPTAIN... CAROL.
BRAND'S BEEN ATTACKED. WALTER FOUND HER. SHE'S IN MEDICAL.
WHAT?
CAPTAIN MARVEL, WE HAVE A NEW CONTACT ON LONG-RANGE SENSORS.

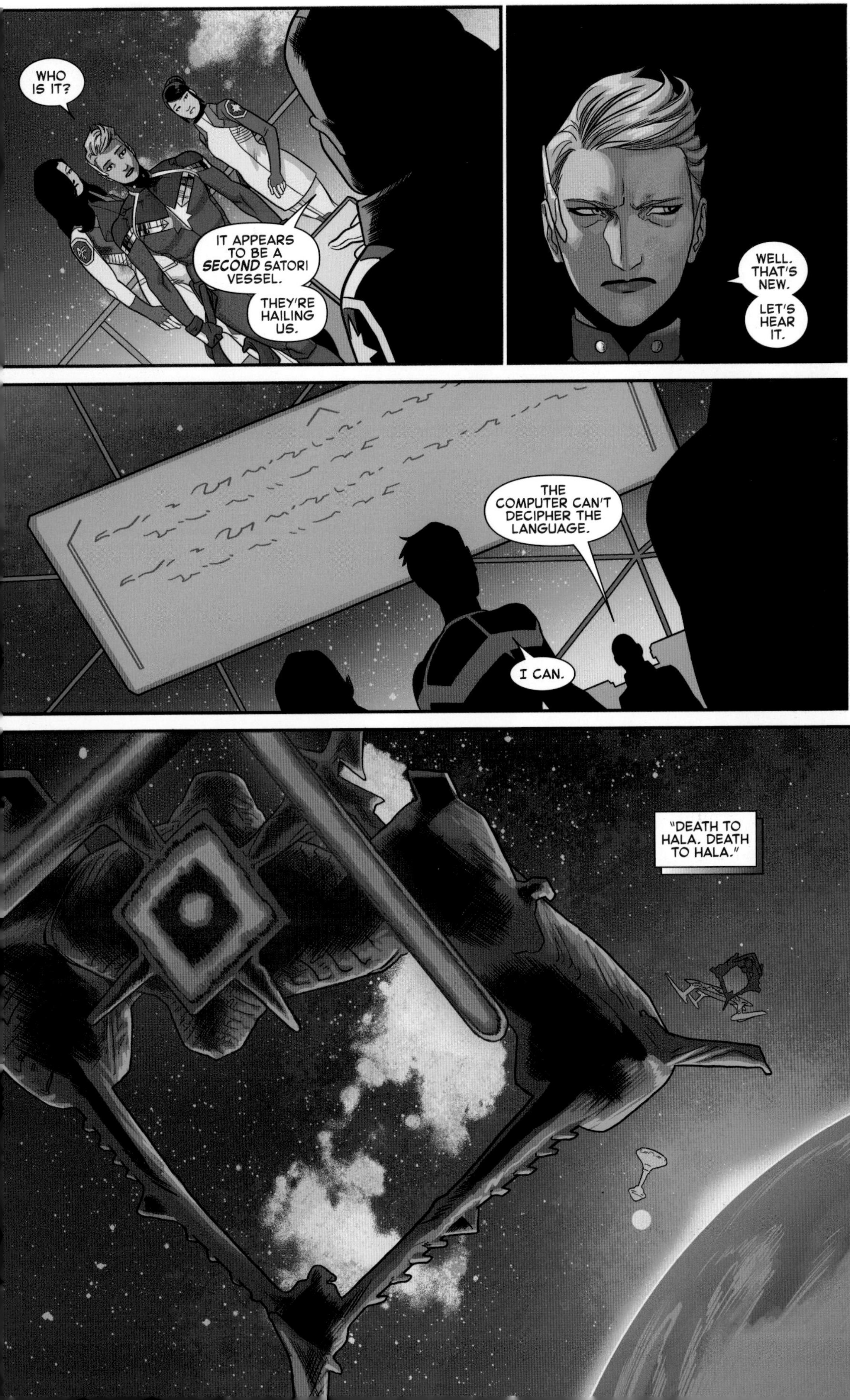
WHO IS IT?
IT APPEARS TO BE A SECOND SATORI VESSEL.
THEY'RE HAILING US.
WELL. THAT'S NEW.
LET'S HEAR IT.
THE COMPUTER CAN'T DECIPHER THE LANGUAGE.
I CAN.
"DEATH TO HALA. DEATH TO HALA."

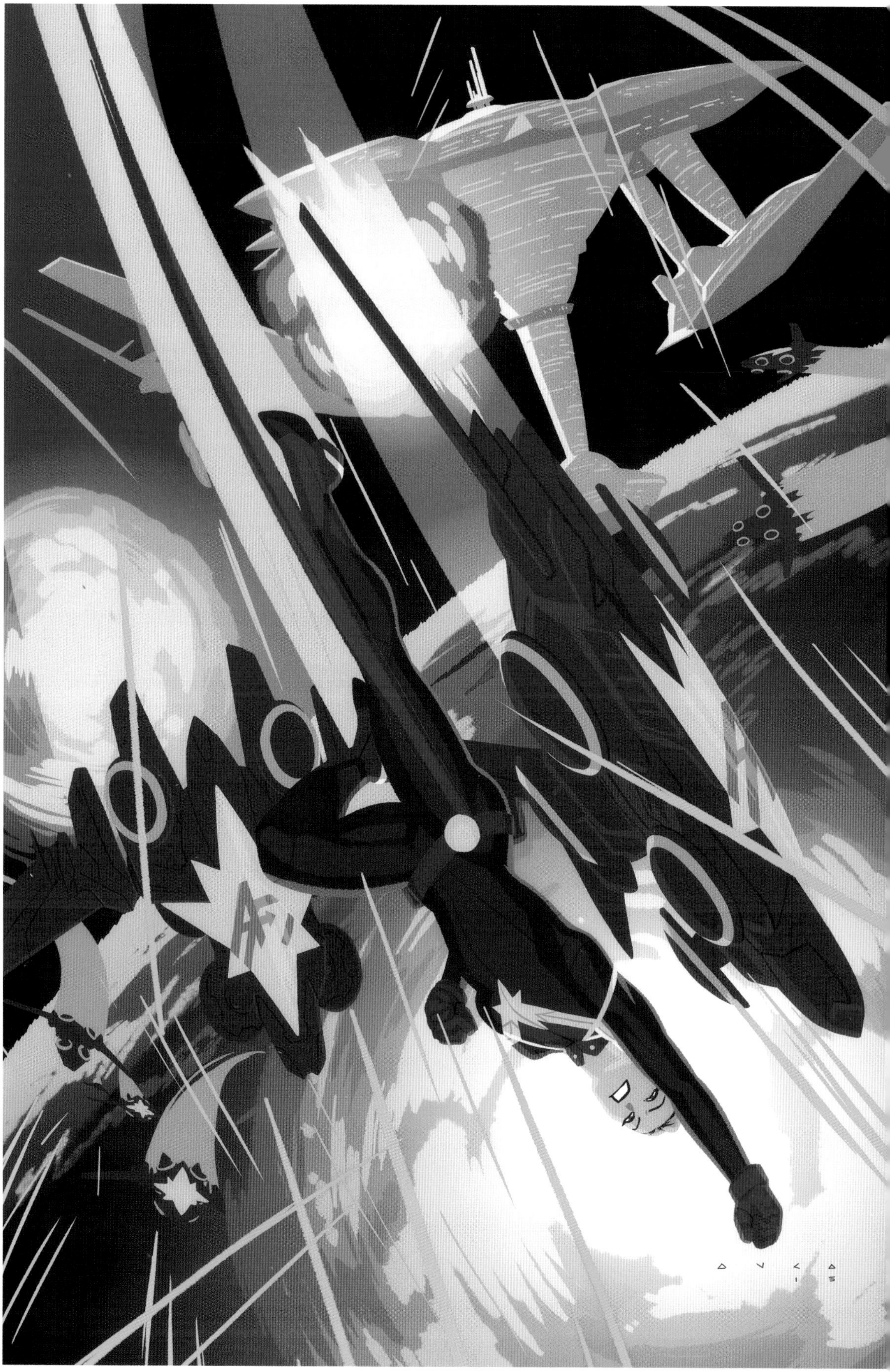

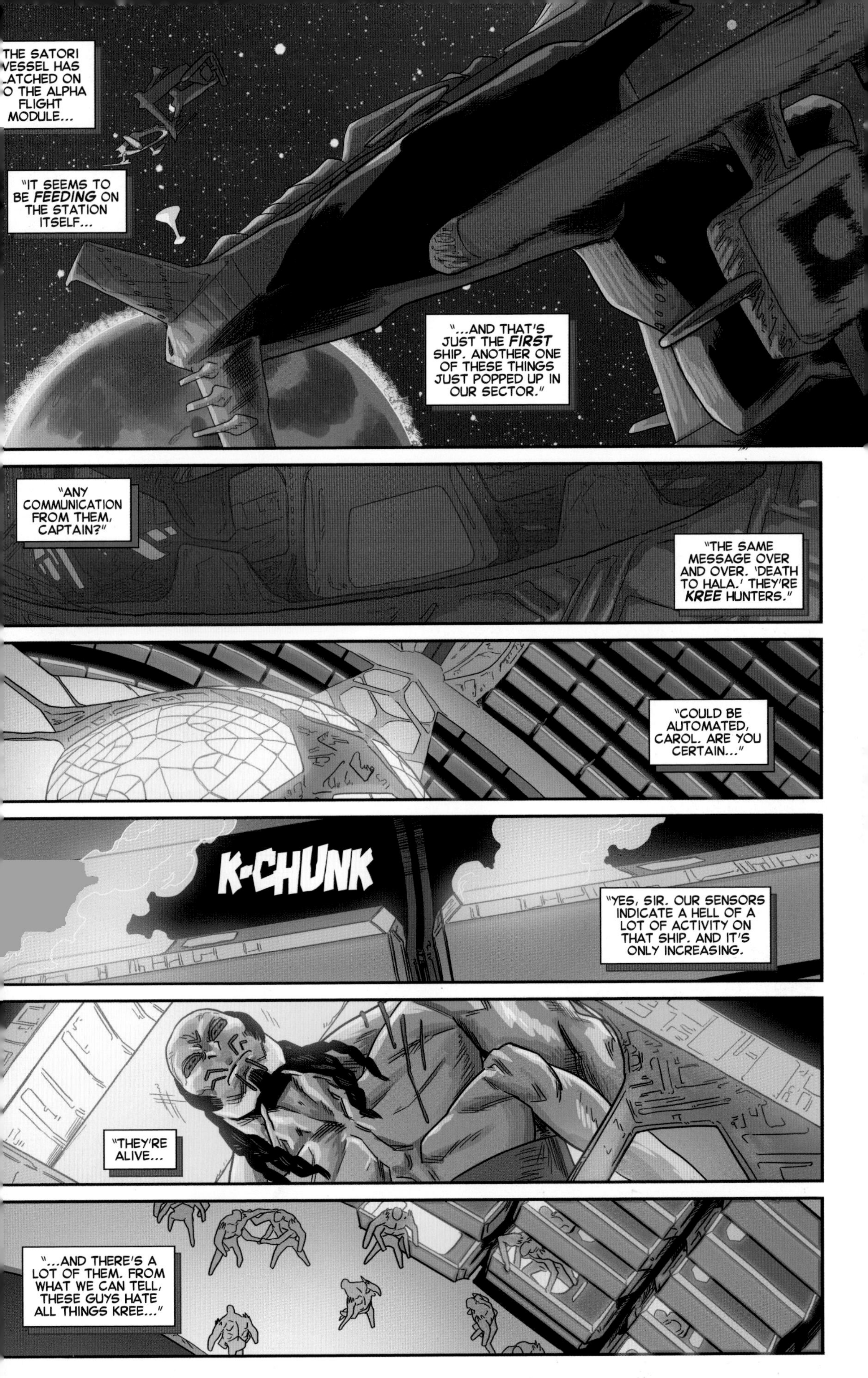
THE SATORI VESSEL HAS LATCHED ON TO THE ALPHA FLIGHT MODULE...
"IT SEEMS TO BE FEEDING ON THE STATION ITSELF...
"...AND THAT'S JUST THE FIRST SHIP. ANOTHER ONE OF THESE THINGS JUST POPPED UP IN OUR SECTOR."
"ANY COMMUNICATION FROM THEM, CAPTAIN?"
"THE SAME MESSAGE OVER AND OVER. 'DEATH TO HALA.' THEY'RE KREE HUNTERS."
"COULD BE AUTOMATED, CAROL. ARE YOU CERTAIN..."
K-CHUNK
"YES, SIR. OUR SENSORS INDICATE A HELL OF A LOT OF ACTIVITY ON THAT SHIP. AND IT'S ONLY INCREASING.
"THEY'RE ALIVE...
"...AND THERE'S A LOT OF THEM. FROM WHAT WE CAN TELL, THESE GUYS HATE ALL THINGS KREE..."

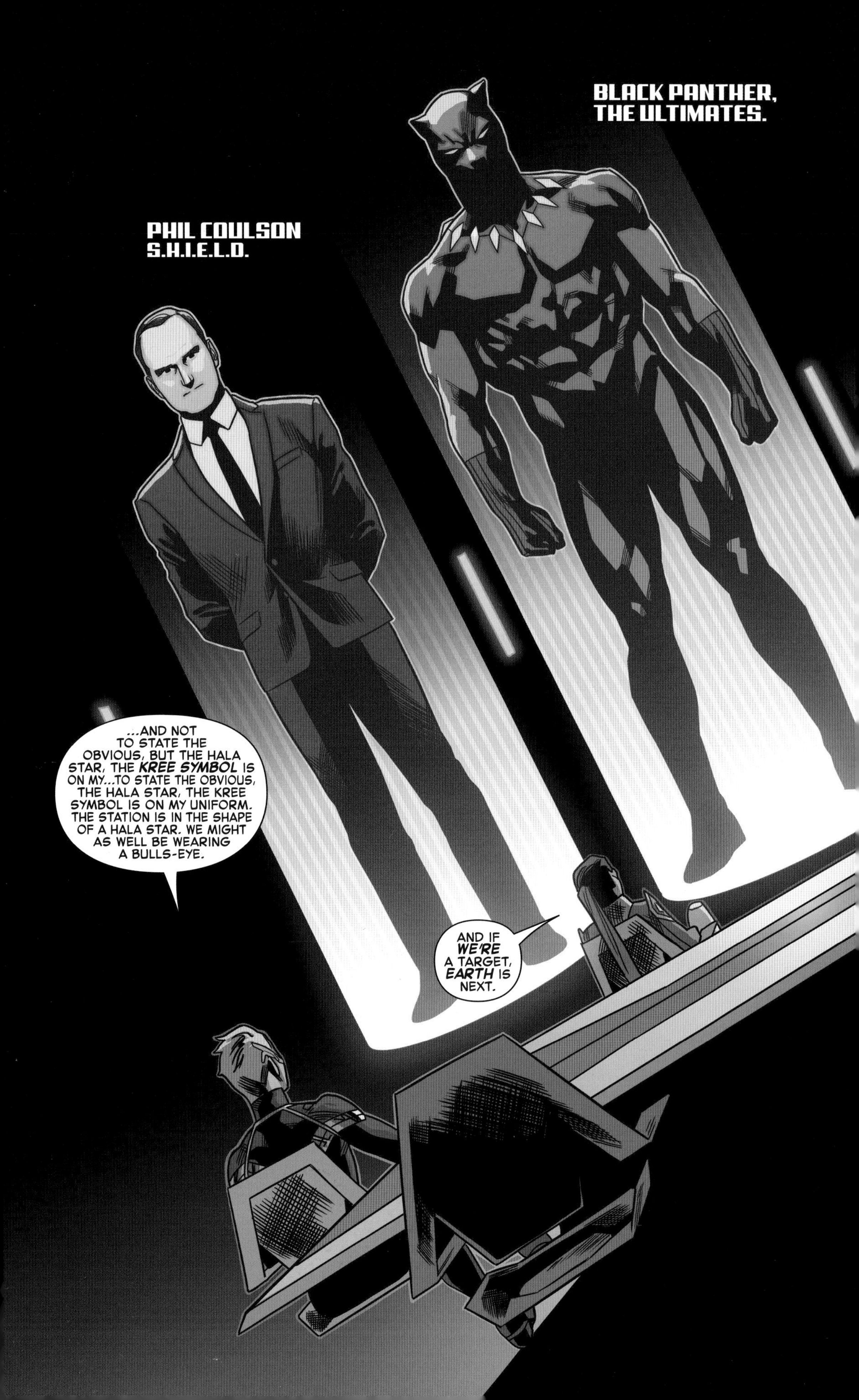
BLACK PANTHER, THE ULTIMATES.
PHIL COULSON S.H.I.E.L.D.
...AND NOT TO STATE THE OBVIOUS, BUT THE HALA STAR, THE KREE SYMBOL IS ON MY...TO STATE THE OBVIOUS, THE HALA STAR, THE KREE SYMBOL IS ON MY UNIFORM. THE STATION IS IN THE SHAPE OF A HALA STAR. WE MIGHT AS WELL BE WEARING A BULLS-EYE.
AND IF WE'RE A TARGET, EARTH IS NEXT.

TELL ALPHA FLIGHT TO GET TO THEIR SHIPS AND PREPARE TO LAUNCH. AND THEN GET YOURSELF BACK TO MEDICAL, BRAND.

NOT A CHANCE, CAPTAIN.

WE'RE A LOT ALIKE, BRAND. AND THAT'S PRETTY OBNOXIOUS.

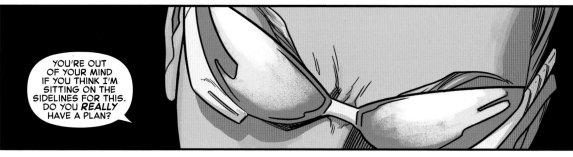

YOU'RE OUT OF YOUR MIND IF YOU THINK I'M SITTING ON THE SIDELINES FOR THIS. DO YOU *REALLY* HAVE A PLAN?

YES. AN INDIRECT PLAN.

AND A TEMPORARY PLAN.

SOMEONE ON THIS STATION IS TRYING TO *SABOTAGE* US. AND RIGHT NOW THAT COULD GET US ALL KILLED.

THEN LET'S GET THEM *OFF* THIS STATION.

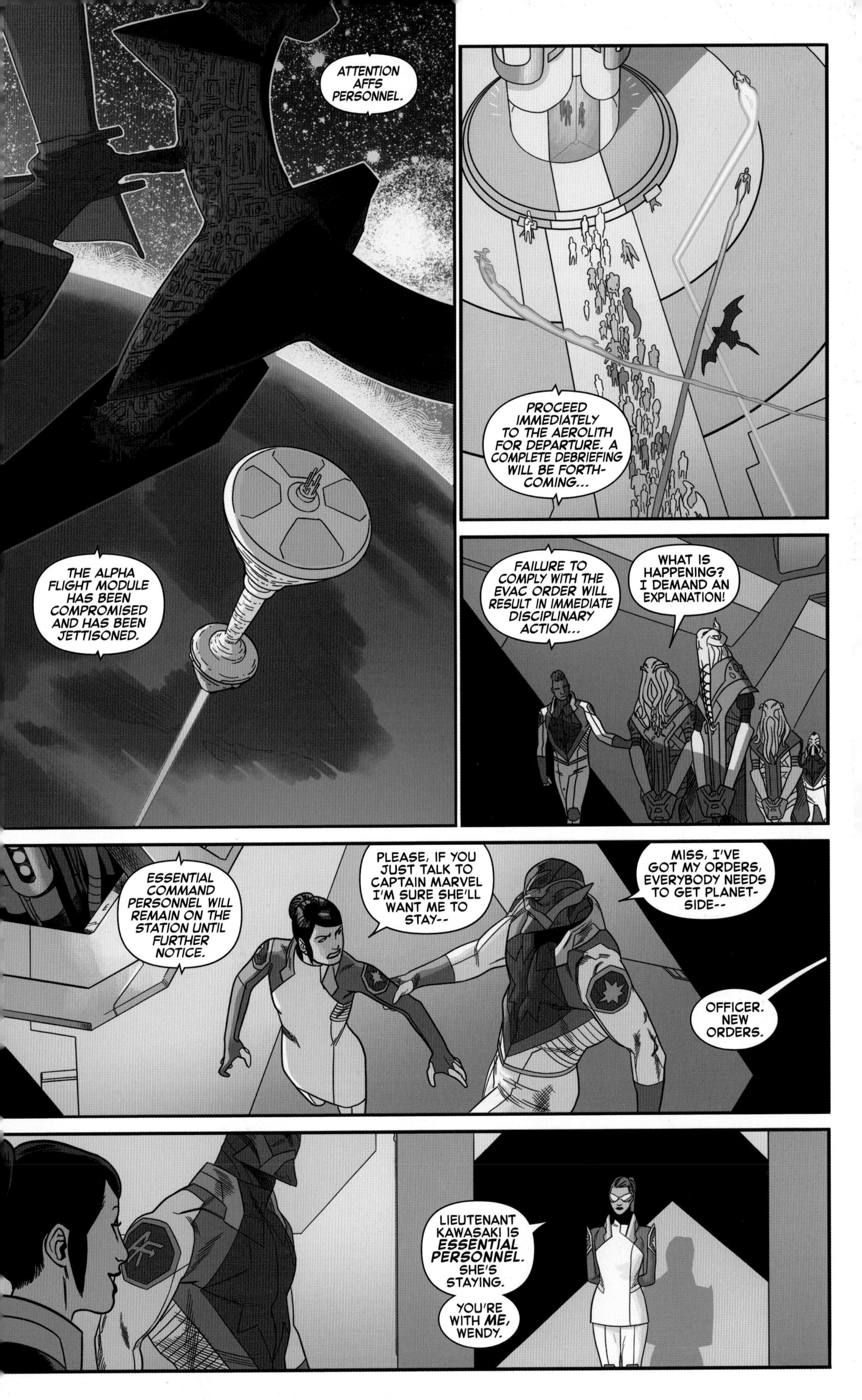
ATTENTION AFFS PERSONNEL.
THE ALPHA FLIGHT MODULE HAS BEEN COMPROMISED AND HAS BEEN JETTISONED.
PROCEED IMMEDIATELY TO THE AEROLITH FOR DEPARTURE. A COMPLETE DEBRIEFING WILL BE FORTH-COMING...
FAILURE TO COMPLY WITH THE EVAC ORDER WILL RESULT IN IMMEDIATE DISCIPLINARY ACTION...
WHAT IS HAPPENING? I DEMAND AN EXPLANATION!
ESSENTIAL COMMAND PERSONNEL WILL REMAIN ON THE STATION UNTIL FURTHER NOTICE.
PLEASE, IF YOU JUST TALK TO CAPTAIN MARVEL I'M SURE SHE'LL WANT ME TO STAY--
MISS, I'VE GOT MY ORDERS, EVERYBODY NEEDS TO GET PLANET-SIDE--
OFFICER. NEW ORDERS.
LIEUTENANT KAWASAKI IS ESSENTIAL PERSONNEL. SHE'S STAYING.
YOU'RE WITH ME, WENDY.

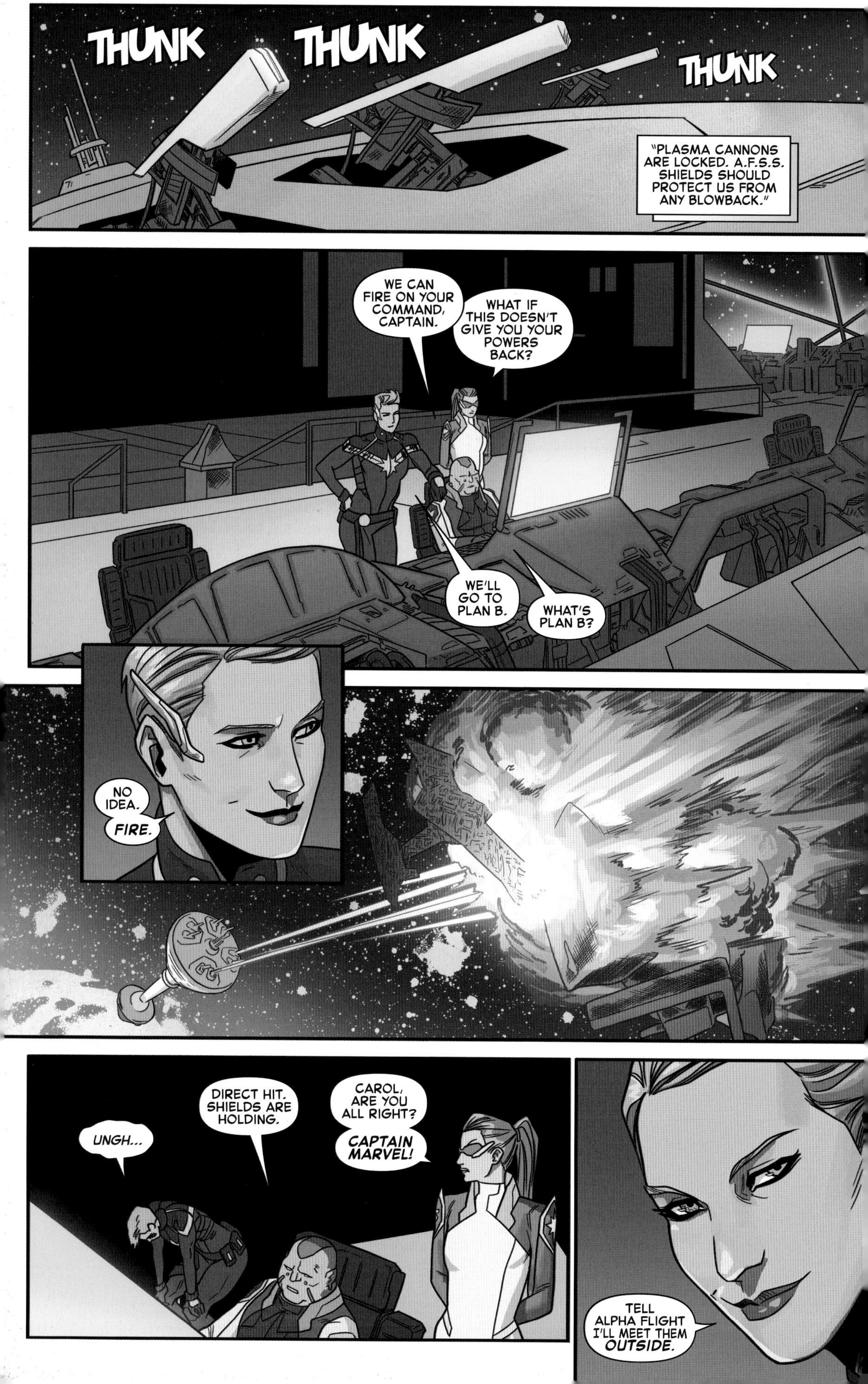
THUNK
THUNK
THUNK
"PLASMA CANNONS ARE LOCKED. A.F.S.S. SHIELDS SHOULD PROTECT US FROM ANY BLOWBACK."
WE CAN FIRE ON YOUR COMMAND, CAPTAIN.
WHAT IF THIS DOESN'T GIVE YOU YOUR POWERS BACK?
WE'LL GO TO PLAN B.
WHAT'S PLAN B?
NO IDEA.
FIRE.
UNGH...
DIRECT HIT. SHIELDS ARE HOLDING.
CAROL, ARE YOU ALL RIGHT?
CAPTAIN MARVEL!
TELL ALPHA FLIGHT I'LL MEET THEM OUTSIDE.

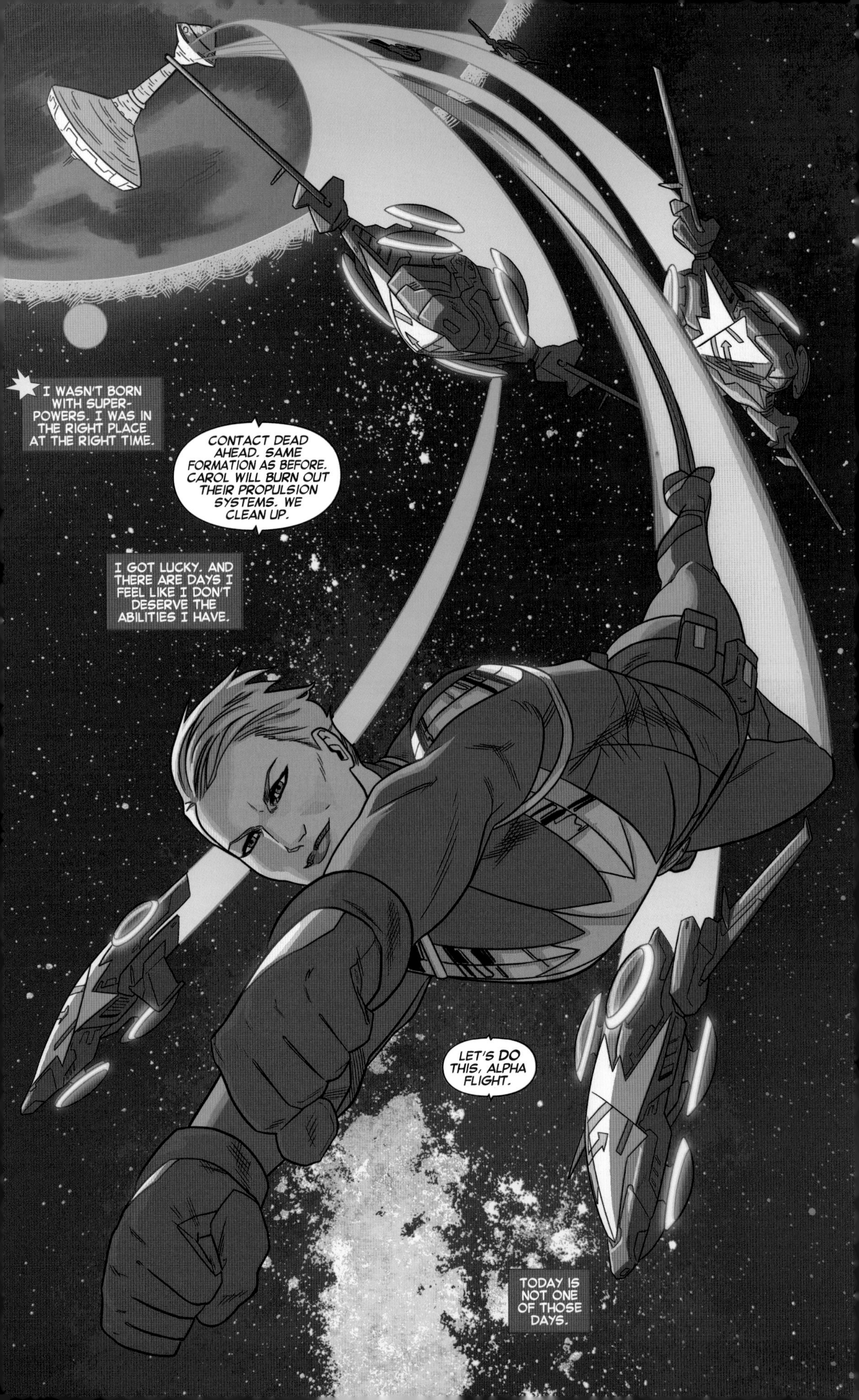
I WASN'T BORN WITH SUPER-POWERS. I WAS IN THE RIGHT PLACE AT THE RIGHT TIME.
CONTACT DEAD AHEAD. SAME FORMATION AS BEFORE. CAROL WILL BURN OUT THEIR PROPULSION SYSTEMS. WE CLEAN UP.
I GOT LUCKY. AND THERE ARE DAYS I FEEL LIKE I DON'T DESERVE THE ABILITIES I HAVE.
LET'S DO THIS, ALPHA FLIGHT.
TODAY IS NOT ONE OF THOSE DAYS.

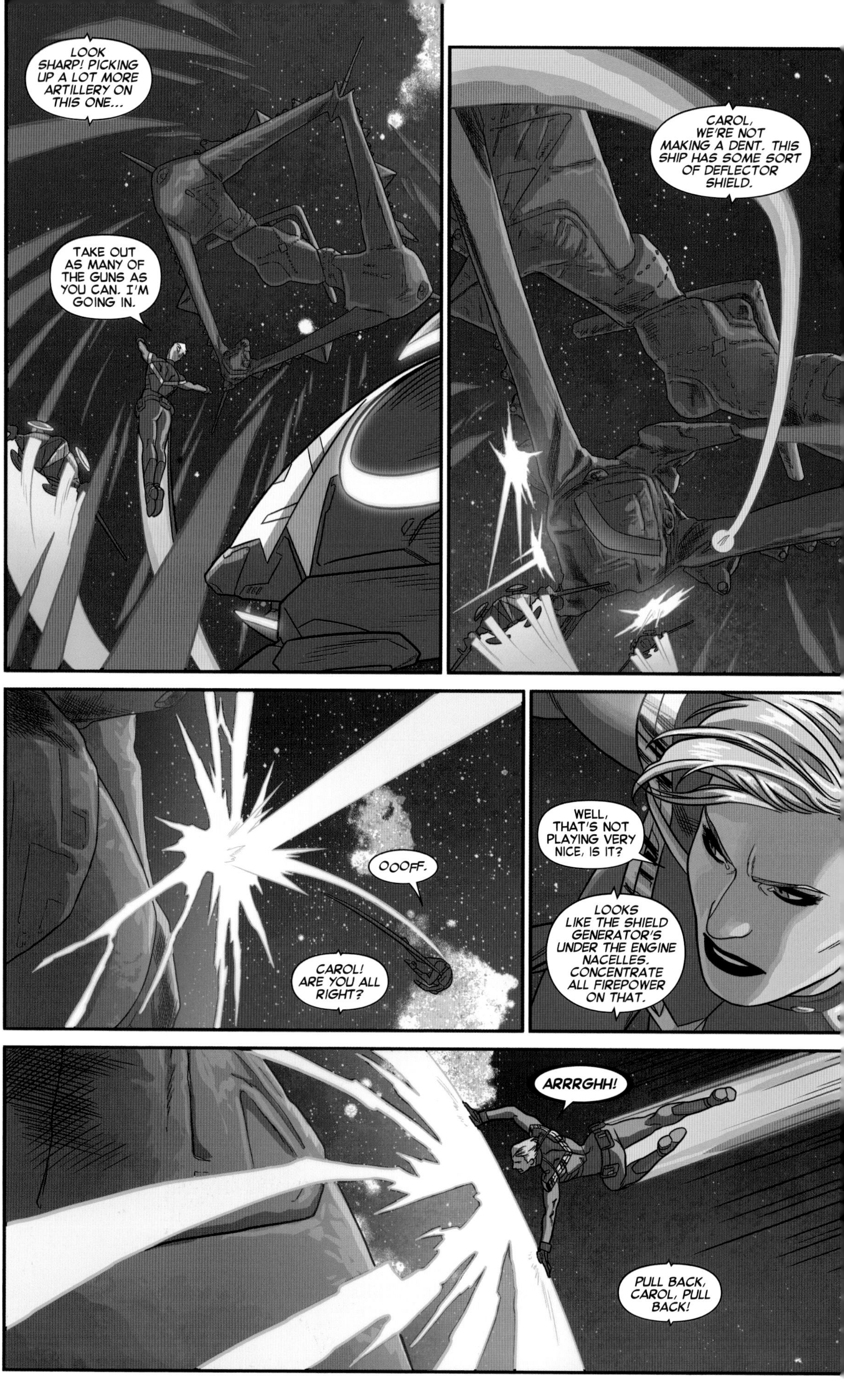
LOOK SHARP! PICKING UP A LOT MORE ARTILLERY ON THIS ONE...
TAKE OUT AS MANY OF THE GUNS AS YOU CAN. I'M GOING IN.
CAROL, WE'RE NOT MAKING A DENT. THIS SHIP HAS SOME SORT OF DEFLECTOR SHIELD.
OOOFF.
CAROL! ARE YOU ALL RIGHT?
WELL, THAT'S NOT PLAYING VERY NICE, IS IT?
LOOKS LIKE THE SHIELD GENERATOR'S UNDER THE ENGINE NACELLES. CONCENTRATE ALL FIREPOWER ON THAT.
ARRRGHH!
PULL BACK, CAROL, PULL BACK!

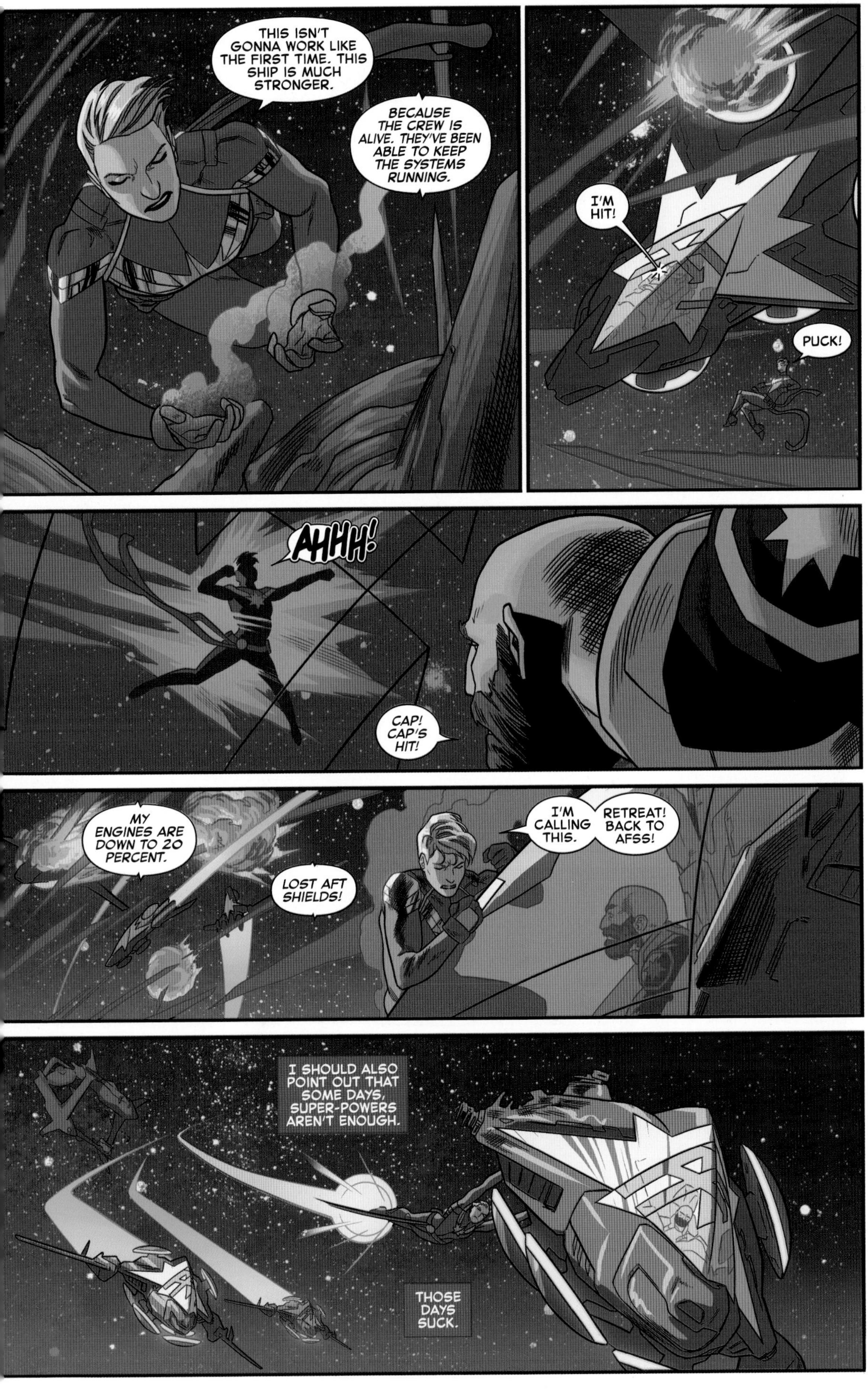
THIS ISN'T GONNA WORK LIKE THE FIRST TIME. THIS SHIP IS MUCH STRONGER.
BECAUSE THE CREW IS ALIVE. THEY'VE BEEN ABLE TO KEEP THE SYSTEMS RUNNING.
I'M HIT!
PUCK!
AHHH!
CAP! CAP'S HIT!
MY ENGINES ARE DOWN TO 20 PERCENT.
LOST AFT SHIELDS!
I'M CALLING THIS.
RETREAT! BACK TO AFSS!
I SHOULD ALSO POINT OUT THAT SOME DAYS, SUPER-POWERS AREN'T ENOUGH.
THOSE DAYS SUCK.

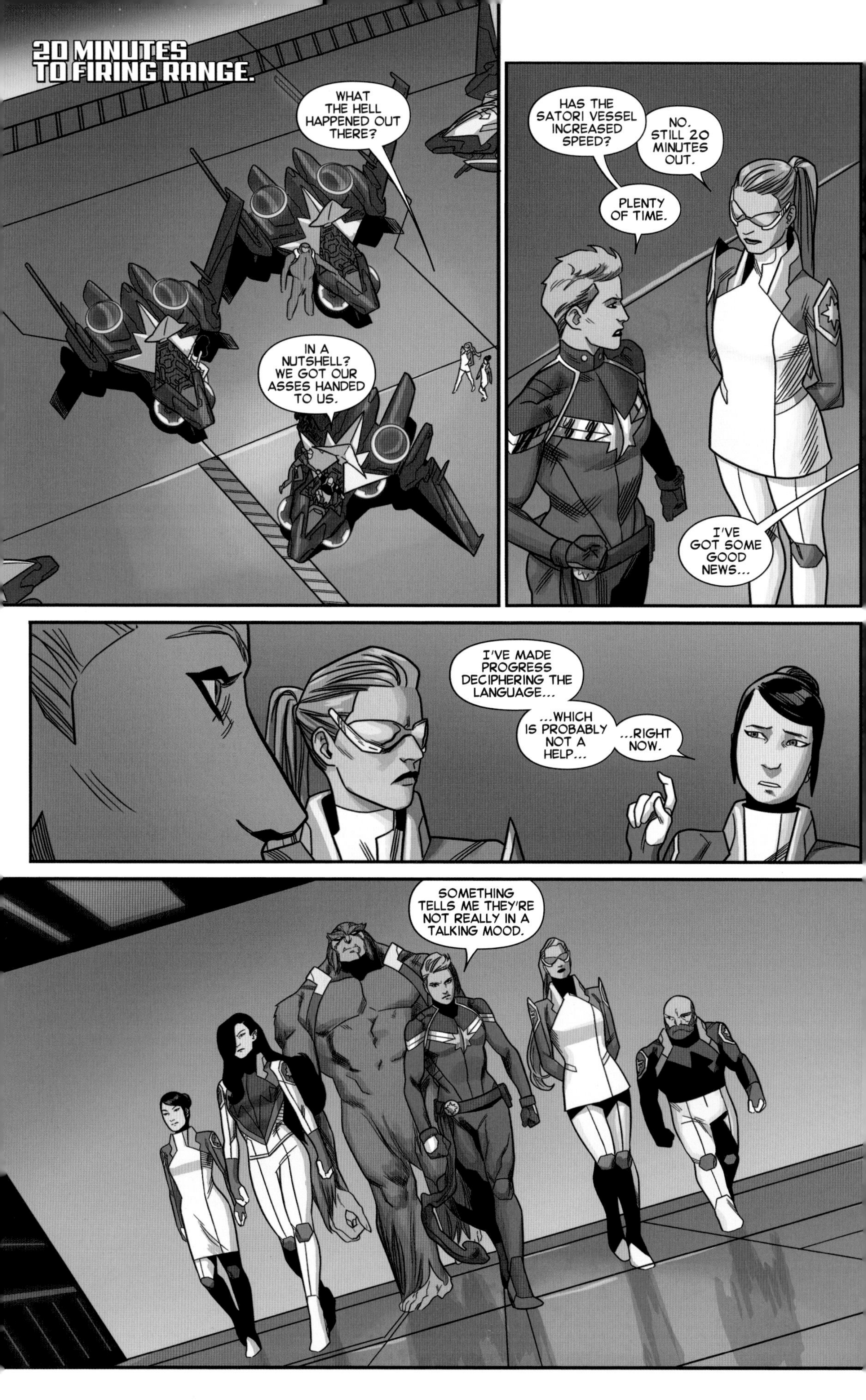
20 MINUTES TO FIRING RANGE.
WHAT THE HELL HAPPENED OUT THERE?
IN A NUTSHELL? WE GOT OUR ASSES HANDED TO US.
HAS THE SATORI VESSEL INCREASED SPEED?
NO. STILL 20 MINUTES OUT.
PLENTY OF TIME.
I'VE GOT SOME GOOD NEWS...
I'VE MADE PROGRESS DECIPHERING THE LANGUAGE...
...WHICH IS PROBABLY NOT A HELP...
...RIGHT NOW.
SOMETHING TELLS ME THEY'RE NOT REALLY IN A TALKING MOOD.

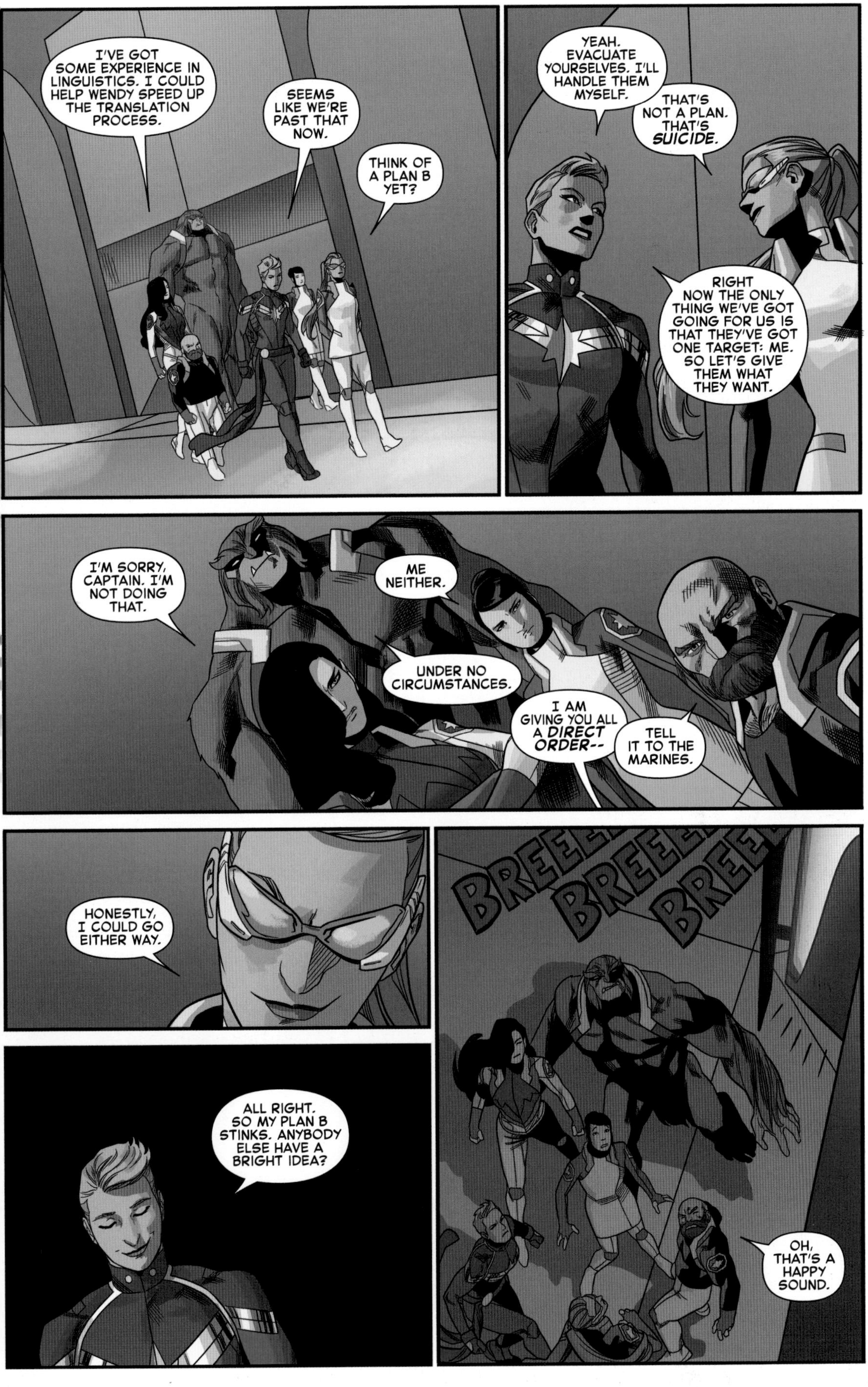
I'VE GOT SOME EXPERIENCE IN LINGUISTICS. I COULD HELP WENDY SPEED UP THE TRANSLATION PROCESS.
SEEMS LIKE WE'RE PAST THAT NOW.
THINK OF A PLAN B YET?
YEAH. EVACUATE YOURSELVES. I'LL HANDLE THEM MYSELF.
THAT'S NOT A PLAN. THAT'S *SUICIDE.*
RIGHT NOW THE ONLY THING WE'VE GOT GOING FOR US IS THAT THEY'VE GOT ONE TARGET: ME. SO LET'S GIVE THEM WHAT THEY WANT.
I'M SORRY, CAPTAIN. I'M NOT DOING THAT.
ME NEITHER.
UNDER NO CIRCUMSTANCES.
I AM GIVING YOU ALL A *DIRECT ORDER--*
TELL IT TO THE MARINES.
HONESTLY, I COULD GO EITHER WAY.
ALL RIGHT. SO MY PLAN B STINKS. ANYBODY ELSE HAVE A BRIGHT IDEA?
BREEE
BREEEE
BREE
OH, THAT'S A HAPPY SOUND.

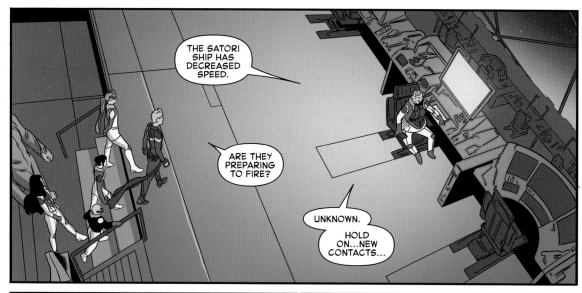

THE SATORI SHIP HAS DECREASED SPEED.

ARE THEY PREPARING TO FIRE?

UNKNOWN.

HOLD ON...NEW CONTACTS...

FIFTEEN SMALL VESSELS DISEMBARKING FROM THE MAIN SHIP AND INCOMING.

ETA?

THREE MINUTES.

LET'S HOPE THE SMALLER ONES ARE EASIER TO HANDLE THAN THE BIG ONE.

ONE CAN DREAM.

I'D LIKE TO STAY BEHIND AND HELP WENDY FIGURE OUT THE LANGUAGE. AT LEAST WE CAN ATTEMPT COMMUNICATION.

TELL THEM I SAID, "HI."

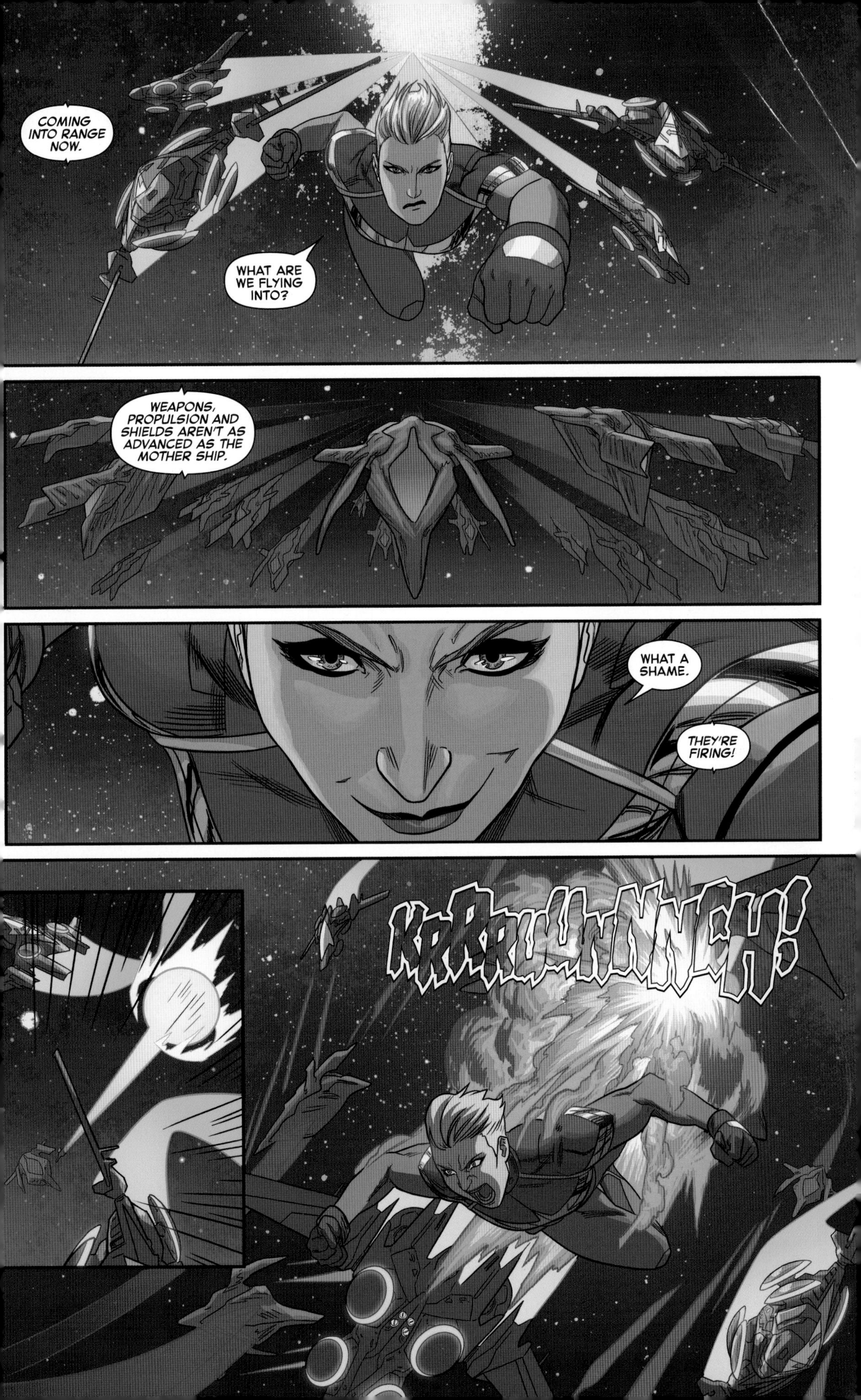
COMING INTO RANGE NOW.
WHAT ARE WE FLYING INTO?
WEAPONS, PROPULSION AND SHIELDS AREN'T AS ADVANCED AS THE MOTHER SHIP.
WHAT A SHAME.
THEY'RE FIRING!
KRRRUNNNCH!

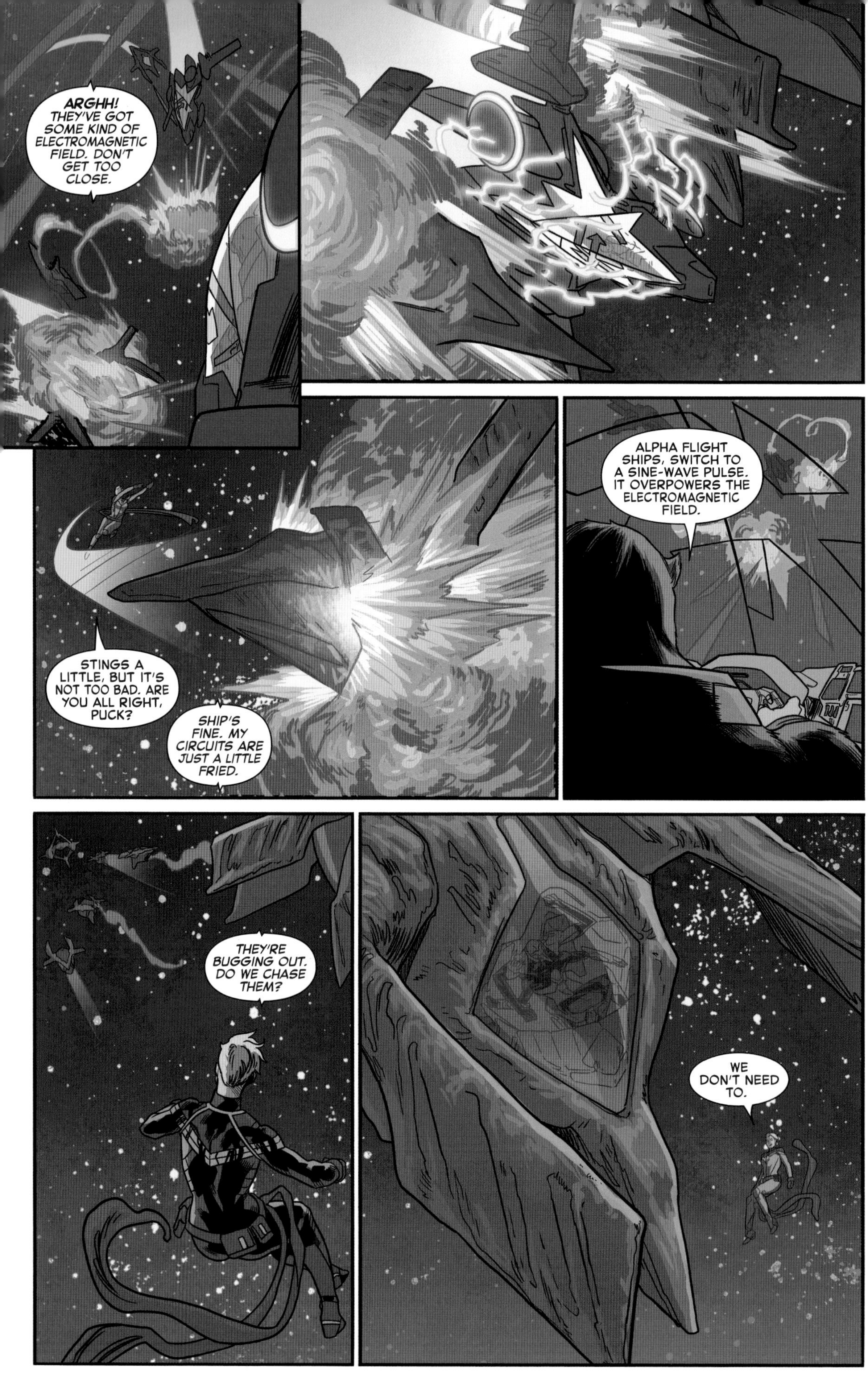
ARGHH! THEY'VE GOT SOME KIND OF ELECTROMAGNETIC FIELD. DON'T GET TOO CLOSE.
STINGS A LITTLE, BUT IT'S NOT TOO BAD. ARE YOU ALL RIGHT, PUCK?
SHIP'S FINE. MY CIRCUITS ARE JUST A LITTLE FRIED.
ALPHA FLIGHT SHIPS, SWITCH TO A SINE-WAVE PULSE. IT OVERPOWERS THE ELECTROMAGNETIC FIELD.
THEY'RE BUGGING OUT. DO WE CHASE THEM?
WE DON'T NEED TO.

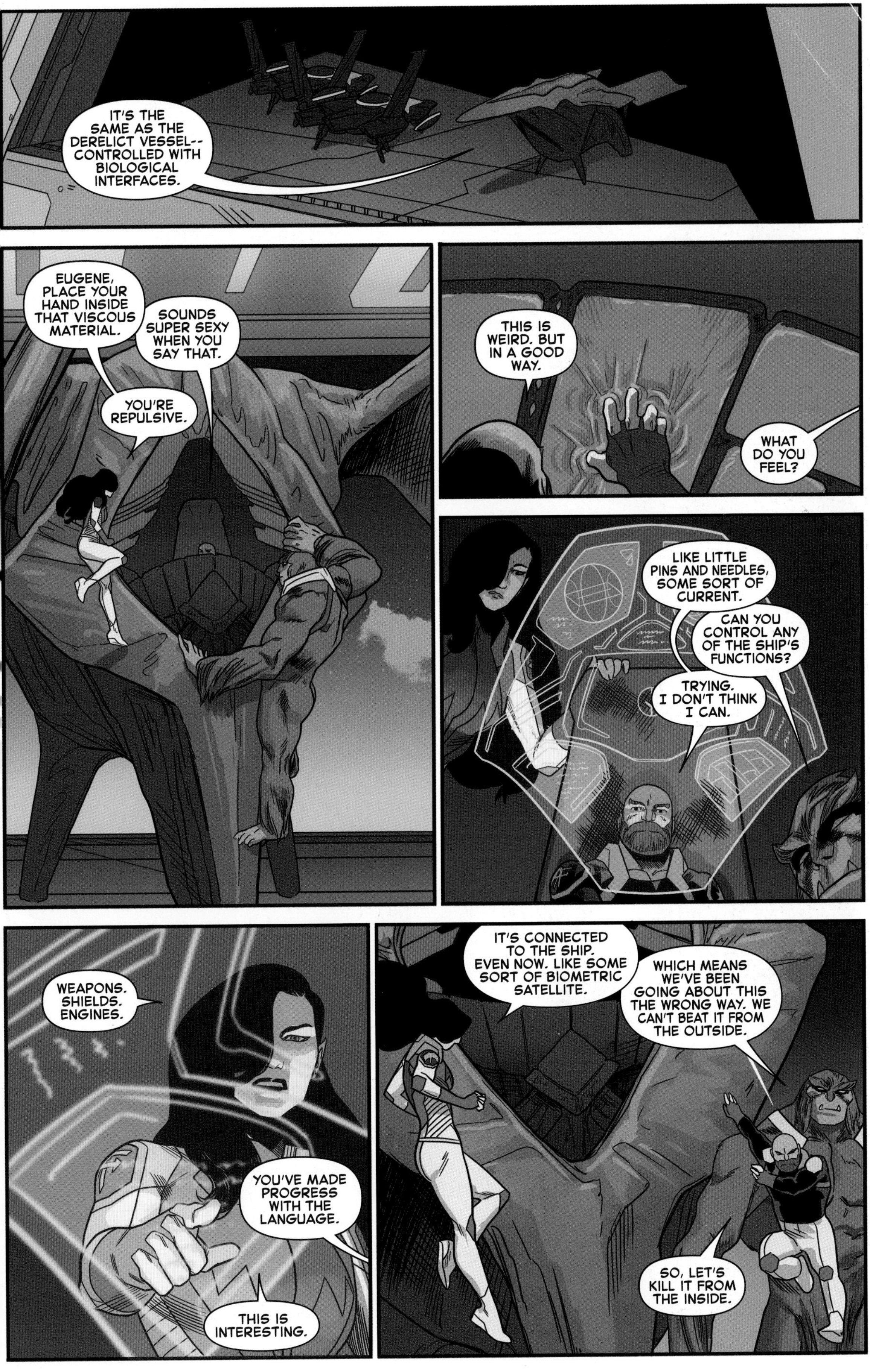
IT'S THE SAME AS THE DERELICT VESSEL-- CONTROLLED WITH BIOLOGICAL INTERFACES.
EUGENE, PLACE YOUR HAND INSIDE THAT VISCOUS MATERIAL.
SOUNDS SUPER SEXY WHEN YOU SAY THAT.
YOU'RE REPULSIVE.
THIS IS WEIRD. BUT IN A GOOD WAY.
WHAT DO YOU FEEL?
LIKE LITTLE PINS AND NEEDLES, SOME SORT OF CURRENT.
CAN YOU CONTROL ANY OF THE SHIP'S FUNCTIONS?
TRYING. I DON'T THINK I CAN.
WEAPONS. SHIELDS. ENGINES.
YOU'VE MADE PROGRESS WITH THE LANGUAGE.
THIS IS INTERESTING.
IT'S CONNECTED TO THE SHIP. EVEN NOW. LIKE SOME SORT OF BIOMETRIC SATELLITE.
WHICH MEANS WE'VE BEEN GOING ABOUT THIS THE WRONG WAY. WE CAN'T BEAT IT FROM THE OUTSIDE.
SO, LET'S KILL IT FROM THE INSIDE.

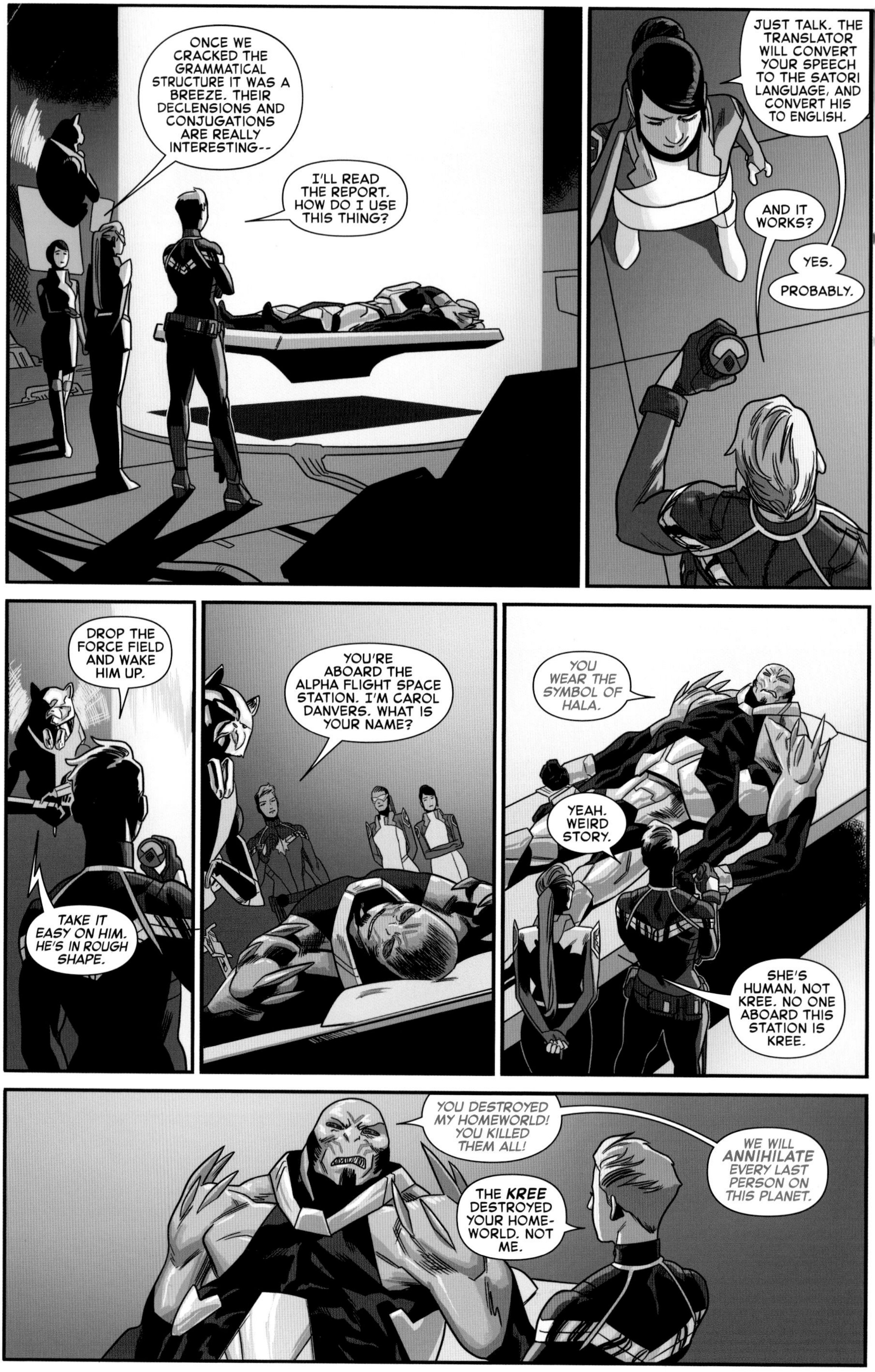
ONCE WE CRACKED THE GRAMMATICAL STRUCTURE IT WAS A BREEZE. THEIR DECLENSIONS AND CONJUGATIONS ARE REALLY INTERESTING--
I'LL READ THE REPORT. HOW DO I USE THIS THING?
JUST TALK. THE TRANSLATOR WILL CONVERT YOUR SPEECH TO THE SATORI LANGUAGE, AND CONVERT HIS TO ENGLISH.
AND IT WORKS?
YES.
PROBABLY.
DROP THE FORCE FIELD AND WAKE HIM UP.
TAKE IT EASY ON HIM. HE'S IN ROUGH SHAPE.
YOU'RE ABOARD THE ALPHA FLIGHT SPACE STATION. I'M CAROL DANVERS. WHAT IS YOUR NAME?
YOU WEAR THE SYMBOL OF HALA.
YEAH. WEIRD STORY.
SHE'S HUMAN, NOT KREE. NO ONE ABOARD THIS STATION IS KREE.
YOU DESTROYED MY HOMEWORLD! YOU KILLED THEM ALL!
THE KREE DESTROYED YOUR HOME-WORLD. NOT ME.
WE WILL ANNIHILATE EVERY LAST PERSON ON THIS PLANET.

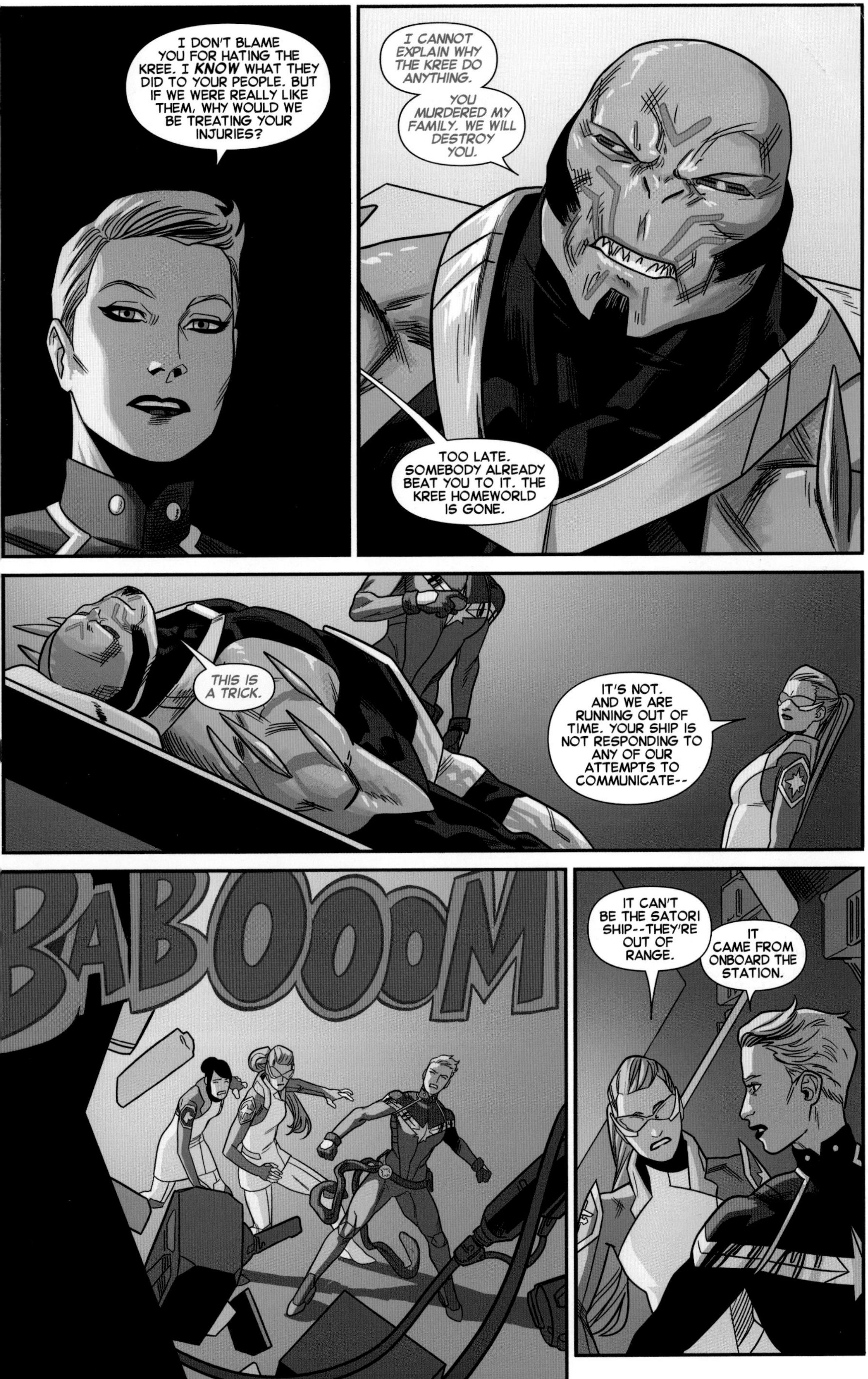
I DON'T BLAME YOU FOR HATING THE KREE. I *KNOW* WHAT THEY DID TO YOUR PEOPLE. BUT IF WE WERE REALLY LIKE THEM, WHY WOULD WE BE TREATING YOUR INJURIES?
I CANNOT EXPLAIN WHY THE KREE DO ANYTHING.
YOU MURDERED MY FAMILY. WE WILL DESTROY YOU.
TOO LATE. SOMEBODY ALREADY BEAT YOU TO IT. THE KREE HOMEWORLD IS GONE.
THIS IS A TRICK.
IT'S NOT. AND WE ARE RUNNING OUT OF TIME. YOUR SHIP IS NOT RESPONDING TO ANY OF OUR ATTEMPTS TO COMMUNICATE--
BABOOOM
IT CAN'T BE THE SATORI SHIP--THEY'RE OUT OF RANGE.
IT CAME FROM ONBOARD THE STATION.

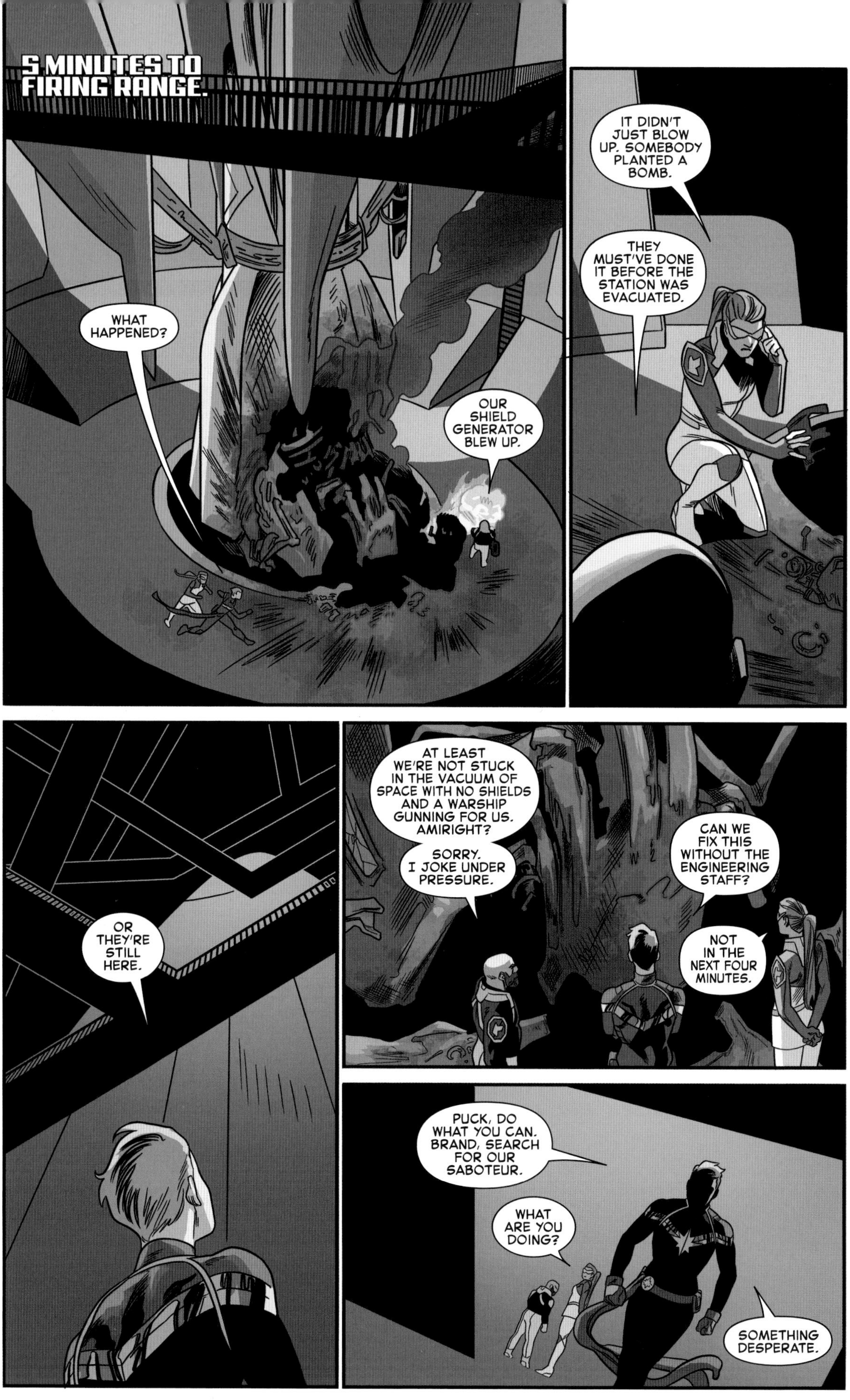
5 MINUTES TO FIRING RANGE.
WHAT HAPPENED?
OUR SHIELD GENERATOR BLEW UP.
IT DIDN'T JUST BLOW UP. SOMEBODY PLANTED A BOMB.
THEY MUST'VE DONE IT BEFORE THE STATION WAS EVACUATED.
OR THEY'RE STILL HERE.
AT LEAST WE'RE NOT STUCK IN THE VACUUM OF SPACE WITH NO SHIELDS AND A WARSHIP GUNNING FOR US. AMIRIGHT?
SORRY. I JOKE UNDER PRESSURE.
CAN WE FIX THIS WITHOUT THE ENGINEERING STAFF?
NOT IN THE NEXT FOUR MINUTES.
PUCK, DO WHAT YOU CAN. BRAND, SEARCH FOR OUR SABOTEUR.
WHAT ARE YOU DOING?
SOMETHING DESPERATE.

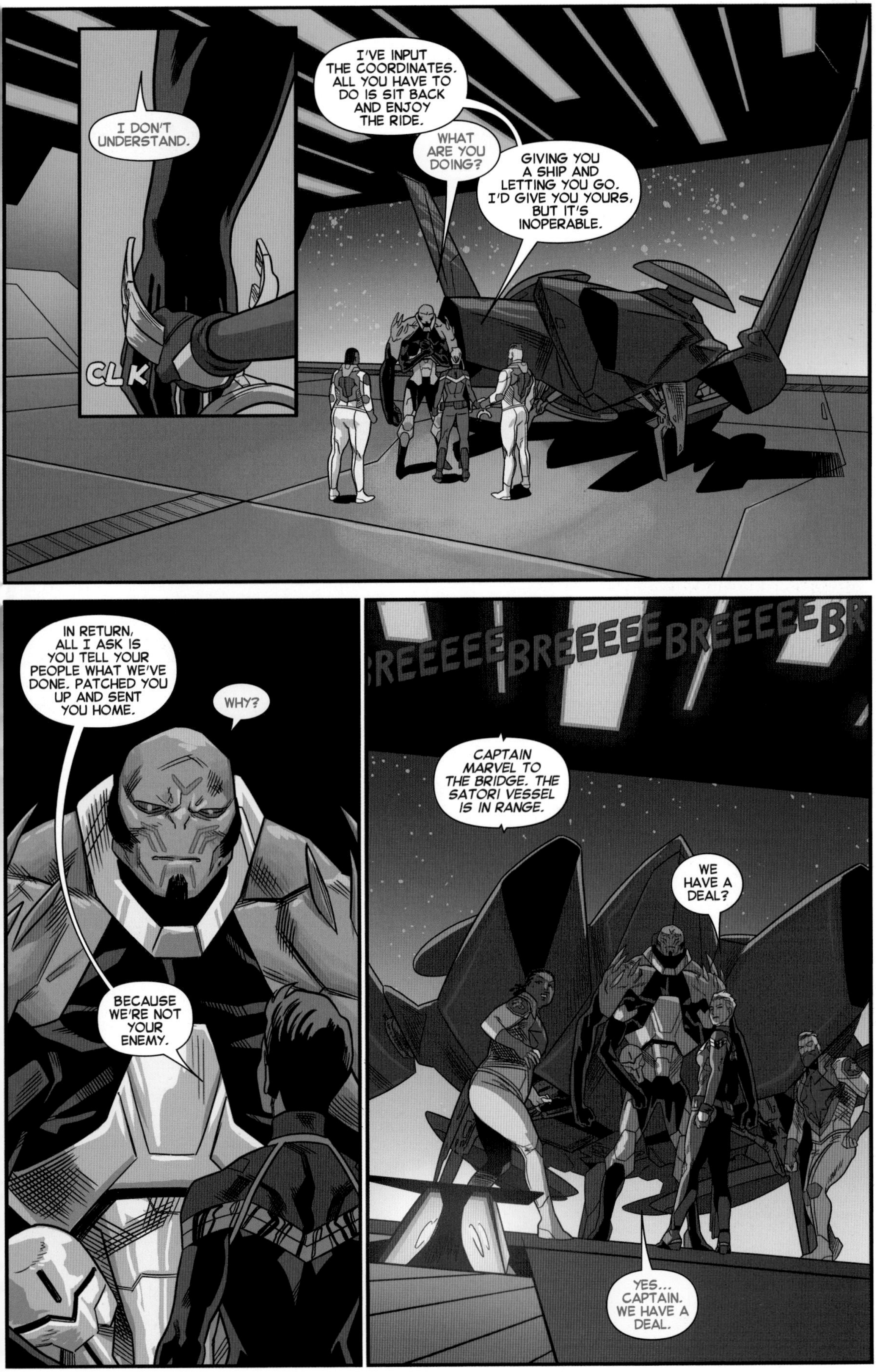
I DON'T UNDERSTAND.
CLK
I'VE INPUT THE COORDINATES. ALL YOU HAVE TO DO IS SIT BACK AND ENJOY THE RIDE.
WHAT ARE YOU DOING?
GIVING YOU A SHIP AND LETTING YOU GO. I'D GIVE YOU YOURS, BUT IT'S INOPERABLE.
IN RETURN, ALL I ASK IS YOU TELL YOUR PEOPLE WHAT WE'VE DONE. PATCHED YOU UP AND SENT YOU HOME.
WHY?
BECAUSE WE'RE NOT YOUR ENEMY.
BREEEEEE BREEEEEE BREEEEEE BR
CAPTAIN MARVEL TO THE BRIDGE. THE SATORI VESSEL IS IN RANGE.
WE HAVE A DEAL?
YES... CAPTAIN. WE HAVE A DEAL.

ENERGY BLOOMS FROM ALL BATTERIES.

WHAT'S THE STATUS OF THE SATORI PILOT?

JUST LAUNCHED AND ON A DIRECT COURSE.

HE'S RADIOING THE VESSEL NOW. HE'S TELLING THEM TO STAND DOWN.

THIS IS GONNA WORK!

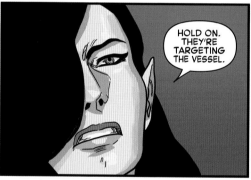

HOLD ON. THEY'RE TARGETING THE VESSEL.

TELL THEM TO POWER DOWN WEAPONS!

SATORI VESSEL, DO NOT FIRE--

TELL THEM IT'S THEIR OWN PILOT!

SATORI VESSEL, WE ARE RETURNING YOUR CREWMAN, I REPEAT, DO NOT--

KBOOOOMMMM

NO!

THEY JUST SHOT DOWN THEIR OWN MAN!

WHAT DO WE DO? CAPTAIN?

WE GO TO PLAN C.

AS SOON AS I FIGURE OUT WHAT IT IS...

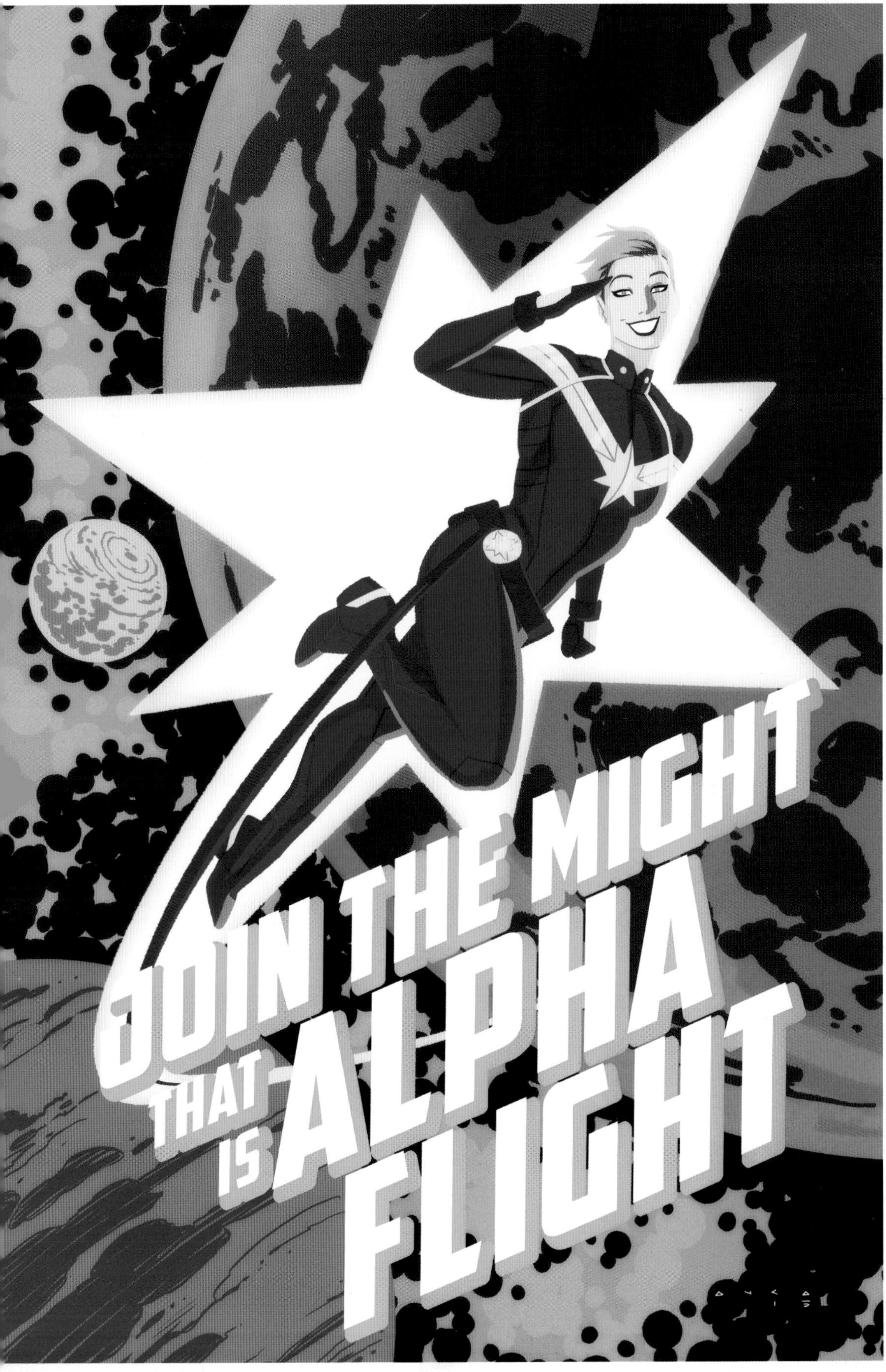
JOIN THE MIGHT
THAT IS
ALPHA
FLIGHT

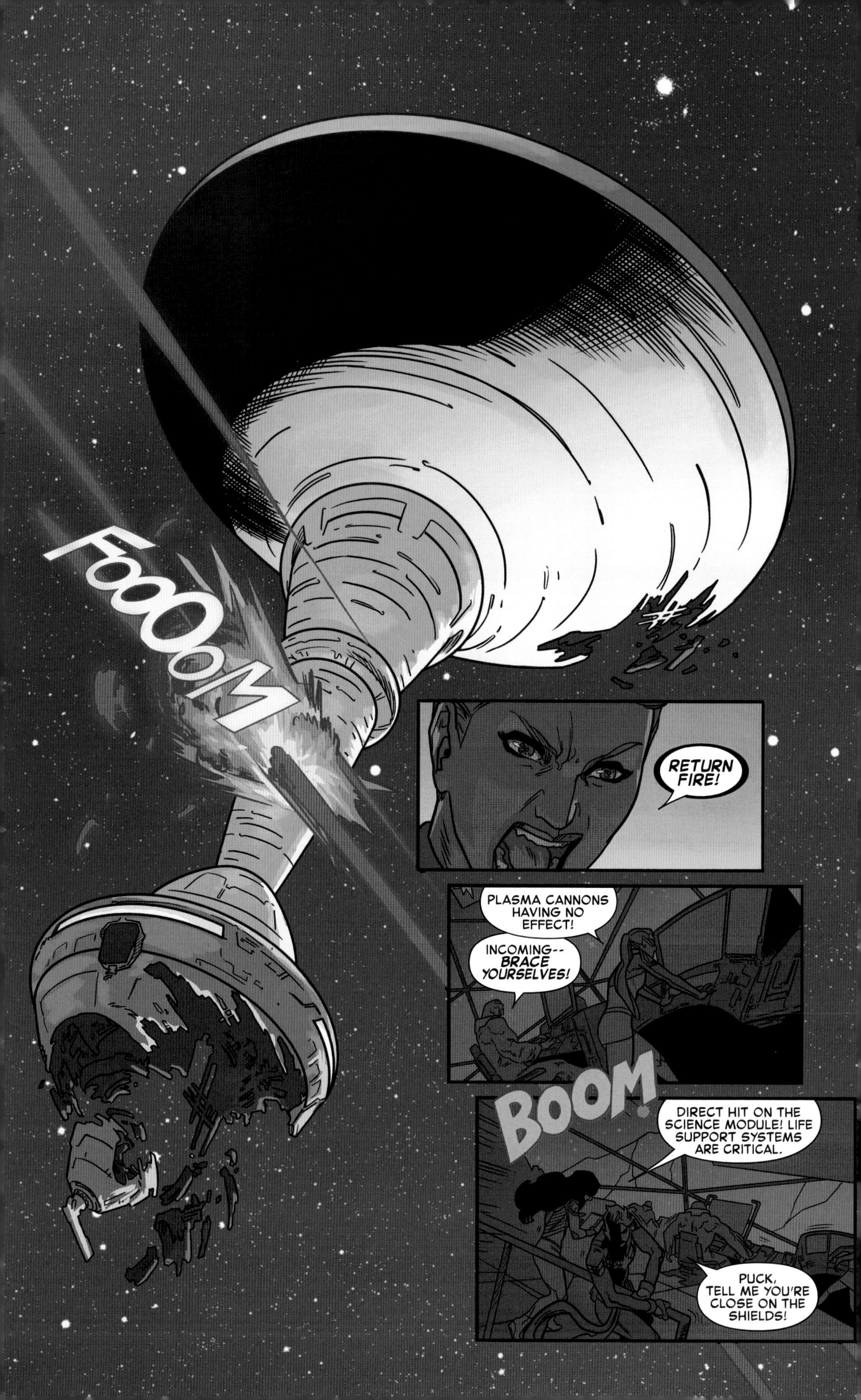
FOOOOM
RETURN FIRE!
PLASMA CANNONS HAVING NO EFFECT!
INCOMING-- BRACE YOURSELVES!
BOOM
DIRECT HIT ON THE SCIENCE MODULE! LIFE SUPPORT SYSTEMS ARE CRITICAL.
PUCK, TELL ME YOU'RE CLOSE ON THE SHIELDS!

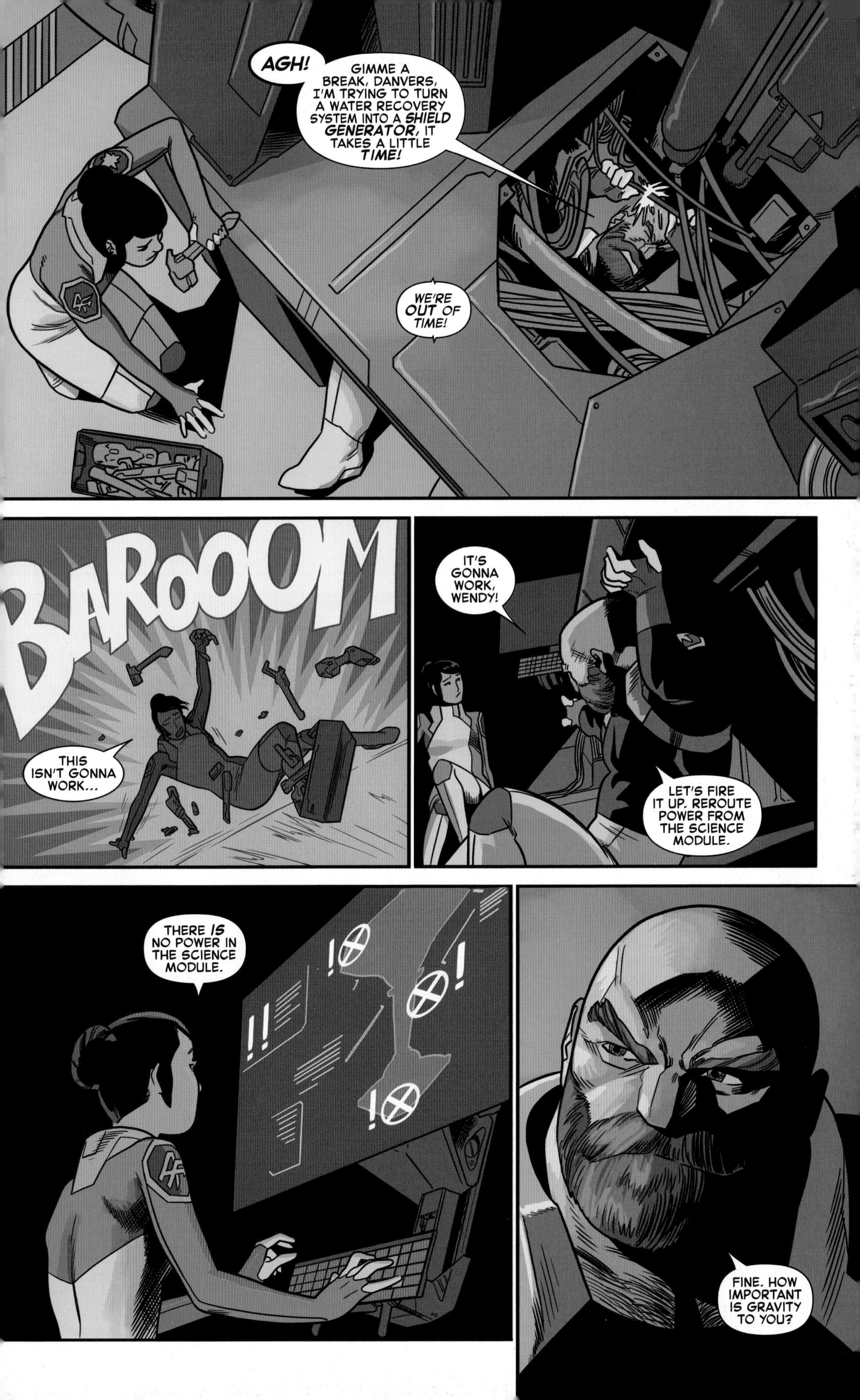
AGH!
GIMME A BREAK, DANVERS, I'M TRYING TO TURN A WATER RECOVERY SYSTEM INTO A SHIELD GENERATOR, IT TAKES A LITTLE TIME!
WE'RE OUT OF TIME!
BAROOOM
THIS ISN'T GONNA WORK...
IT'S GONNA WORK, WENDY!
LET'S FIRE IT UP. REROUTE POWER FROM THE SCIENCE MODULE.
THERE IS NO POWER IN THE SCIENCE MODULE.
FINE. HOW IMPORTANT IS GRAVITY TO YOU?

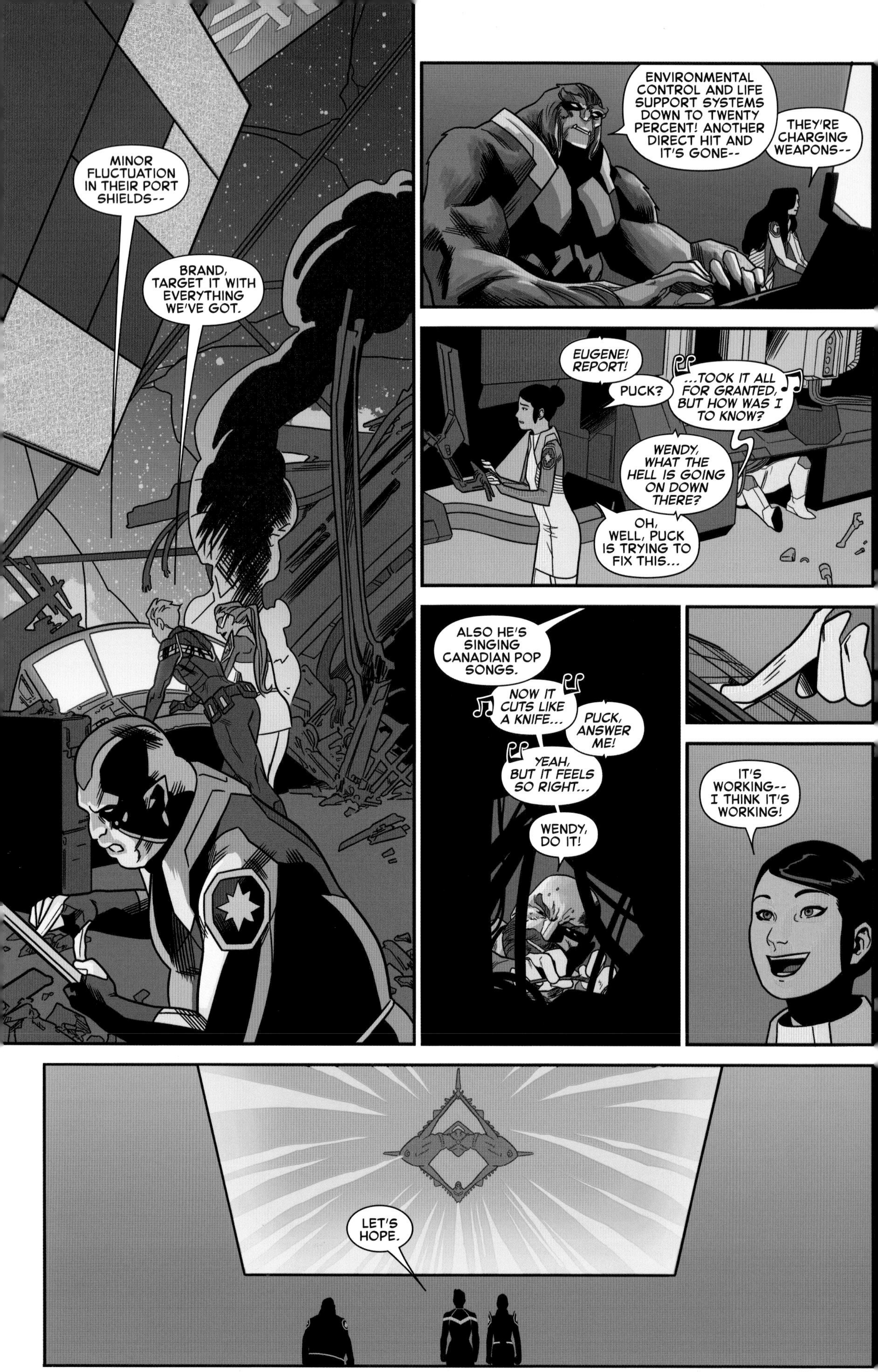
MINOR FLUCTUATION IN THEIR PORT SHIELDS--
BRAND, TARGET IT WITH EVERYTHING WE'VE GOT.
ENVIRONMENTAL CONTROL AND LIFE SUPPORT SYSTEMS DOWN TO TWENTY PERCENT! ANOTHER DIRECT HIT AND IT'S GONE--
THEY'RE CHARGING WEAPONS--
EUGENE! REPORT!
PUCK?
...TOOK IT ALL FOR GRANTED, BUT HOW WAS I TO KNOW?
WENDY, WHAT THE HELL IS GOING ON DOWN THERE?
OH, WELL, PUCK IS TRYING TO FIX THIS...
ALSO HE'S SINGING CANADIAN POP SONGS.
NOW IT CUTS LIKE A KNIFE...
PUCK, ANSWER ME!
YEAH, BUT IT FEELS SO RIGHT...
WENDY, DO IT!
IT'S WORKING-- I THINK IT'S WORKING!
LET'S HOPE.

SHRAAM

SHIELDS ARE HOLDING.

GOOD WORK, PUCK AND WENDY.

AND BRYAN.

THIS ONLY BUYS US TIME, AND NOT A LOT. WE'RE NEVER GOING TO BEAT THEM WITH FIREPOWER.

BUT WE MAY BE ABLE TO USE THEIR OWN TECHNOLOGY AGAINST THEM.

THEIR SHIPS ARE LINKED--ALMOST LIKE ORGANISMS WITHIN AN ECOLOGICAL SYSTEM.

WE BELIEVE THAT IF WE AFFECT ONE ORGANISM, THE OTHER WILL BE EQUALLY AFFECTED.

FOR INSTANCE, WITH A *VIRUS*. SPECIFICALLY DESIGNED TO DISRUPT THE VESSEL'S SYSTEMS.

SOUNDS LIKE YOU'RE DESCRIBING A *BIOLOGICAL WEAPON*.

NO. IT AFFECTS THE SHIPS. NOT THE CREW. HOW QUICKLY CAN THIS HAPPEN?

IMMEDIATELY.

DO IT.

WARSHAUER AND I WILL HOLD DOWN THE FORT HERE.

AND WHAT AM I SUPPOSED TO BE DOING?

MAKING SURE WHOEVER TOOK OUT OUR SHIELDS DOESN'T DO IT AGAIN.

TAKE THE SCENIC ROUTE-- STAY OUT OF MAIN CORRIDORS. THEY'LL BE LOOKING FOR YOU.

USE ANY NECESSARY FORCE. IF THEY CAN GET AT OUR SHIELDS, THEY CAN GET AT ANYTHING.

CLANG
CLANG
CLANG

COME ON, BRAND, YOU'VE BEEN ON ME SINCE DAY ONE ABOUT BEING IN A *COMMAND* POSITION.

CLANG CLANG C

I'M DELEGATING. YOU SHOULD BE HAPPY.

RATATAT
TATAT

YEAH. I'M *THRILLED.*

IT'S ESSENTIALLY AN ALIEN VERSION OF THE HANTAVIRUS.

AN RNA STRAND THAT LEADS TO APOPTOSIS-- CELLULAR DEATH.

DANGEROUS TO US?

NO.

I MEAN, DON'T LICK IT.

NOTED.

ALL COMMUNICATION PATHWAYS TO THE MOTHERSHIP ARE FUNCTIONING. THE SHIP HAS ALMOST ENTIRELY REPAIRED ITSELF.

GOOD. LET'S KILL IT.

WILL THAT BE ENOUGH?

HOPE SO. I COULD ONLY ENGINEER A LIMITED SUPPLY.

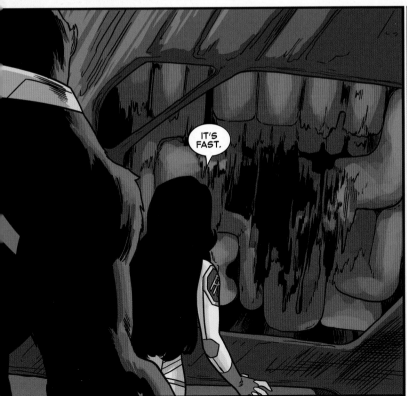

IT'S FAST.

BA BOOM

TOO FAST.

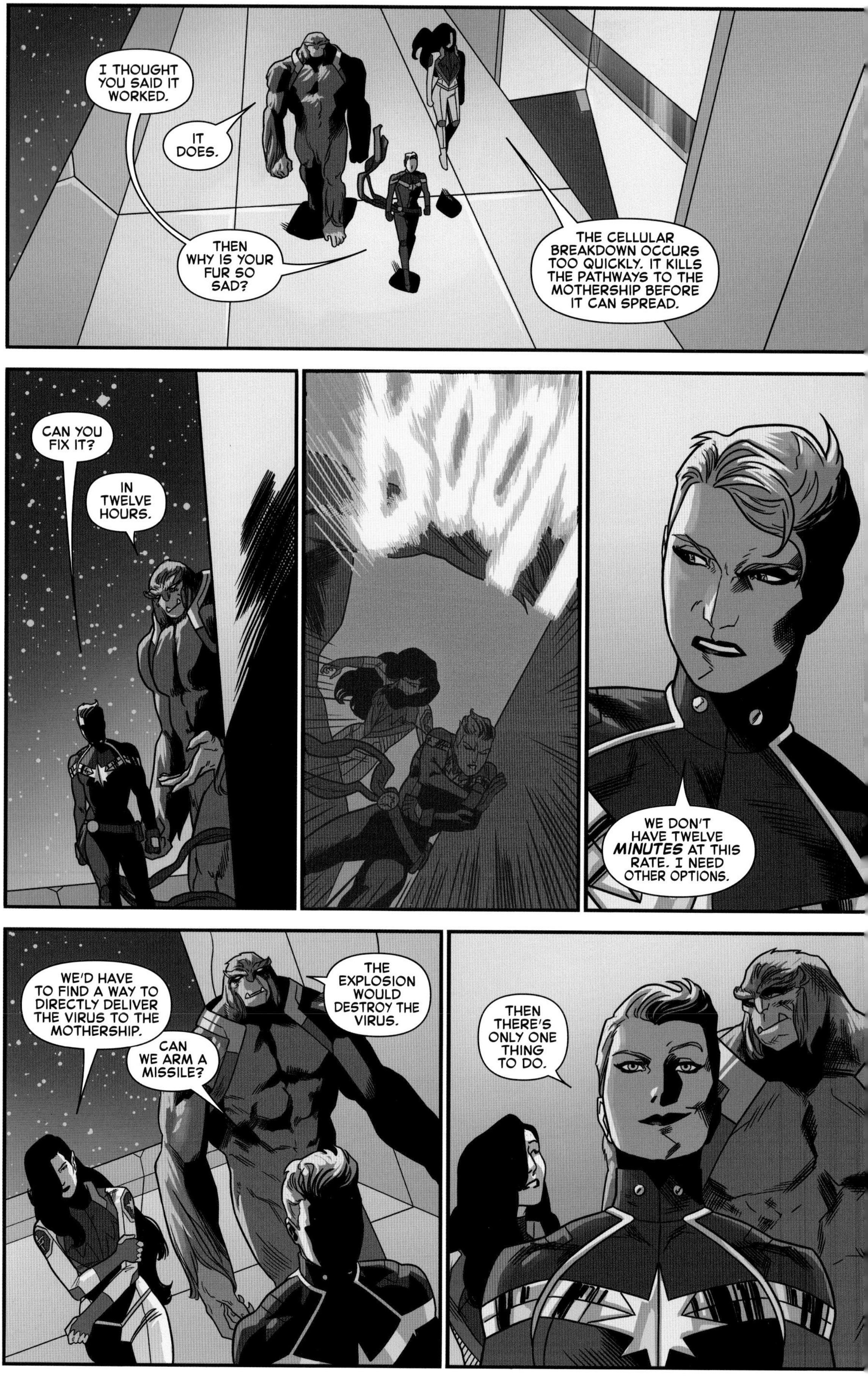
I THOUGHT YOU SAID IT WORKED.
IT DOES.
THEN WHY IS YOUR FUR SO SAD?
THE CELLULAR BREAKDOWN OCCURS TOO QUICKLY. IT KILLS THE PATHWAYS TO THE MOTHERSHIP BEFORE IT CAN SPREAD.
CAN YOU FIX IT?
IN TWELVE HOURS.
WE DON'T HAVE TWELVE *MINUTES* AT THIS RATE. I NEED OTHER OPTIONS.
WE'D HAVE TO FIND A WAY TO DIRECTLY DELIVER THE VIRUS TO THE MOTHERSHIP.
CAN WE ARM A MISSILE?
THE EXPLOSION WOULD DESTROY THE VIRUS.
THEN THERE'S ONLY ONE THING TO DO.

OPEN A LINE TO THE SATORI VESSEL.

THEY HAVEN'T BEEN RESPONDING TO--

THEY'LL RESPOND TO THIS.

bbrruumbbll

THAT WAS A BIG ONE. OUR SHIELDS DROPPED BACK TO FIFTY PERCENT--

THE CHANNEL IS OPEN TO THE SATORI VESSEL, CAPTAIN.

SATORI VESSEL. THIS IS...

...THIS IS MAR-VELL. OF THE KREE IMPERIAL MILITIA.

WHAT DID SHE SAY?

DANVERS, WHAT THE HELL ARE YOU DOING?

IF YOU CEASE FIRE IMMEDIATELY AND LEAVE THIS SYSTEM...

I WILL SURRENDER MYSELF TO YOUR CUSTODY.

NO--!

SHUT DOWN THE LINK! SHUT IT DOWN NOW!

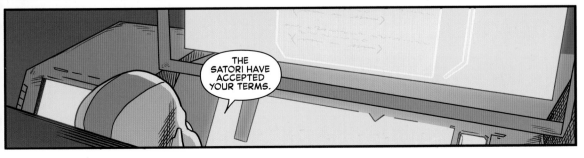

THE SATORI HAVE ACCEPTED YOUR TERMS.

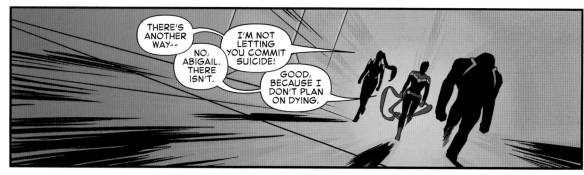

THERE'S ANOTHER WAY--

NO, ABIGAIL. THERE ISN'T.

I'M NOT LETTING YOU COMMIT SUICIDE!

GOOD, BECAUSE I DON'T PLAN ON DYING.

THE SATORI JET YOU INFECTED. WILL IT FLY?

NO.

GUESS I'LL HAVE TO GIVE IT A GOOD PUSH.

YOU'RE GOING TO USE IT TO INFECT THE MOTHER SHIP. LIKE A *TROJAN HORSE*--BUT YOU'RE THE HORSE. CLEVER.

RECKLESS.

I ACCEPT BOTH OF THOSE AS *COMPLIMENTS*.

WHAT IF IT DOESN'T WORK? WHAT IF THEY FIGURE IT OUT? WHAT IF THEY *BLOW* YOU OUT OF THE SKY BEFORE YOU GET THERE? WHAT DO YOU EXPECT US TO DO THEN?

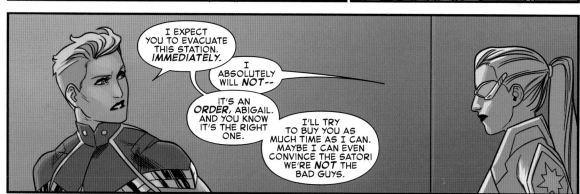

I EXPECT YOU TO EVACUATE THIS STATION. *IMMEDIATELY.*

I ABSOLUTELY WILL *NOT*--

IT'S AN *ORDER*, ABIGAIL. AND YOU KNOW IT'S THE RIGHT ONE.

I'LL TRY TO BUY YOU AS MUCH TIME AS I CAN. MAYBE I CAN EVEN CONVINCE THE SATORI WE'RE *NOT* THE BAD GUYS.

YOU'RE INSANE.

AGREED. BUT LET'S HOPE I'M MORE OF A DIPLOMAT THAN I LOOK.

I'M NOT LOVING THE ODDS.

YEAH. ME NEITHER. GET EVERYONE TO SAFETY.

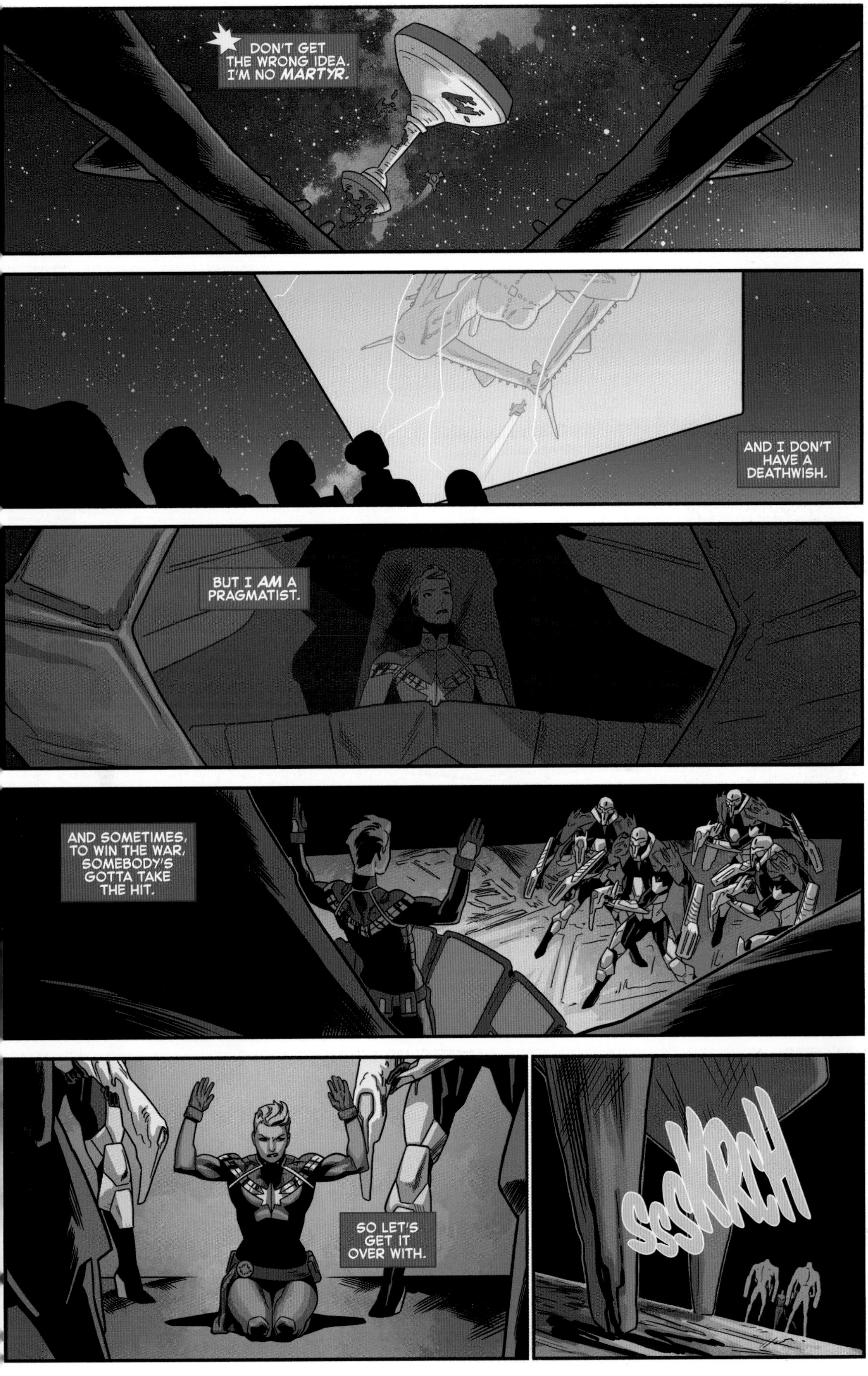
DON'T GET THE WRONG IDEA. I'M NO MARTYR.
AND I DON'T HAVE A DEATHWISH.
BUT I AM A PRAGMATIST.
AND SOMETIMES, TO WIN THE WAR, SOMEBODY'S GOTTA TAKE THE HIT.
SO LET'S GET IT OVER WITH.
SSSKRCH

WE CANNOT *ABANDON--*

WE *AREN'T* ABANDONING ANYBODY, WE CAN COORDINATE FROM THE GROUND.

THEY'RE GOING TO KILL HER!

WE DON'T KNOW THAT THEY CAN KILL HER.

THOUGH, GIVEN THEIR TECHNOLOGY, THERE IS A HIGH PROBABILITY.

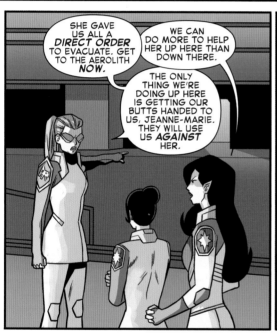

SHE GAVE US ALL A *DIRECT ORDER* TO EVACUATE. GET TO THE AEROLITH *NOW.*

WE CAN DO MORE TO HELP HER UP HERE THAN DOWN THERE.

THE ONLY THING WE'RE DOING UP HERE IS GETTING OUR BUTTS HANDED TO US, JEANNE-MARIE. THEY WILL USE US *AGAINST* HER.

brrru mble!

WHAT THE HELL WAS THAT?

THEY'RE FIRING AT US AGAIN!

NO WEAPONS FIRE.

WHERE?

THERE'S BEEN AN EXPLOSION ONBOARD THE STATION.

LIEUTENANT BRADNER. HE WAS SUPPOSED TO HAVE EVACUATED WITH THE FIRST WAVE.

OUR SABOTEUR KILLED HIMSELF IN THE PROCESS.

HE HAD A SECONDARY COMMUNICATOR. HE WAS WORKING WITH SOMEONE ELSE.

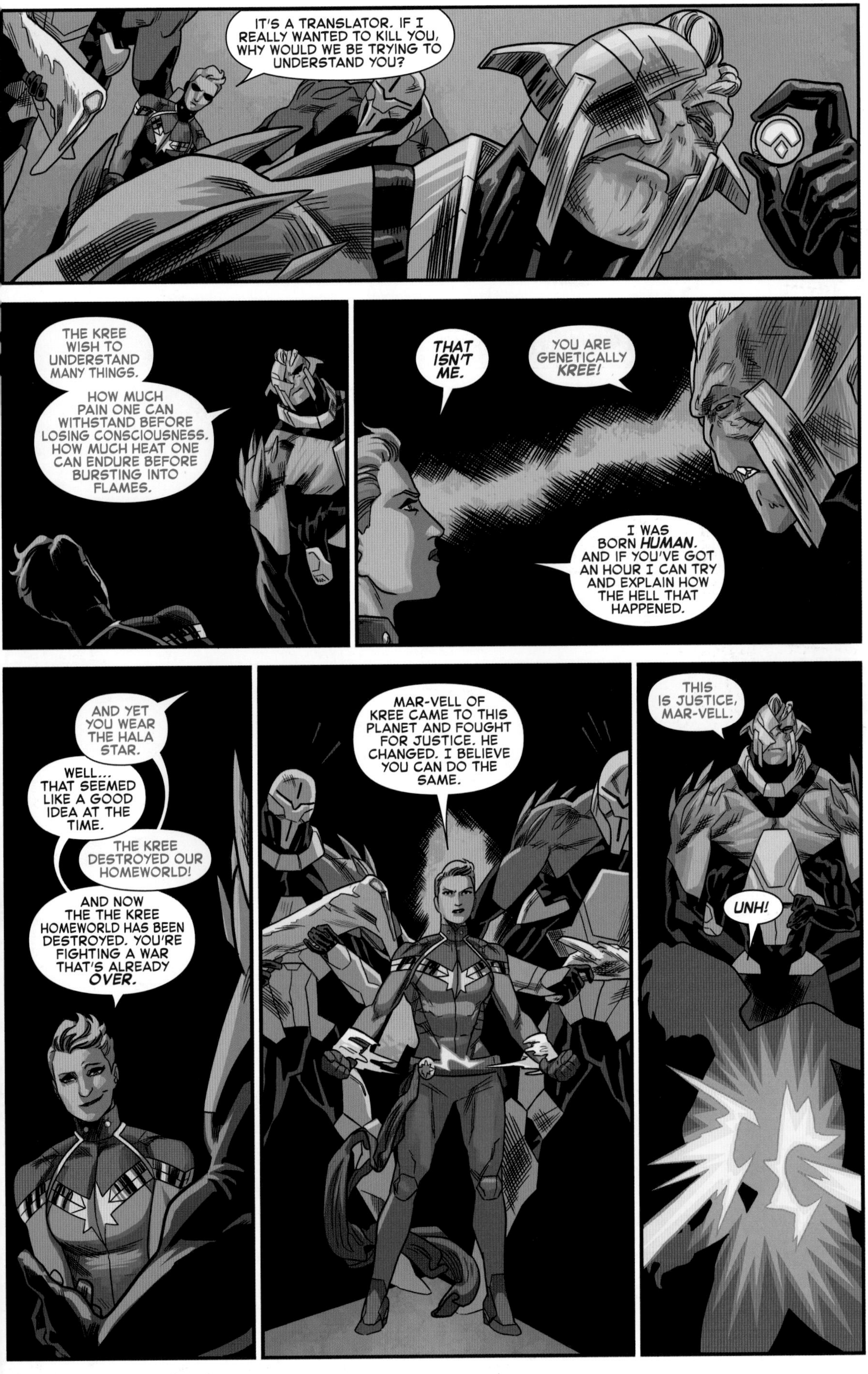
IT'S A TRANSLATOR. IF I REALLY WANTED TO KILL YOU, WHY WOULD WE BE TRYING TO UNDERSTAND YOU?
THE KREE WISH TO UNDERSTAND MANY THINGS.
HOW MUCH PAIN ONE CAN WITHSTAND BEFORE LOSING CONSCIOUSNESS. HOW MUCH HEAT ONE CAN ENDURE BEFORE BURSTING INTO FLAMES.
THAT ISN'T ME.
YOU ARE GENETICALLY KREE!
I WAS BORN HUMAN. AND IF YOU'VE GOT AN HOUR I CAN TRY AND EXPLAIN HOW THE HELL THAT HAPPENED.
AND YET YOU WEAR THE HALA STAR.
WELL... THAT SEEMED LIKE A GOOD IDEA AT THE TIME.
THE KREE DESTROYED OUR HOMEWORLD!
AND NOW THE THE KREE HOMEWORLD HAS BEEN DESTROYED. YOU'RE FIGHTING A WAR THAT'S ALREADY OVER.
MAR-VELL OF KREE CAME TO THIS PLANET AND FOUGHT FOR JUSTICE. HE CHANGED. I BELIEVE YOU CAN DO THE SAME.
THIS IS JUSTICE, MAR-VELL.
UNH!

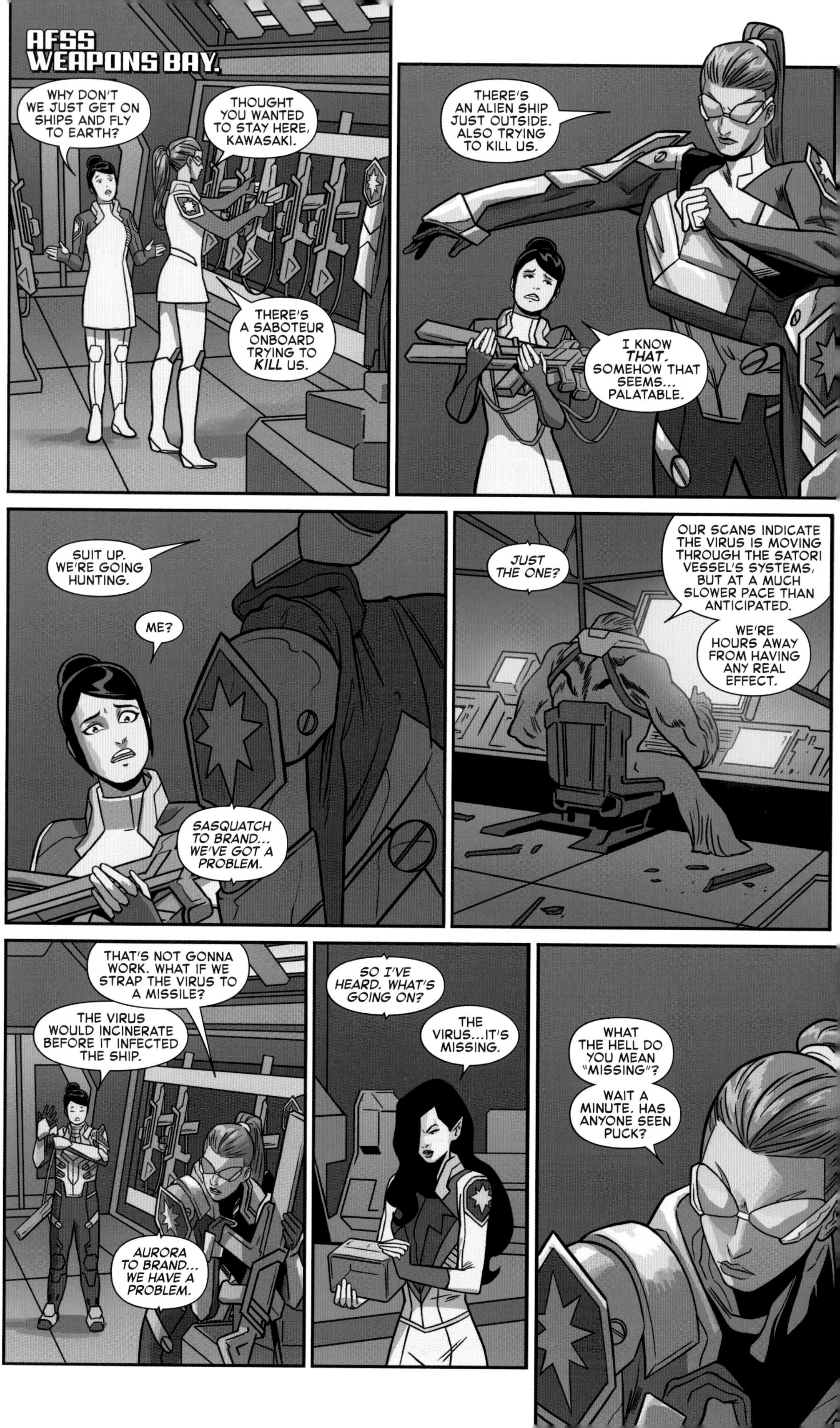
AFSS WEAPONS BAY.
WHY DON'T WE JUST GET ON SHIPS AND FLY TO EARTH?
THOUGHT YOU WANTED TO STAY HERE, KAWASAKI.
THERE'S A SABOTEUR ONBOARD TRYING TO KILL US.
THERE'S AN ALIEN SHIP JUST OUTSIDE. ALSO TRYING TO KILL US.
I KNOW THAT. SOMEHOW THAT SEEMS... PALATABLE.
SUIT UP. WE'RE GOING HUNTING.
ME?
SASQUATCH TO BRAND... WE'VE GOT A PROBLEM.
JUST THE ONE?
OUR SCANS INDICATE THE VIRUS IS MOVING THROUGH THE SATORI VESSEL'S SYSTEMS, BUT AT A MUCH SLOWER PACE THAN ANTICIPATED.
WE'RE HOURS AWAY FROM HAVING ANY REAL EFFECT.
THAT'S NOT GONNA WORK. WHAT IF WE STRAP THE VIRUS TO A MISSILE?
THE VIRUS WOULD INCINERATE BEFORE IT INFECTED THE SHIP.
AURORA TO BRAND... WE HAVE A PROBLEM.
SO I'VE HEARD. WHAT'S GOING ON?
THE VIRUS...IT'S MISSING.
WHAT THE HELL DO YOU MEAN "MISSING"?
WAIT A MINUTE. HAS ANYONE SEEN PUCK?

chunk

C'MON,
CAROL.

IT'S THE LACK
OF TRUST THAT
REALLY TICKS
ME OFF.

LIKE ALPHA FLIGHT IS SO
INCOMPETENT THAT
YOUR ONLY CHOICE IS TO
SACRIFICE *YOURSELF*
TO SAVE *US*?

THAT HURTS
ME. THAT
HURTS ME A
LOT.

AND WHEN
I'M HURT, I WILL
SOMETIMES
MAKE DECISIONS
THAT COULD BE
DEEMED RASH.

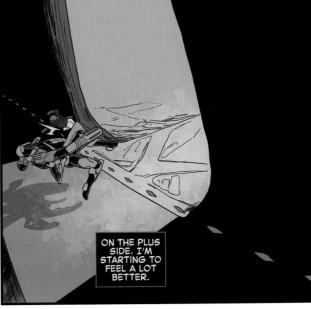

ON THE PLUS
SIDE, I'M
STARTING TO
FEEL A LOT
BETTER.

DELETING SELECTED FILES
REQUIRES PASSWORD
*****_

DON'T DO IT, GARCIA.

IT PROBABLY GOES WITHOUT SAYING, BUT YOU ARE VERY FIRED.

FOR DOING MY DUTY? FOR PROTECTING THE EARTH?

HOW 'BOUT FOR BEING A *TRAITOR?*

HEH, YOU'LL HAVE TO PROVE IT FIRST.

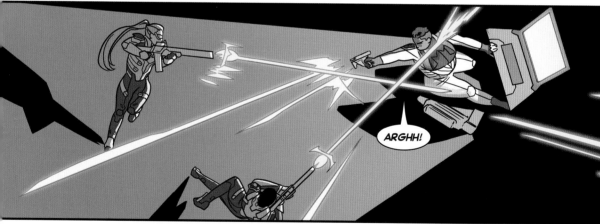

ARGHH!

WHERE'D YOU LEARN TO SHOOT LIKE THAT, KAWASAKI?

UM... MOSTLY LASER TAG.

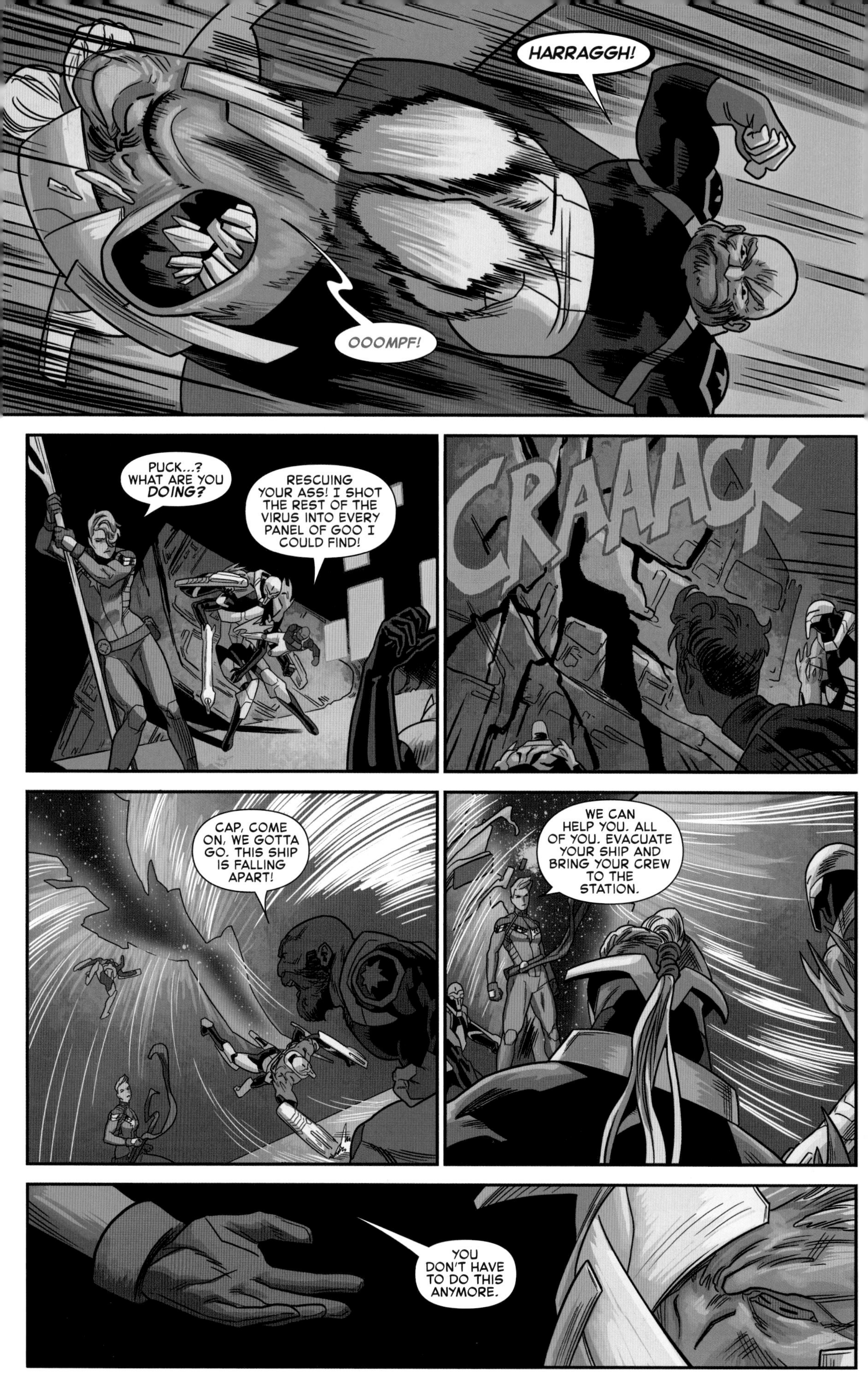
HARRAGGH!
OOOMPF!
PUCK...? WHAT ARE YOU DOING?
RESCUING YOUR ASS! I SHOT THE REST OF THE VIRUS INTO EVERY PANEL OF GOO I COULD FIND!
CRAAACK
CAP, COME ON, WE GOTTA GO. THIS SHIP IS FALLING APART!
WE CAN HELP YOU. ALL OF YOU. EVACUATE YOUR SHIP AND BRING YOUR CREW TO THE STATION.
YOU DON'T HAVE TO DO THIS ANYMORE.

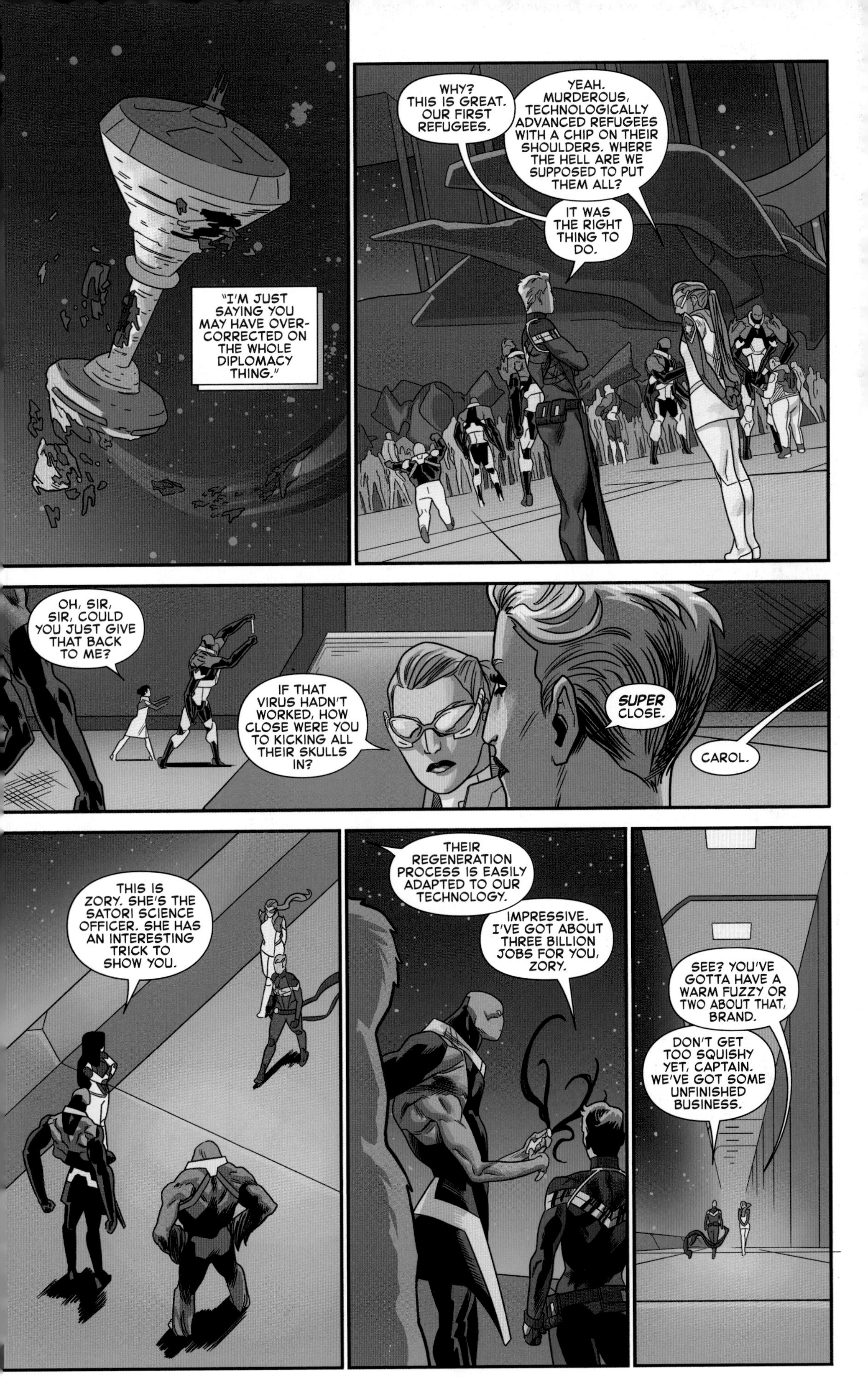
"I'M JUST SAYING YOU MAY HAVE OVER-CORRECTED ON THE WHOLE DIPLOMACY THING."
WHY? THIS IS GREAT. OUR FIRST REFUGEES.
YEAH. MURDEROUS, TECHNOLOGICALLY ADVANCED REFUGEES WITH A CHIP ON THEIR SHOULDERS. WHERE THE HELL ARE WE SUPPOSED TO PUT THEM ALL?
IT WAS THE RIGHT THING TO DO.
OH, SIR, SIR, COULD YOU JUST GIVE THAT BACK TO ME?
IF THAT VIRUS HADN'T WORKED, HOW CLOSE WERE YOU TO KICKING ALL THEIR SKULLS IN?
SUPER CLOSE.
CAROL.
THIS IS ZORY. SHE'S THE SATORI SCIENCE OFFICER. SHE HAS AN INTERESTING TRICK TO SHOW YOU.
THEIR REGENERATION PROCESS IS EASILY ADAPTED TO OUR TECHNOLOGY.
IMPRESSIVE. I'VE GOT ABOUT THREE BILLION JOBS FOR YOU, ZORY.
SEE? YOU'VE GOTTA HAVE A WARM FUZZY OR TWO ABOUT THAT, BRAND.
DON'T GET TOO SQUISHY YET, CAPTAIN. WE'VE GOT SOME UNFINISHED BUSINESS.

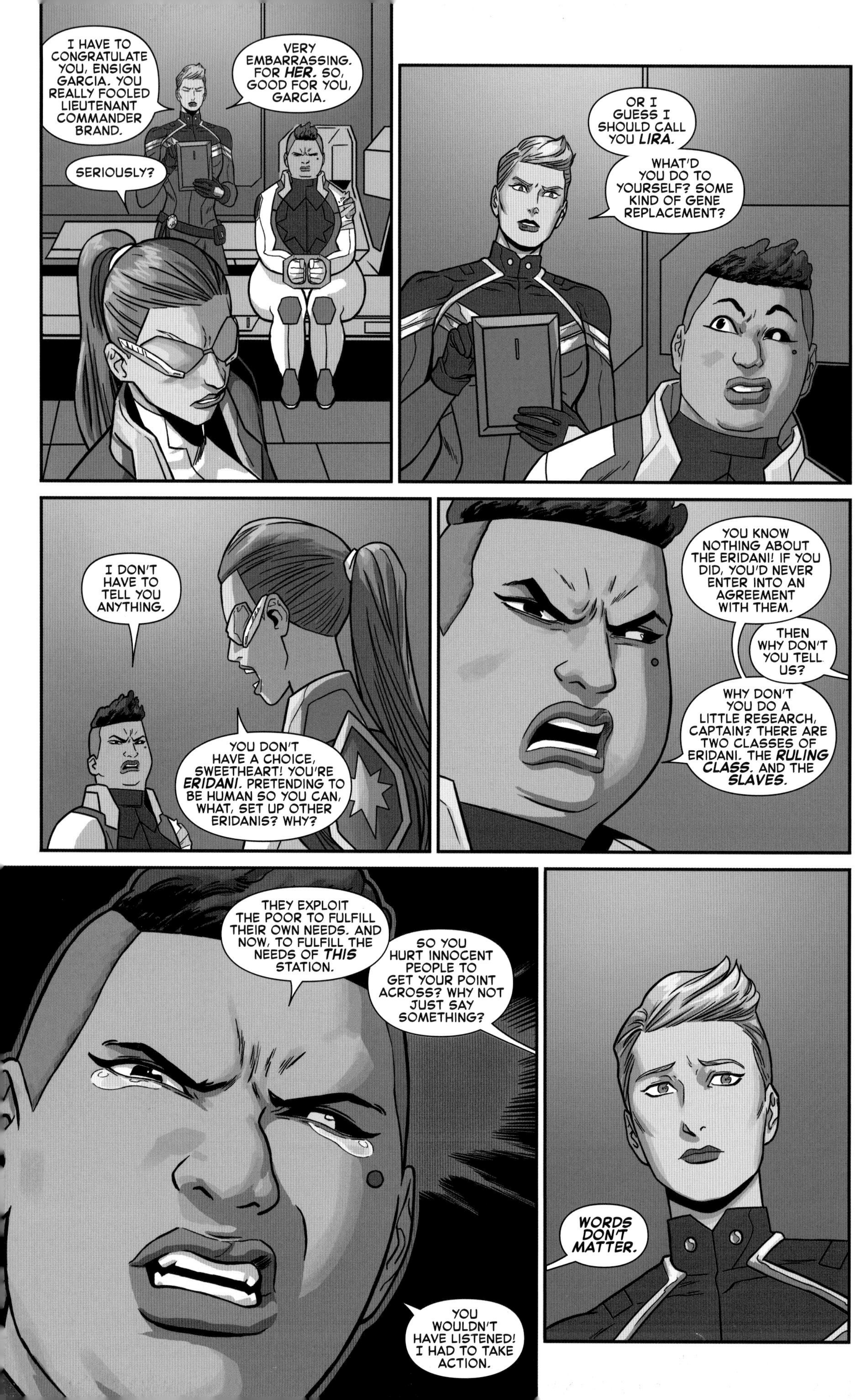
I HAVE TO CONGRATULATE YOU, ENSIGN GARCIA. YOU REALLY FOOLED LIEUTENANT COMMANDER BRAND.
SERIOUSLY?
VERY EMBARRASSING. FOR HER. SO, GOOD FOR YOU, GARCIA.
OR I GUESS I SHOULD CALL YOU LIRA.
WHAT'D YOU DO TO YOURSELF? SOME KIND OF GENE REPLACEMENT?
I DON'T HAVE TO TELL YOU ANYTHING.
YOU DON'T HAVE A CHOICE, SWEETHEART! YOU'RE ERIDANI. PRETENDING TO BE HUMAN SO YOU CAN, WHAT, SET UP OTHER ERIDANIS? WHY?
YOU KNOW NOTHING ABOUT THE ERIDANI! IF YOU DID, YOU'D NEVER ENTER INTO AN AGREEMENT WITH THEM.
THEN WHY DON'T YOU TELL US?
WHY DON'T YOU DO A LITTLE RESEARCH, CAPTAIN? THERE ARE TWO CLASSES OF ERIDANI. THE RULING CLASS. AND THE SLAVES.
THEY EXPLOIT THE POOR TO FULFILL THEIR OWN NEEDS. AND NOW, TO FULFILL THE NEEDS OF THIS STATION.
SO YOU HURT INNOCENT PEOPLE TO GET YOUR POINT ACROSS? WHY NOT JUST SAY SOMETHING?
YOU WOULDN'T HAVE LISTENED! I HAD TO TAKE ACTION.
WORDS DON'T MATTER.

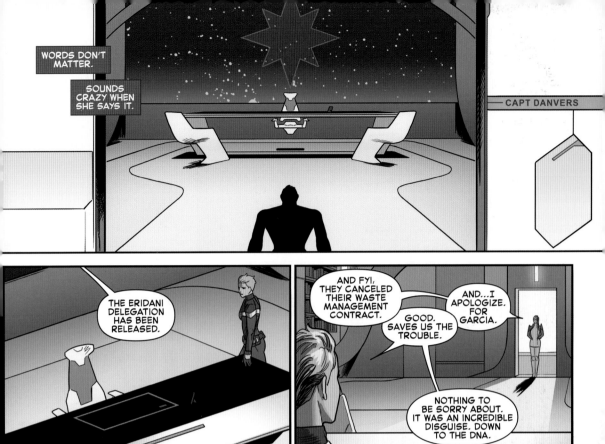

WORDS DON'T MATTER.

SOUNDS CRAZY WHEN SHE SAYS IT.

CAPT DANVERS

THE ERIDANI DELEGATION HAS BEEN RELEASED.

AND FYI, THEY CANCELED THEIR WASTE MANAGEMENT CONTRACT.

GOOD. SAVES US THE TROUBLE.

AND...I APOLOGIZE. FOR GARCIA.

NOTHING TO BE SORRY ABOUT. IT WAS AN INCREDIBLE DISGUISE. DOWN TO THE DNA.

YOU'RE BEING VERY UNDERSTANDING.

STOP IT.

YOU ONLY HAVE YOURSELF TO BLAME. ALL THAT DIPLOMACY GARBAGE IS REALLY SPEAKING TO ME NOW.

YOU BELIEVE THIS IS THE FIRST TIME I'VE EVEN *SEEN* THIS DESK?

YEAH? WHAT DO YOU THINK?

NOT BAD. PRETTY COMFORTABLE--

BREEEE BREEEE BREEEE

OH, THANK GOD...

CAPTAIN MARVEL

Variant Covers

Captain Marvel #1
by Judy Stephens

Captain Marvel #1
by Kris Anka

CAPTAIN MARVEL
THE NEW COMMAND

Captain Marvel #1
by Marguerite Sauvage

Captain Marvel #1
by Adam Hughes

Captain Marvel #2
by Phil Jimenez